Acknowledgement

The book, Northeast India Before and After Partition: Issues and Experiences, is an outcome of an ICHR sponsored two day National Seminar on 'Northeast India: Before and After Partition" held on 14-15 February 2015 at Swami Vivekananda Mahavidyalaya, Mohanpur, West Tripura. We are Grateful to ICHR, New Delhi for extending financial support to organize the seminar. The proceeding contains many of the papers presented in the seminar by academic persons and research scholars. We are grateful to the paper contributors without whose cooperation, this volume would not have been possible. We regret to those whose papers have not been considered in the volume. We also regret for being extremely delayed in bringing out the book. We are thankful to the contributors for their patience.

We are also grateful to the colleagues of the Swami Vivekananda Mahavidyalya for their whole hearted support and cooperation, the resource persons and speakers who have addressed the seminar. Special thanks to Professor A. K. Thakur, Department of History, NEHU. He has kindly delivered the Key Note Address on the theme of the seminar. We are also equally thankful to Professor Satyo Deo Podder, Department of History, Tripura University and Dr. Dipannita Chakraborti, Principal, Bir Bikram Memorial College, Agartala for addressing the seminar during the inaugural and valedictory sessions. Finally we are thankful to all those individuals who have provided useful support, ideas and encouragement for successful conclusion of the seminar and bringing out the proceedings in the form of this book. We shall remain deeply delighted if the book finds a place in epistemic debate and discussion and become an important literary source on the study of partition of India and refugee studies as well. We are indebted to Shivalik Prakashan, Delhi for agreeing to publish the book.

Dr. Nirmal Bhadra

Dr. Bindu Ranjan Chakma

Introduction

The British departure in August 1947 bifurcated India with emergence of two independent sovereign nations-the Peoples Republic of India and Islamic Republic of Pakistan. The British colonial administration used the politics of 'divide and rule' to prolong its colonial rule and interests in India. They showed the seeds of communalism and encouraged communal divisions especially between the Hindus and Muslims. The partition of Bengal on communal basis in 1905 was a clear indicative in this regard. Such policy continued till conclusion of their colonial rule. Islamic Republic of Pakistan was born on 14 August 1947 out of such communal politics. The partition of India produced many problems and challenges in the process of post independent national reconstruction. It marked the beginning of strained Indo-Pakistani hostility that still persists even after 70 years of British's departure from India. Displacement and trans-border migration of people inflicted untold sufferings among people in the midst of strained and antithetical bilateral relations between the two belligerent neibhours. The birth of Pakistan with presence of territory (East Pakistan, now Bangladesh) having geographical contiguity with Northeast India had serious security (social, political, economic, military and strategic) underpinnings in the Northeast India. Although economic and infrastructural underdevelopment figured greatly in the Northeast before partition, yet it did not experience problems such as sub nationalism, ethnic insurgency and ethnic conflicts, uneven growth of population, and politico-military security emanating from overt and covert involvement of many regional, extra regional national and sub-national actors. Partition of India is responsible for generating many of such problems in the post partition era in the Northeast. The primary objective of the seminar is to unravel, explain and analyse the implications of partition in the Northeast India. The book, an outcome of this seminar, includes articles that have dealt with different critical problems which are greatly figured now in the politics, academic and non academic literature in the Northeast India.

Professor Amrendra Kr Thakur dealt with partition and experiences in the Northeast with some thematic issues. Dr. Binayak Dutta explained the impact of decolonization and partition on the politics beyond Punjab and Bengal with special emphasis on Assam and Tripura. He argues that despite the transfer of power, partition continues to affect the lives of the people in Northeast India. The unresolved boundary question in Northeast India and the continuous acrimony over the legality of migration has become a pointer to the assertion that partition is not an event but a process which is far from its closure. Faith Elwin Kharbuli in his paper tried to locate Khasi and Jaintia people in Partition Scholarship. The paper argues that multiple experiences and voices of the Khasi and Jaintia people have for so long been hidden and is striving to be heard in the partition history. The Partition for them brought with it a mass exodus of refugees who came from East Pakistan and settled here. These refugees drastically changed and affected the demography of the Khasi and Jaintia state. The Partition of 1947 also paralyzed their economic progress and growth. Dr. Atom Sunil Singh in his paper on 'Geopolitics behind the Migration in the Northeast India' states that Northeast as frontier zone is the heaven for illegal migration. Most illegal migration is happened in the frontier zones. Such illegal migration is also very difficult to check it. Exclaveness makes Northeast India the heartland of migration in India. The paper argues that illegal migration in the Northeast from Bangladesh is visible due to racial and cultural differences between the Bangladeshi illegal migrants and the people of the Northeast India. But, illegal migrations from China, Nepal, Bhutan and Myanmar, also existed extensively, remains comparatively not easily visible because they are very difficult to identify due to cultural and ethnographic proximity. Dr. Nirmal Bhadra in his paper explained how partition caused non tribal migration in Tripura and how the communal politics and religious discrimination against the minority Hindus in East Pakistan and Bangladesh instigated migration of Hindu population in Tripura and other parts of India. Dr. Pradeep Kumar Deepak explained how the tiny state Tripura faced multi-faceted problems in the post Partition of India in 1947 and how the tribal population of the state declined from majority to minority. Dr. Bindu Ranjan Chakma explained linkage between partition and growth of Islamic fanaticism in East Pakistan and Bangladesh and how the process of Islamization penetrates into India's immediate and long term political, economic and geo-strategic interests in South Asia in general and the Northeast India in particular. Dr. Monoranjan Das in his paper narrated the journey of development and changes of the Tripura's tribal languages, particularly Kakborok, before and after partition. He argues that Kakborok, which remained deeply neglected during the pre partition era, has been recognized as official language in 1979 in Tripura. As the government of Tripura has put highest priority on improving education and development of tribal languages, it is expected that Kakborok will be on the door gate of national recognition at a full-fledged level in the near future. Dr. Md. Mojahid Rahman in his paper explained how the liberation war of Bangladesh was debated in the Tripura's Legislative Assembly and despite the refugee population overtaking the number of Tripura total population, how the people of Tripura cutting across of political, religious, linguistic and cultural affiliation wholeheartedly supported the liberation war of Bangladesh. The reason for such whole hearted support was due to presence of linguistic and cultural proximity between a large section of people of Tripura and Bangladesh and also because they wanted to see bring down on the burden of partition in Tripura. Some papers included in the volume although did not have direct linkage with partition history, yet some pertinent issues discussed in those paper attach significance and relevance in explaining the pre partition and post partition history of the Northeast India.

Partition and Experiences in the Northeast: Some Thematic Issues
Revised version of the Keynote Address for publication which was Delivered during the ICHR sponsored seminar on "North-East India: Before and After Partition with Special Reference to Tripura" Organised by Dept. of History, Swami Vivekananda Mahavidyalaya, Mohanpur, Agartala, Tripura (West) 14-15 February 2015.

(1)
History and the Partition of India: Probing Northeast India

Amrendra Kr Thakur

The process of historical reconstruction has been directed either towards finding generalities in development patterns or towards the detailed study of development patterns in a particular area. Interest in conceptual and methodological questions of history, uses and its misuses for surveys of social and political purposes, novelty and critical assessments of various historical trends is quite widespread. Interventions and subsequent debates *vis- a- vis* historical reconstruction, focus on finding out what actually is and what is not. While the larger discourse of partition manages to guide us to its impact on northeast India, it also makes us overlook the peculiarities in the region.

Concern for the conceptual and methodological questions of historical research also occupy an important place in the study of impact of partition in the region. The surveys, critical assessments of various historical trends and intervention in related debates, undertaken with different approaches, also influence historical writings. Thus, it is often seen that writings of history are either based on moulded historical facts or on their purposeful reinterpretation, with the aim of achievement of particular political goals. This problem has also been highlighted by Eric Hobsbawm in his book *On History*, in which he writes, "...history is the raw material for nationalist or ethnic or fundamentalist ideologies, as poppies are the raw material for heroin addiction. The past is an essential element, perhaps the essential element, in these ideologies. If there is no suitable past, it can always be invented". He further writes "I used to think that the profession of history, unlike that of, say, nuclear physics, could at least do no harm. Now I know it can. Our studies can turn into bomb factories."[1]

I have indulged in the analysis of this problem in the historical reconstruction of the past of India has been elsewhere and hence, I don't intend to repeat the same here.[2] Nonetheless, in the recent months of 2015, this problem has assumed a new dimension and historians are voicing their concerns. Prof. D. N. Jha "... explains how popular myths about the cow and beef-eating were systematically etched into the nation's memory by Hindutva extremists and speaks about their larger political interests in rewriting history."[3] Prof. Badri Raina has also expressed his concern on the issue, he writes, "That project [of Hindu Rightwing] aims with devious energy to propagate the myth that beef was never eaten by Hindu, and that only the invading Mussalman wrought the calamity of cow slaughter. And, taking cue from the ideological mentors of the current power structure, to make it known that the righting of that and other "wrongs" will no longer be left just to law-enforcement but taken up by committed factious basking in the knowledge of a friendly state."[4] Prof. Harbans Mukhia in his article "Distorting History Won't Help" clearly mentions that "In reality, every society, every religion, has mythologies that are cultural constructs meant to impart certain lessons and moral values, these are not reconstructions of factual information. Mythologies have a much wider reach in society than knowledge of history has. ... It [history] is strictly bound by its methodological discipline. History and mythology belong to two different genres of knowledge and culture, not inferior or superior to each other. ... the past gets constantly constructed and reconstructed by the present in accordance with its needs, and it gets constructed differently according to each segment's needs – like the Sangh's needs."[5]

The *Frontline* writes that "In the last few months, the Bharatiya Janata Party (BJP)-led Union government has stepped up its efforts to steer the Sangh Parivar's Hindutva agenda by changing the nature of public institutions. ... such as the Indian Council of Historical Research (ICHR), the Nehru Memorial Museum and Library (NMML) and the Lalit Kala Akademi, to carry out research only on topics that are in line with the Sangh Parivar's doctrines. Many scholars claim that in the process the government is high-handedly promoting unethical and unscientific research practices in various disciplines."[6] In the interview to *Frontline*, Prof. Irfan Habib states that "Thankfully, history itself will not change however much it may be falsely presented. But the nation's mental make-up may grievously suffer thereby." He further asserts, "Religious mythologies, whether of the Brahmanical, Judaic or Islamic traditions, have no place in history for the events they relate, though how these myths themselves arose is often an interesting question for the historian to inquire into." Explaining further, he observes, "There is psychological difficulty with RSS men. Though they shout of 'nationalism', they do so now when, after 1947, it has become safe to do so. They contributed no 'heroes' to the national movement themselves at the time it meant going to jail or suffering otherwise. They kept on the good side of the British while seeking to undermine the national movement by shouting 'Hindu-Hindi-Hindustan' or 'Hindu Raj Amar Rahe'. Did these activities not contribute to Partition, the blame for which they now lay at the door of Gandhiji and Nehru? Thus they have to invent a false history in which they can paint themselves as nationalists while defaming the principal freedom fighters."[7]

The Union Home Minister, Rajnath Singh, while having succeeded in creating an unseemly controversy over the Nehru Library and the contrived resignation of its Director, Mahesh Rangrajaan, entered triumphantly the Nehru Library accompanied by other stalwarts of the BJP, and said that there should be a full debate on all subjects and highlighted BJP leader Din Dayal Upadhyay's "Integral Humanism". The suggestion is welcome, though the attitude is divisive. But then this debate should be open to all the view."[8] The other suggestion towards revamping the NMML came to have a separate gallery for the partition history. Is this going to show violence of partition permanently? What purpose is it going to serve, needs to be observed.

Our responsibilities towards historical reconstruction of the past are many fold. And the first is to base our research on historical reality and its facts. Anything other than the objective narration of truth of the past should not be accepted. This is important for the researches working on any event of history but it is all the more vital for the historical researches pertaining to partition, as it involves the politics of religion, region, ethnicity and loss of lands and property. Partition ushered in an era of mistrust, hatred and unending rivalry in all the affected regions. Particularly in the case of northeast India the legacy of the partition of 1947 continues even today, as the issue of migration of people across the border and its legality is widely discussed. Emphasis should also be laid on criticising the politico-ideological misuse of history. Seemingly in India these days, orienting history in relation to a particular faith and 'abuse' of history to suit such idea is growing. The history of partition should not be made a victim of the same. We should not invent what happened and thus not indulge in subjective analysis. Our researches should be based on credible archaeological, textual and oral sources and our writings must convey historical reality without any bias.

II

Partition created a harvest of bitterness and unleashed an untold misery. An enormous human tragedy of loss of lives and property occurred as millions of Hindu and Muslim refugees fled either to Pakistan or to India. The Partition was accompanied by violence, trauma, displacement, widespread sexual savagery and fear, uncertainty, created by the drawing of borders. The violence of 1947 still continues to haunt the lives of the people.

For a long period of time, Partition studies mainly dwelled on the question of 'why' it occurred and 'who' was responsible for it. A plethora of literature on modern India, produced by Indian scholars, fixed the responsibility of the Partition of India on Jinnah, the Muslim League and the British. Similarly, the works undertaken by Pakistani scholars blamed the Congress and its leaders for the Partition of the country. A new genre of partition historiography has brought into light a new way of looking at and trying to understand what Partition means. Today different scholars have become interested in studying different issues that were associated with the aftermath of Partition. Thus, of late, the human dimension of the experiences of Partition rather than the questions of 'who' was responsible and 'who' caused it, has dominated most of Partition scholarship. The human sufferings and struggles of women, children, and men has come to the forefront, which gives one a better and clearer perspective of what the partition actually brought about.

However, even this new historiography of partition, primarily focuses on the experiences of people of Punjab and Bengal. Initially, scholars concentrated more on the experiences of Punjab and subsequently, Bengal was brought into the picture. Most of the scholars have tried to understand the process, pattern, violence and impact of migration on families and caste. As a result, the study of Partition seems to be lacking as it fails to include the experiences of the people of northeast India, who were as much effected by the Partition and Independence of India in 1947. Northeast India has not been studied as extensively as Punjab and Bengal, in terms of the history of Partition. The writings which do exist on the subject only look into the economic impact of Partition and the inflow of refugees into this part of the country. However on the bright side, today a few scholars have managed to bring Assam into partition historiography. Thus, in order to understand Partition in its complete terms, attempts have to be made to include the north-eastern part of the country.

The Partition of India has paradigm shift in the Nehruvian policy from the pre-Partition days. The Indian federalism was weakened in the Post-Independence and Post-Participation era. In the Nehruvian policy the central intervention increased and resulted in centralisation of power, as the dismissal of the elected communist government of Kerala, the introduction Planning Commission to monitor and control the finance of the states, the developments in Jammu and Kashmir and Nagaland etc, occurred. How all of this affected the course of history of Independent India has to be examined. In the future these dimensions should form the focus of our research as the discourse on Partition. The acts of undertaking of smuggling in spite of the formation of heavily guarded borders between the countries should also be analysed. And the outcome of these new researches should be incorporated in the textbooks for schools and colleges. Analysis of the causes of changes in Post- Independence India and narratives based on the experiences of people should become a part of Historical research. And to some extent the new researches are now finding place in the textbooks. The change is reported under the heading, "NCERT text blame on Jinnah for portion".[9] It states that in a departure from the tone of political correctness, the NCERT history textbook for class XII for the first time has identified the villains of partition, putting the blame on Mohammad Ali Jinnah for sowing the seeds of antagonism.

After Partition communalism was heaving along with religious nationalism. These led to many incidents of sexual violence, abductions and forceful settlement of people in their ne lives. Atrocities against women were also on the rise as their trafficking, rapes and abductions took place on both sides. About 33,000 and 50,000 Hindu and Sikh women were abducted in India and Pakistan, respectively. According to estimates, 30,000 women were 'recovered', overall 22,000 Muslim women in India and 8,000 Hindu and Sikh women in Pakistan, in an operation ended as late in 1954. Even the relatives of the abducted women refused to talk them back. Both the government were insensitive to the complexities of human relationships.

Most studies pertaining to partition have been focussed on its aftermath in Punjab and the region of North East India remains neglected. The second partition which occurred in 1971 again brought in refugees and followed the legacy of the partition of 1947. Various communities of people including the Chakma Hajongs, Drus, Hindus and Muslims were again subjected to the tragic fate of Partition. Rabindra Nath Tagore's words seem opt to be quoted as another dimension of the Partition problem. Gurudev writes, "Strangers you have become in your own land…shall we live like this? Shall our ultimate salvation be the right to vote?"[10] Partition brings about fresh border cuts across a national homeland.15 million people were displaced in the migration surge that followed, this was the largest forced migration in the 20th century. A figure of 2lakhs to 20 lakhs having being dead is obtained, which however is a matter of dispute. Nearly 1lakh women were kidnapped on both side of the border. Women were victimised because they symbolised community honour.

The historiography of Partition has gone through a sea change during the recent years, particularly after the golden jubilee year of India's Independence, as the researchers are now more interested in reconstructing the aftermath of Partition, which has brought the high cost associated with the process and radical changes in the societies of Eastern and North-Eastern India, rather than the causes of the landmark event and the 'high politics' behind it.[11] It is largely related to the process of evaluating the achievements and failures of the nation-state after fifty years of its Independence. Remarkably, so long very little is known about the socioeconomic impact of Partition on different localities and individuals.

Hence, the human dimension of the experience of Partition has become the major content of the new Partition historiography.

Bipan Chandra in his book *India After Independence* (Penguin Books, New Delhi, 1999), states that a large number of Muslims, Christians and Buddhists were forced to migrate and seek shelter in West Bengal, Assam and Meghalaya in India from East Pakistan. Vazira Fazila Yacoobali Zamindar in her work, *The Long Partion and the Making of Modern South Asia: Refugees, Boundaries, Histories* (Oxford University Press, New Delhi, 2007), makes an important point that Partition means that India and Pakistan were not like other ex-colonial new states, in that their institutions and practices were not a continuation of their colonial arrangements but rather the result of complicated new arrangements. Partition also created a flow of refugees who were not really at home in either of the two new states.

Sanjib Baruah in his book, India Against Itself, Assam and the Politics of Nationality traces the history of the economic and political history of Assam. He states that the post-partition riots led to more migration of minorities from East Pakistan to India and from India to East Pakistan. The work offers an important contribution to the study of ethnic conflict. Dilip Kumar Chattopadhyay in a work, History of the Assamese Movement Since 1947 (Minerva Publications, Calcutta, 1990) demonstrated that since independence and partition in 1947, growing immigration had led to conflicts among different ethnic groups and that the Assamese, who constituted the majority group feared that the unending stream of migration might turn them into a minority.

Mahadev Chakravarti in his above quoted book shows how the memory of the partition triggered further fragmentation and conflict in the society and the partition resulted in the abrupt severance of inland water, road and railway communication, as well as the loss of access to the Chittagong Port, crippling crucial economic linkages and driving up cost of all commodities. He also stated that partition brought with it increasing waves of migration that disrupted the traditional way of life, and how people were cut off from their traditional markets. Due to its geographical location, and great distance from New Delhi, the people of this region often suffer from a feeling of neglect and feel that the central government does not have much time or concern for their security, priorities and needs. This feeling has, at times, been exacerbated by responses from New Delhi which did not take into account the feelings and sensitivities of the people inhabiting this area. Referring to the other side of the picture regarding the social position of "settler Bengali" in Meghalaya in a world of "ethnicised modernity" after sixty years of Partition, Rajesh Dev points out in the words of Mahadev Chakravari, The `settlers' who came basically in two phases-one group before the partition and the other as victims of a gory partition-are being ever more represented as the adversarial `other' within the new state……... Every ethnic group in the region, especially those that derive the legitimacy of their agency from `indigenity' is simultaneously engaged in narrativising its past in a fashion that valorises difference and the articulation of collective action that grants political recognition of this difference. The same story is repeated in the other states of the North-East.

Joya Chatterjee, over and above her celebrated work *Bengal Divided*, has developed a standard criticism against the 'Radcliffe Line' drawn between the two parts of Bengal and North-East India. In her words it was 'a hastily and ignorantly drawn line' by a man who had 'no background in Indian administration, nor did he have any prior experience of adjudicating disputes of this sort'. Before his appointment, Sir Cyril Radcliffe, a reputed barrister, had never visited India and knew no-one in India. Paradoxically, to the British and feuding politicians alike, this liability was looked upon as an asset; on the theory that ignorance of India would equal impartiality, and he was considered to be unbiased toward any of the parties, except of course Britain. Britain's action in 1947-condemned as a "shameful flight" by Winston Churchill (who predicted that India would break up in just ten years, though his forecast proved wrong)--had a catastrophic effect particularly on the North-East. Stanley Wolpert's new book -- *Shameful Flight,* published in 2006, is an account of the Partition story which lays the blame for one of the most horrific episodes of the 20th century squarely on Mountbatten, the flamboyant cousin of the king, who rushed the process of nationhood along at an absurd pace. Radcliffe Award was the outcome of an official plan announced by Lord Mountbatten. The partition, according to the Radcliff Award, was followed by a massive influx of Bengali Hindu refugees from East Pakistan to different parts of the country. The migration virtually started before the partition, particularly after the Noakhali riot in 1946. Partition brought with it unceasing waves of migration that disrupted, and continue to disturb, existing demographic equations in different parts of North-Eastern region, particularly the present Assam, Tripura, Meghalaya,

Arunachal Pradesh and Mizoram. Wolpert's main contention is that the United Kingdom abandoned India in a reckless and headlong retreat - a retreat that left India and Pakistan in a chaotic bloodbath that left perhaps a million dead and 12 million refugees.

In the work *Encyclopaedia of Meghalaya* (Amol Publications, New Delhi, 2009) Kumud Borthakur, has demonstrated that the transfer of power and the change of administration, brought a tremendous upset in the economic life of the people living across the borders due to the closure of the border trade and commerce immediately after 1947. Hamlet Bareh's work *Meghalaya* (North-Eastern India News and Reature Service, Shillong, 1974) and David Syiemlieh's article, 'Trade and Markets in the Khasi Jaintia Hills – Changed Conditions in the 19th and 20th Centuries', in D.R.Syiemlieh and Manorama Sharma (eds.), *Society and Economy Vol.3,* (Regency Publications, New Delhi, 2008) show how trade and commerce was severely affected due to partition. Armstrong Swer, in an article 'Border Hats in Khasi-Jaintia Hills: The Historical Perspective' (*Proceedings of North East India History Association*, 33rd session, Itanagar, 2012, pp.254-258) examines how after partition, the prosperous economy of the border areas came to a standstill with the progress of plain areas of Sylhet and Mymensingh, and as a result the Khasi, Jaintia and Garo were deprived of the traditional sources of income as well as access to markets. Similarly, L. S. Gassah in a paper, 'Effects of Partition on the Border Marketing of Jaintia Hills' in J. B. Ganguly (ed.), *Marketing in North-East India* (Omsons Publications, New Delhi, 1984) demonstrated how 1947 brought a heavy attack on the economic life of the War Jaintia, their relations in trade and commerce with their counterparts in the plains and also a setback in the exchange of goods and essential commodities in the border markets. Faith Elwin Kharbuli and Lasoborki Pyrngap have also started working on the partition history and socio-economic impact of the same in the region.

As stated earlier, initially Punjab centric study of partition history dominated the landscape and only in the 1950s did the research of Partition pertaining to Bengal come up. All the states of Northeast India in general and the state of Tripura in particular have not been broadly studied in terms of Partition. Also the initial works focussed on the role of communalism and its reasons. Only in the later studies did the focus shift to the sufferings of the people during partition and the issues of forced migration and displacement. Even though the region of Northeast remains largely neglected within the region the focus has been on the valley areas of Brahmaputra and Barak Surma, the hill states and Tripura have faced sheer neglect. The Socio-economic and human impact of partition on the historical processes in Northeast India is the other neglected area. In the case of Northeast India the legacy of 1947 has continued and was rejuvenated in 1971. Following partition was the disruption of Socio-economic life. Population of some of the border areas depends mostly on the other side of the border than the side they belong to.

Issues of violence and other matters continue to haunt the states of the region. In 1964 the establishment of the Kaptai Hydro-Electric project in Chalawa and other such policies, deprived the people of their land. The refugees that came in during partition and after continue to struggle for their voting and other rights to achieve equality of status in the country. In Mizoram, Mizos and their relations with the Mara, Chokma and Bru are still debated. In Tripura, as well the issue of the Brus remains unresolved. Thus, even in the 21st century the tragic aftermath of the Partition remains problematic. Historians with constructive and credible researches must fulfil their responsibilities in the matter. Migration from across the border in the aftermath of partition disrupted the demographic pattern of the states, adversely affected the psyche of the people of the Region and led to various other problems including that of security.

III

This section tries to keep the Partition histories into perspective mainly for the benefit of the emerging scholars on Partition histories of Northeast India.

Historical Accounts:

Mushirul Hasan ed. *India's Partition: Process, Study, and Mobilisation,* OUP, 1993- the book recreates the events surrounding the Partition through extracts, memoirs, and essays; Joya Chatterji *Bengal Divided: Hindu Communalism and Partition 1932-47,* Cambridge University Press, 1994- the book focusses on the disillusionment that creeps in the larger society when a certain majoritarian identity politics is followed and promoted; Sucheta Mahajan *Independence and Partition: The Erosion of Colonial Power in India*, Sage Publications, 2000- the book evaluates the interactions of imperial, national, and communal conflicts as it examines the role of the Britishers, the Congress, the

Muslim League, and the Hindu 'nationalists' in the Partition of India; Yasmin Khan *The Great Partition: The Making of India and Pakistan*, Yale University Press, 2007- The book reconstructs the painful narrative of the creation of the nations of India and Pakistan through a bloody history of the Partition; Ayesha Jalal- *The Pity of Partition- Manto's Life, Times, and Work Across the India-Pakistan Divide,* Princeton University Press, 2013- The book is a good attempt at an intellectual biography of the celebrated Urdu writer Saadat Hasan Manto. Manto's work, along with those of the likes of Ismat Chughtai and Rajinder Bedi is often read as highlighting the human cost of the Partition; Nisid Hajari *Midnight's Furies: The Deadly Legacy of India's Partition*, Houghton Mifflin Harcourt, 2015- It is one of the rare books that traces some of the major problems being faced by India today on the socio-political front such as communal tension, religious polarisation etc. to the legacy of the Partition; Urvashi Butalia ed. *Partition: The Long Shadow*, Zubaan/Viking, 2015- The book is one of more comprehensive takes on the legacy of the Partition. It takes the Partition of the 1971 War into account. It also includes essays that cover new ground such as gender, migration, and memory. Some essays also cover Laddakh, Kashmir, and the North East (Assam).

Literary Accounts:

Compared to the historical accounts of Partition that tend to focus on the facts of the situation, the causes, and impact of the Partition, literary recollections, reconstructions, and rememberings have tended to highlight the human cost of the Partition of the subcontinent. Millions of people were affected, thousands killed, displaced or rendered homeless. Literature, in both English and the 'regional' languages of India, has responded to the Partition in a variety of ways. Most writers have tended to question the logic of a process that makes new nations but destroys peoples' lives and memories. Manto, Chughtai, and Bedi are the most prominent names that are noteworthy in this regard. There are individual works such as Khuswant Singh's *Train to Pakistan* (1956), Yashpal's *Jhootha Sach* (1958), Bhisma Sahni's *Tamas* (1972), and Bapsi Sidhwa's 1988 novel *Cracking India* whose narratives deal with the Partition very directly. There are also anthologies that present creative pieces (in English and other Indian languages) along with critical essays that deal with the various aspects of Partition such as violence, trauma, and memory. Suvir Kaul ed. *The Partitions of Memory: The Afterlife of the Division of India,* Permanent Black, 2001 is a collection of letters and essays that deals with, among other things, the legacy of Partition in present day Pakistan and the Dalit claims on Partition memory. Similary, Ravikant and Tarun K. Saint eds. *Translating Partition: Stories, Essays, Criticism,* Katha, 2001 presents to the reader translated pieces by Gulzar, Manto, Sahni, Surendra Prakash, Joginder Paul and others along with critical pieces on Partition Literature by Deeba Zafir, M Asaduddin, Arjun Mahey, and Bodh Prakash. Quite apart from the interrogations of the Partition conducted through the written word, there are three books that deal with Partition in fresh ways and they do not concentrate on the written word. Tarun K. Saint's 2010 work *Witnessing Partition: Memory, History, Fiction,* Routledge, 2010 focusses on the (crises of) witnessing and the need for testimonials that the Partition gave rise to. It focusses on novels and short stories that act as self-reflexive testimonials on the tragic event. Similarly, Vishwajyoti Ghosh in 2013 (Yoda Press) curated an anthology of graphic narratives on the Partition with contributions from India, Pakistan, and Bangladesh. It is called *This Side, That Side: Restorying Partition.* Anam Zakaria in *The Footprints of Partition: Narratives of Four Generations of Pakistanis and Indians* (Haper Collins India, 2015) presents the memories, mental trauma, exhaustion, and forgetting related to the Partition as recounted, in oral narratives, by four generations of men and women in India and Pakistan.

Accounts from Alternative Perspectives:

Urvashi Butalia's 1998 book *The Other Side of Silence: Stories from the Partition of India* has been the pioneering work in this field (Penguin India). Butalia highlights the fact that a narrative about the Partition from a strictly politico-historical lens will always be incomplete as it will elide the human cost of the tragedy. Struggling with historical amnesia, the book recovers the otherwise marginalised voices of those nameless thousands who were displaced, raped, and killed during the Partition. She highlights for the reader the impact of the Partition carried out on communal lines on the women and thus attempts to see the Partition from a feminist lens. She explores the ways in which communal ideology colludes with patriarchal ideology in such circumstances. Similarly, Ritu Menon and Kamla Bhasin in *Borders and Boundaries: Women In India's Partition* (Rutgers University Press, 1998) refuse to see the thousands of women who were raped, killed, and displaced during the Partition as victims and rather seek to recover their voice by highlighting their courage in such circumstances. The book presents such courageous narratives, stories, and testimonials by women. In a similar vein, Jasodhara Bagchi and Subhoranjan Dasgupta's *The Trauma and the Triumph: Gender and Partition in Eastern India* (Stree, 2005) focuses on the Partition of India along its eastern areas such as Bengal and presents the various ways in which women were oppressed and yet emerged triumphant then. The book also serves as a necessarily corrective endeavour as much of Partition literature and history has focussed on the western side of India.

Notes and References:

1. Eric Hobsbawm, *On History*, Abacus, London, 1998, pp.6-7.
2. For details, see Amrendra Kr Thakur, "The Curriculum in History in Modern India: An Overview", in Sagar Boruah (ed.), *Historical Studies in the Context of Globalisation: Rationale for Restructuring Curriculum*, Khagarijan College, Nagaon, Assam, 2011, pp.9-34 and Binayak Dutta's review of the book in *The NEHU Journal*, Vol. XI, No. 2, July, 2013, pp.97-101.
3. D. N. Jha, "The cow was neither unslayable nor sacred in the Vedic period", *Frontline*, October 30, 2015, pp.16-18.
4. Badri Raina, "The Lynchings", *Mainstream*, October10, 2015, pp. 5-6.
5. Harbans Mukhia, "Distorting History Won't Help", *India Today*, October12, 2015, p. 16.
6. For details, see *Frontline*, October 16, 2015, pp.40-44.
7. *Ibid.*
8. Rajindar Sachar, "Don Not Play With Fire", *Mainstream*, October17, 2015, p. 3.

9. *The Times of India,* September 27, 2007.
10. *Mainstream*, Dec 25, 2010.
11. For details, see Mahadev Chakravarti "Redcliff Award and Partition Historiography: Assam and Tripura", *SOCIAL CHANGE IN NORTH-EAST INDIA Partition, Ethnicity, Revivalism, Globalization*, NEIHA, Shillong, 2008, pp.16-39 and David R. Syiemlieh, *RESPONSE OF THE NORTH EAST HILL TRIBES OF INDIA TOWARDS PARTITION, INDEPENDENCE AND INTEGRATION: 1946-1950*, Pratibha Devi Memorial Lectures, Gauhati University, Guwahati, 2003. I have extensively used Mahadev Chakravarti's writing for this part of my lecture.

(2)
De-colonization Politics beyond Punjab and Bengal: The Story of Assam and Tripura

Binayak Dutta

"I began to realize that partition was not, even in my family, a closed chapter of history"

Urvashi Butalia

Introduction: Some Practical Concerns

Partition of colonial India, often referred to as 'the partition of Punjab and Bengal' [i] in academic discourse is probably the most defining moments of Indian life in the twentieth century. While it is common knowledge that it marked the creation of two state-nations, Pakistan and India, its role in disrupting the lives of millions of people in the Indian sub-continent has not received adequate attention. Though figures could probably generate contest, some estimates point out that over a million people lost their lives and over fifteen million people were uprooted from their homes and became displaced. Over the years, though official pronouncements and pedagogy in India continued to glorify Indian nationhood partition continued to be alive in the lives of the people at the subconscious. With the Anti Sikh riots of 1984 and with riots that have broken out ever since scholars like Urvashi Butalia[ii] Gyan Pandey, Paul Brass and Ian Talbot, to name a few have worked through riots and genocides in contemporary India to revive debates on partition of India. Over the years, many more scholars have joined the debate.[iii]

This unease of the Indian state to engage with violent interludes in its history and emphasise the syncretic peaceful life through statist pedagogy led to miscarriage in history, as silence was often misinterpreted as absence. Parts of its history which were seen as undesirable to national interests of 'unity' and 'integrity', [iv] were quickly subverted, a process often sanctioned by those who occupied the highest echelons of power since independence. [v] Even Jawaharlal Nehru, went to the extent of denying the magnitude of post partition violence and displacement in the Eastern borders of India in 1948 on the plea that it would disturb the secular character of the Indian state and cause unprecedented upheaval in India.[vi] Scholars who have committed themselves to the ideological moorings of Nehruvian politics have often found partition stories undesirable and anti-national. Some have even gone to suggest that, "[W]here communal historians can only see the hard lines of the boundaries that separate communities, secular historians have emphasized the porosity and open-endedness of these boundaries"[vii]. Such attitudes were not only un-objective and polemical but also greatly problematic as it created academic ambivalence reflected across the political and academic spectrum [viii] and contributed to subversion of partition history in Indian eastern frontier. The emergence of scholarship on Eastern India has been a recent phenomenon. Despite the recovery of Punjab and Bengal in terms of narratives of partition and post partition displacement, Assam, especially Sylhet still remained an unexplored tract. Though some sporadic scholarship exists on Sylhet partition, they are limited only to its political dimension and singularly characteristic of the absence of popular ongoing experiences that Partition really is. For those communities who had lost their homelands to map making in 1947, the situation continued to be critical. Partition as divorced from transfer of power was a story of anxiety and pain. The sudden transformation of a familiar space into an unfamiliar terrain was traumatic. Partition in colonial Assam was not a simple realignment of cartographic contours but an event that metamorphosed the life of the people who fell on the 'wrong' side of the boundaries.

But most scholars in India and abroad have not taken a serious cognizance of the north-eastern experience and continued to locate partition in Punjab and Bengal only. Thus Assam as the third site of Partition experience suffered from lack of visibility. While recent years have been marked by the publication of a plethora of texts which attempted re-examine the history of partition to articulate the question of victimhood,[ix] they have only succeeded in exposing the fragmentary nature of the statist project of Indian Partition history. Historians have only recently entered this campaign to counter statist historical project by shifting from causal to experiential history through the use of memory in the reconstruction of historical narratives. Historical imagination has thus become integrated with memorial consciousness as the hiatus has enlarged between the nation and the popular and between history and memory. In the words of Pierre Nora, History and Memory–imagination are today in a binary relationship, existing within the State-Nation Discourse in oppositional terms. If the Indian nation tried to homogenize harmony, a million histories rose to tell tales of the uncomfortable reality of discord leading to the transfer of power. Such explosion of popular voice gave a lion's share to their imagination of what historians such as Dipesh Chakraborty calls the discourse of ancestry, partiality and the sacred.

Coloured by their angst against post-colonial Indian state, these counter narratives nurtured a deep seated idea of betrayal, as they often relapsed into tales of their 'glorious past' and their collapse into an uncertain future. A central part of these stories was of partition, and the discourse on the moment of rapture and displacement that was imposed on the lives of the displaced - a moment when they were torn away from their home and *desh* and were uprooted. Pierre Nora's observations that, "History's goal and ambition is not to exult but to annihilate what has in reality taken place"[x] could probably sum up the northeast situation well. As the partition displaced fought against statist attempts at subverting their victimhood, nostalgia became a script on which they wrote their history of partition experiences and memory of migration. Debates within partition history have thrown up varied themes of research. Power play and elite politics, displacement and migration, refugee issues, community conflict and violence, gender rights and violations, trauma and memory studies, etc. have all enriched this debate. But despite its intensity and variety, Assam has been peripheral to Indian Partition debates till recent times In fact, the Assam story, as part of lost eastern experiences in partition history [xi], continue to cast its shadow on the lives and politics of the people in north east India despite the passage of more than six and a half decades since the 'independence of India'. It is sad that even the few scholars who have engaged with partition and post-partition experiences in the east have systematically worked to deny the victimhood of the partition displaced from colonial Assam.[xii] But partition scholarship that seemed to be fixated on Punjab and Bengal for long have now moved beyond these sites to engage new areas. Assam in this sense is an integral part of Indian partition history and an emerging site for partition scholarship. But Assam was not alone. The other site was Tripura. It is important to integrate both these areas into partition scholarship in India to give the story a comprehensive character.

The Case of Assam and Tripura

When the partition proposals came in May-June 1947, the situation in the Assam Congress and the attitude of the Assamese leaders had not undergone any change.* Sylhet, a district of colonial Assam, was predominantly Bangla speaking. Since 1874, it continued as a part of the province of Assam till the partition of 1947, except for a brief period when it was made a part of Eastern Bengal and Assam (1905-1911). When negotiations began to partition the Indians subcontinent, between the Colonial state on the one hand and the Indian National Congress and the Muslim League on the other, to create a 'Pakistan', the Colonial Government in its wisdom, decided to partition Punjab and Bengal and hold a referendum in the Mussalman majority district of Sylhet, in Assam. Thus, despite being part of Assam, which was a non-Mussalman majority province, of the district of Sylhet was drawn into the vortex of partition politics and campaigns. Though the Government of Assam was opposed to be a part of the same group with Bengal in Group C as proposed by the Cabinet Mission, they had no opposition to the partition of Sylhet and its merger with East Bengal.† When Lord Mountbatten announced the decision of the Colonial state to organize a referendum in the district of Sylhet on the 3rd of June the contending parties, the Congress, the Communists and Jamiat-ul-ulama- i- Hind on the one side and the Muslim League and the Jamiat-i-Islami on the other, jumped into the campaign. It was this battle which decided Sylhet's fate after 14th of August 1947. While the first group was in favour of retaining Sylhet within Assam and in India, the second were in favour of detaching Sylhet from Assam, which was predominantly a non-Muslim province and was not part of proposed Pakistan. In view of this peculiar position of Assam and Sylhet, it was decided that the question of partition of Assam and Sylhet's joining Pakistan would be settled by a referendum. Both the sides were allotted symbols that represented their position before the voters, as they cast their vote in the referendum. While the Pro-Partitionists, ie., those who

---

* See the Report of the Governor of Assam, Hydari to Viceroy Mountbatten,dated 5th June, 1947, Acc No.5123, NAI.

† P.Moon, Wavell The Viceroy's Journal, OUP, Delhi,1973,p.233

favoured Sylhet joining Pakistan were allotted the 'AXE', those that opposed partition were given the symbol of the 'HUT'. The Muslim League leadership represented by Abdul Matin Choudhury was originally desirous to have the 'Crecent moon' as their symbol, which was resented by the nationalist Muslims as it "nourished a communal feeling".* Aggressive campaigns accompanied by rhetorical slogans were constructed around these symbols. Rhetoric and slogans of either side rent the air as the days of the referendum drew close. Contrary to most official narratives, the Referendum Campaign had a vibrant cultural dimension reflected in songs, poems and slogans mired in their unique sense of history, culture and even geography. There was little doubt that by 1947, the Pakistan Movement had become predominantly communal, with religion playing an important part in the campaign. As Muslim League leaders arrived in Sylhet from Bengal, they were determined to espouse and establish the case for Pakistan at their campaigns.

Despite being the last, it was not an even battle; contest was keen and the battle lines were clearly drawn. But there was little doubt in minds of people on the field, including colonial official that the Muslim League had an upper hand in this battle.† While the Congress-Communist-Jamiyati volunteers spared no effort at getting their message across to the voters of the Referendum, their message was lost in the hustle-bustle of the campaign on most occasions.‡ Though in perceptions shared by the officials, the demography of the District was overwhelmingly against the Congress led combine; there was no letup in the enthusiasm of the anti-partitionists, who kept their hope that the referendum could be won by them by ensuring the overwhelming turnout of the Hindu voters and the votes of a substantial section of the Mussalmans who had voted in favour of the Congress supporters in the elections of 1946. Despite the efforts of

---

* Governor of Assam's Report to the Viceroy dated 28th June, 1947, Mountbatten Papers, acc no. 5123 NAI

† Annexure C to Referendum Commissioner's report on the Sylhet Referendum in Private Secretary to the Viceroy Papers acc. No. 3471, National Archives of India, New Delhi.

‡ Peter Hardy in his *The Muslims of British India* (p.245) argues that despite building up a viable critique of the Pakistan proposal, the Jamiat ul Ulama i Hind failed to transmit their nuanced arguments to the masses.

the Congress and the Anti Partition campaigners, the referendum resulted in the victory of the Pro Partition group led by the Muslim League. The Referendum was mired in an enormous amount of violence and intimidation. As against the 15000 Muslim League volunteers who had moved into the interiors of the district,* well in time for the Referendum, the Police force was only about 2850. The Referendum report pointed out, "the national guards penetrated into the remotest villages and created panic in the minds of non Muslim villagers"† The administration was extremely apprehensive about the situation and there could be little doubt that the administration was hopelessly unprepared to meet the situation. A report sent to the Viceroy by the Governor in the end of May, pointed out that "present armed strength at disposal of the province will not be sufficient to deal with the situation effectively. This amounts to 2850 armed police including Rail Force and 5 Batalions ie. 62 platoons of Assam Rifles."‡ The report was honest in admitting that the security was inadequate and there was apprehension of "widespread loss of life and destruction of property."§

With many serious short comings Sylhet moved into the Referendum on the 6th and 7th of July, 1947.There was rampant cases of violence and intimidation and the Referendum Commissioner in his report honestly reported that, "there were numerous allegations of intimidation of voters, nearly all of intimidation of Hindu voters by Muslim voters and volunteers, and a few cases of intimidation of Muslim voters…"** Though the official report tried to down play the level of intimidation there was no denial of the same. The Report noted that," No doubt some non violent intimidation by League Muslims had begun but not to the extent claimed by the Hindus."†† While the extent of the violence and intimidation in the Sylhet Referendum became a bone of contention for the contending parties, the results of the referendum came to be notified by the Colonial Government as the Viceroy telegraphed the report of the Referendum

---

* Star Of India, July 8th, 1947, NMML
† Referendum Commissioner's Report , Mountbatten Papers, Acc No. 5123
‡ Mountbatten Papers, Acc No. 5123, NAI
§ Ibid
** Referendum Commissioner's Report, Ibid.
†† Annexure C, Referendum Commissioner's Report, Ibid

Commissioner to the Government at London. But there was no doubt that the magnitude of the violence and intimidation indulged in by the League volunteers necessitated the intervention of the security forces. Firing was resorted to and it caused the death of one League volunteer and the injury of three others among the Leaguers and invited violent retaliation on the Congress workers of the area. An IB Report of the incident sent to the Secretary of State reported," Referendum in Sylhet completed fairly peacefully but fire opened on riotous Moslem crowd in South Sylhet July 7th: one killed three wounded. Leaguers attacked Congress workers near Sylhet twelve injured of whom eight taken to hospital"[*] The firing on the 7th let loose a reign of terror at Sylhet and became the metamorphic moment of Sylhet partition.[†] When the result of the Referendum was made public, it came to light that the difference of votes between the two sides was only 50,000. Sylhet was ready to be put on the dissection table of the Boundary Commission. Both the sides in the contest were apprehensive about the Bengal Boundary Commission. Many Congress leaders both at the level of the province and Central Leadership felt that the Bengal Commission would not to justice to the cause of Assam - the relations between the Bengalis and the Assamese elite being extremely antagonistic in Assam. Nehru raised this apprehension with the Viceroy Lord Mountbatten and demanded that a separate Boundary Commission be constituted for Sylhet.[‡] The Viceroy, on his part, dismissed these apprehensions and rejected the Congress demand for paucity of time.[§] Therefore in the post-Referendum situation, the Sylhet question was placed before the Bengal Boundary Commission with the contending sides making detailed presentations. On the 14th of August, Sylhet except three and a half thanas became a part of East Pakistan. What remained in India became part of the Cachar district of the composite state of Assam in post-colonial India.

Tripura, unlike Assam was a unique case in northeast India as it was a princely state. Compounding the complexity of the Tripura situation

---

*. Political History of Assam, File No. 169, ASA

† See my article on this incident in Binayak Dutta, From History to Lore: An Interesting Anecdote from the Sylhet Referendum,1947, in Janakristi, Vol.3,1-3,2009-10, pp.78-86.

‡ Transfer of Power Vol XII, pp. 167-68.

§ Transfer of Power Vol XII, p. 168

that came as a result of its status was its topographical diversity. Comprising of the hills and the plains, it presents for the partition historians an unprecedented situation. Contrary to claims made in most standard texts, the princely state of Tripura was also partitioned as its territories located within East Bengal were taken away from it with the creation of East Pakistan. The Tripura Kings were the rulers of both the hills and some areas in the plains of eastern Bengal since the fifteenth century. Entire Comilla and parts of Sylhet, Noakhali and Chittagong districts. These plains areas came under the sway of the colonial control in 1761 after an operation led by Lieutenant Mathews on behalf of the Chittagong Council, which was in charge of the operations in Tripura and " thus the English flag was hoisted over the plains of Tripura. Marriot the collector was sent from the Chittagong Council on 15th march to settle and receive the revenues of Tripura…the paying part of Tripura lay on plains and was known as Chakla Roshnabad." A reference to the plains is significant in the context of partition as hills Tripura became the home for a multitude of people who migrated to from their homes in East Bengal since the eve of partition till 1970s.

Tripura was an integral part of the politics of decolonization in the Indian sub-continent. Tripura decided to join the Constituent Assembly. When the Cabinet Mission discussed the fate of the princely States on decolonization, Tripura, as a part of the Chamber of Princes was also a signatory to the resolution which stated that "the princely states shared the general desire in the country for the immediate attainment by India of her full stature and will make every possible contribution towards the settlement of Indian constitutional problem."[xiii] Tripura therefore decided to join and participate in the deliberations of the Constituent Assembly. Accordingly Shri G.S. Guha, who was a minister in the Tripura government, was nominated to the Constituent Assembly. The Maharaja of Tripura was also clear about Tripura joining the Indian union.[xiv] Probably he had already indicated his decision to the Government of India about his decision. In a letter written to G.S. Guha, Dewan B.K. Sen, Advisor to the Ruler of Tripura, dated the 22nd of April, 1947, one can find attached the copy of the format of the Instrument of Accession that was sent to the government of the Princely state of Tripura for the purpose of signature by the government of India. But despite all the political arrangements being relatively certain on the eve of partition, the political situation became extremely fragile with the passing away of Maharaja Bir

Bikram Kishore Manikya on the 17th of May, 1947. His son then was still a minor and therefore a Council of Regency was formed with maharani Kanchan Prava Devi as President and Satyavrata Mukherjee as the Chief Mukherjee as the Chief Minister. The proposals for decolonization had by then almost finalized and the then viceroy, Lord Mountbatten proceeded to London to give the final shape to the decolonization plans. The final declaration about decolonization was made on the 3rd of June, 1947 which announced that the Indian subcontinent would be divided into the two dominions of India and Pakistan and the Princely states of India would be given an option to join either of the dominions. A boundary Commission was also constituted with Sir Cyril Radcliffe as the chairman to demarcate the boundary between India and East Bengal, subsequently forming the core of East Pakistan. Though the Maharani, as the President of the Regency Council signed the Instrument of Accession to the Indian Union on the 13th of August, 1947[xv] the award of the Boundary commission formalized the process of partition and accordingly the estates of Chakla Roshnabad which belonged to the Maharaja of Tripura as a zamindar found itself within East Pakistan. Thus with the partition of India, princely Tripura, along with Punjab, Bengal and Assam also experienced the process of Partition and the people living in the princely state of Tripura were also exposed to the vicissitudes of post partition trauma and displacement. Dependant on the wisdom of the rulers, the Hindu subjects of Chakla Roshnabad "did not submit any memorandum to the Radcliffe Commission for inclusion of the Zamindary into the post partition Tripura though they were an inalienable part of the territorial possessions of the king of Tripura much before the onset of colonial rule. The silence of the Maharani and the silence of the Hindu subjects of the area emboldened the Muslim ryots of the Zamindary to assert their claims for including the areas of Chakla Roshnabad into Pakistan and keep it as such. With the creation of East Pakistan, these subjects led a fast growing movements began to grow in support of the merger of Chakla Roshnabad into Pakistan. Though the Maharani, as the President of Council of Regency declared that the princely state of Tripura had acceded to the Indian Union according to the wishes of the late Maharaja and called upon the people of Chakla Roshnabad to celebrate the 'historic occasion', a few members of the royal family who harboured designs to take the throne, began to organize agitations for the merger of Tripura with East Pakistan.[xvi] These members of the royal family had a close relationship with the leaders of the Anjuman Islamia, which was an ally of the Muslim League. A wave of propaganda was carried on in the areas of Chakla Roshnabad by the Anjuman and the Muslim League National Guard which had a field day in those areas as a result of the patronage it enjoyed from the government of East Pakistan. Intelligence reports observed that

"...the Muslim League National Guards in East Bengal are carrying on open propaganda that Tripura State belongs to East Pakistan and that preparations are being made to invade Tripura." [xvii]

Similar reports were also received from ground based officers of the Tripura government which informed the government about meetings and mobilization campaigns and resolutions in favour of the merger of Tripura with Pakistan and about the threats by the Muslim League supporting ryots to withhold payment of rent if their request of Tripura's merger with Pakistan was not acceded to.

...it is that the Muslim National Guards from East Bengal, Tippera district , have started an agitation against accession of Tripura State to the Indian Union and they may well have raids. Tripura is very feeble and the Raj family is itself divided...[xviii]

But despite these movements which continued in some areas of Eastern Pakistan, the Instrument of Accession signed on the 13th August, 1947 was only reinforced by the support extended to Tripura by the Government of India to overcome the political crisis that arose in the administration during between 1947 and 1949. The signature of the Maharani on the Merger Agreement on the 9th of September, 1949 sealed all doubts about Tripura's fate as part of the Indian union and ensured the transfer of administration from the regency council to the Indian government. Tripura was made a Chief Commissioner's province and Chakla Roshnabad became "the absolute private property" [xix] of the Tripura royal family but in reality lost on transfer to East Pakistan despite the protests by the Hindu subjects and the subordinate zamindars.[xx]

Violent Parting: Violence on Partition and After

Contrary to the experiences of displacement and violence from Punjab and Bengal which has now been officially acknowledged, northeast is an unredeemed terrain. The story of the Punjab has emphasized that violence was endemic to construction of victimhood in India since 1947 and claims for rehabilitation. But the Government of

India began to engender an ambivalent approach towards the East. Contrary to Punjab, displacement in the east was indeed a gradual affair. But like the Punjabis from West Punjab and the Bengalis from East Bengal the people of Sylhet and Tripura too had their experience of violence and violation that forced them to leave their ancestral homes and seek refuge in post-colonial India. Meghna Guha Thakurta' assertion that, 'violence is not always to be measured by external acts of murder loot or abduction. Fear itself could be a physical and psychological violation,"[xxi] seems to hold good to justify their claims of violent experience. Post partition East Pakistan was a fertile ground of opposing emotions. While the first set of emotions were fear, suspicion and hate, the other emotion was one of jubilation, victory celebrations. Violence and depravity found expression in licentious behaviour of League supporters. While the League supporters celebrated on the streets with processions and fireworks and observed 'Thanks giving Day', as a public expression of jubilation,[xxii] at the grassroots, the League supporters shouted provocative slogans and intimidated the minorities. One could again revert to the recordings of one of the Congress political activists from East Pakistan from Sylhet, who observed,[xxiii]

> **"19.7.1947... the law and order situation was worsening. The exuberance of the Muslim League at the creation of Pakistan sounded like threats to the minority community".**

Few of the displaced could understand the intricacies of the transfer of power but most realized its ominous implications. Numerous similar notes and letters indicate the extent of intimidation and harassment that the Hindus which ensured their displacement to India. The launch of a witch hunt to punish the opponents of the Muslim League, by the Muslim League leadership with the active participation of the Muslim League National guards led to almost all the prominent pro-India campaign leaders fleeing East Pakistan. Lawlessness had become the law of the day and the minority civil society lay terrorised and marginalised. The 'concept of honour' was intimately connected to women and hence threatening the women and their honour was the best way to intimidate an already traumatised society, as the men area were engrossed in their worry of "protecting the women folk".[xxiv] Memories of Noakhali swept across minds as the men folk made hurried moves to move to safe locations to save the honour and life of the women in the family, [xxv] as one of my respondents, in course of my interview told me that "we the Hindus felt that something terrible as in Eastern Bengal earlier should not befall us".

Threats and intimidations of the non Muslim minorities were a part of both official and popular programmes and it took various forms. Jogendra Mandal , in his resignation letter addressed to Liaquat Ali Khan specifically refers to the cases of violence against the Hindus, especially the Scheduled Castes who had stayed on at Sylhet after Partition. For instance, the life of the Scheduled Caste Hindus of Habiganj district was brutally insecure. Jogendra Nath Mondol informs us that,

> **Their "women were ravished, their houses raided and properties looted by the police and the local Mussalmans. The military pickets posted in the area not only oppressed these people and took away foodstuff forcibly from Hindu houses but also forced the Hindus to send their womenfolk at night to the camp to satisfy the carnal desire of the military."** [xxvi]

Apart from physical violence, violation would also extend to indiscriminate requisition of Hindu houses at the towns. Dacoity, forced conversions, forced marriages and abductions had become a part of life, especially in the rural areas. Raids and violation of Hindu Houses were also common. While these violations were indulged at the local levels, the largescale requisition of Hindu property, across East Pakistan, left no doubt about official support towards creating discomfort in the lives of urban Hindus and conveying a message to them to leave their homes and hearth. By the close of 1949 and beginning of 1950, the communal situation in East Pakistan was volatile and precarious.

Partition's Post-Script:

When partition finally took place, it physically separated northeast India from the rest of the country save through a small passage of 22 km commonly known as the chicken neck. Assam lost 4,769 square miles of territory and a population of 2,825,282 persons. But the loss of territory was not as significant as was the loss in paddy fields, lime and cement industries and tea gardens of Sylhet. [xxvii] The adverse impact of the transfer of the Sylhet district to East Pakistan was noted in the Census Report of 1951 which observed that, "the far reaching effects of this loss will continue to be felt by Assam as well as India for many years to come." [xxviii] As the situation became critical as the initial trickle of people wanting to migrate to India from East Pakistan became a flood by 1950 as the political atmosphere in East Pakistan became increasingly hostile to the minority communities. The Census Report for Assam, Manipur and Tripura, 1951 observed, that, "the recent influx of Hindu refugees from Pakistan constitutes the biggest migration stream into Assam during the last decade. Following the Noakhali Riots, in October, 1946, and the Partition of India, there has been an almost steady and continuous exodus of the Hindus of Pakistan into Assam and Tripura. According to a census taken in July 1949, there were 24,600 families of displaced persons in Assam or approximately 114,500 persons" [xxix] The migration situation aggravated further as riots broke out in various other parts of East Pakistan in 1949 and 1950.[xxx] The Census Report 1951, observed that, "Soon after the 1949 Refugee Census occurred the incidences of Soneswar and Habiganj, the oppression of the Hajongs in Northern Mymensingh and the atrocities committed on the Santhals in Rajshahi, in East Dinajpur, etc. Then came the gruesome incidents over large areas of East Pakistan in February-March 1950, especially Dacca. These led to the inevitable result, viz, the desertion by hundreds and thousands of Hindus in East Pakistan of their hearths and homes to seek shelter in the neighboring districts of West Bengal and Assam whichever was nearer..."[xxxi] The number of displaced almost touched about half a million people by April, 1950. The grave situation led the Prime Ministers of India and Pakistan to meet in April and come up with an agreement, popularly known as the Nehru - Liaquat Pact. But despite the pact there was no improvement in the situation on the ground and a large number of displaced preferred to settle down in Assam. The Census of 1951 revealed that as many as 274,455 persons were settled in Assam, predominantly in the plains. While 259,946 persons settled in plains areas, only 14,509 persons moved into the hill areas. [xxxii] The political situation in East Pakistan only contributed to the inflow of more Hindu refugees into Assam. As against 273000 refugees in the Census of 1951, the number of refugees returned in 1961 Census was 628000. The influx of refugees contributed to social tension in Assam. Assamese elites feared danger to their economic political and cultural life. Situation became more critical as the Census Superintendent observed in his report of 1961 that "[A]fter independence the Bengali Muslim immigrants into the Assam Valley have, almost to a man returned their mother tongue as Assamese whether they know the language or not". [xxxii] The culture conscious Assamese middle class who initially welcomed these immigrants subsequently began to be wary of them. As these immigrants became vote-banks of the ruling partiy in power, [xxxiv] they became more assertive. In 1962, they flew Pakistani flag with cries of Pakistan Zindabad in villages near Tezpur and Morajar area of the Nagaon district.In the backdrop of the Chinese invasion, the government launched the Prevention of Infiltration from Pakistan Scheme (PIP) to check and deport infiltrators from Assam. Though the government of Shri B.P. Chaliha began to vigorously implement the scheme, cries of harassment by the Jamiat-ul-Ulama-e-Hind and opposition from two of the cabinet ministers of Assam, viz, Fakhruddin Ali Ahmed and Moin-ul-Haque Chaudhury ensured the slow death of the scheme. [xxxv] The birth of Bangladesh on the partition of Pakistan in 1971 made the situation worse. It added the 'Bangladeshi' dimension to the 'foreigners' imbroglio. By late 1970s, the issue of foreigners in electoral rolls had come to become a major issue in Assam politics. The Assam Anti-Foreigners Agitations were launched in 1978 and which came to a close with the signing of the Assam Accord in 1985. The question of presence of foreigners of Bengali origin in Assam had, despite the signing of the Accord never dissipated from Assamese popular imagination, taking the form of anti-Foreigner demonstrations from time to time. The threat to Assam from across its eastern border never really disappeared from popular and administrative debates in north East India and the ghost of partition, Pakistan and Bangladesh came back to haunt the politically sensitive population in Assam who felt that despite the prolonged movement, the foreigners issue had never really been buried for good.

In Tripura, the partition of Tripura and the loss of Chakla Roshnabad only contributed to aggravation of a social and political crisis. One of the pioneering scholars, Tripur Chandra Sen, in his *Tripura in Transition*, pointed out that "[h]ad the zamindary been included in the State of Tripura, the refugee problem would not have been so acute and injurious to the people of this country." [xxxvi] This was similar to the situation in Assam where the loss of Sylhet deprived the Brahmaputra Valley of a buffer zone for absorbing the partition displaced from East Pakistan and exposed the Brahmaputra valley to refugee inflow. Partition also exposed Tripura to an enormous inflow of refugees. As a relatively peaceful state contiguous to East Pakistan and as an area that had welcomed the settlement of Bengalis from East Bengal under the patronage of the Maharajas, Tripura was perceived as a safe haven for the displaced Bengali Hindus from the various districts of East Pakistan. After Partition, Tripura witnessed a spurt in Bengali immigration, especially after 1951. The Census of 1951 indicates a direct relationship between violence in Eastern Pakistan and refugee inflow into Tripura. In 1950-51, the number of refugees who migrated to Tripura was as high as 1, 84,000. With violent anti-minority movements breaking out in East Pakistan in The second high point of refugee inflow was in 1964-65, when Census data recorded the inflow of as many as 1,00,340 persons. Gayatri Bhattacharyya very aptly summed up the post Partition scenario when she recorded that, "[b]efore the partition the progress of settlement of the Bengalees was slow and steady. But after partition especially from 1951there was a sudden spurt in immigration of the minority community of East Pakistan, now Bangladesh. At times the inflow of displaced persons slowed down but following communal troubles in East Pakistan and introduction of the passport system it again quickened. Today the displaced persons far outnumber the Tribal population. [xxxvii]

In Lieu of a Conclusion:

Despite the passage of more than six decades since the transfer of power, partition continues to affect the lives of the people in northeast India. Over years, the unresolved boundary question in north east India and the continuous acrimony over the legality of migration across the created state-nation boundaries has become a pointer to the assertion that partition is not an event but a process which is far from its closure. Though the impact of partition, 1947 persists on the lives of the land and the people of India, there are few attempts to negotiate with it. Probably official apathy and antagonism aggravated by violations and violence faced by the Bengali Hindus in the Brahmaputra Valley at the grassroots, since 1947 itself, led to the adoption of denial of partition experience among the Bengali Hindus as a survival technique. However it is sad that Political expediency and short term strategies often, contributed to 'memo side' and resulted in the loss of thousand testimonies, through the death of witness/participants of Sylhet referendum or on their senility on age. Though some attempts have been made for an academic engagement with it in recent years, these have been far from adequate and lack a comprehensive character. We can only conclude by emphasising that the partition story in northeast India is a complex story far from the possibility of a definitive conclusion. Here, "partition is a living history...yet to be discovered which we are still only beginning to remember."[xxxviii]

Notes and References:

1. Brendan O'Leary, Analysing Partition: Definition, ClassificationAnd Explanation, Working Paper 27, Queen's University, Belfast, 2006, p.6.
2. The Other Side of Silence Voices from the Partition of India, 2000
3. See works of scholars like, Anita Inder Singh, Veena Das, Madhav Godbole, Stanley Wolpert, Patricia Gossman, Pradip Dutta, Suranjan Das and Ashutosh Varshney, to name a few
4. N. Bhattacharyaa, Predicaments of Secular Histories, Public Culture Vol. 20, No. 1
5. See the debates on writing History in India in Krishna Kumar, Prejudice and Pride, R. C. Majumdar, History of the Freedom Movement, Vol. I & III
6. G. Parthasarathi (ed) Letters to Chief Ministers, Vol.1, p. 225
7. Neeladri Bhattacharyaa, *Predicaments of Secular Histories*, Public Culture, Vol. 20, No. 1
8. Ashoka Gupta, East is East,West is West, Seminar, No.510, 2002.
9. Anita Inder Singh, Partition of India, Stanley Wolpert, Shameful Flight(2006), Madhav Godbole, The Holocaust of India's Partition,(2006) Bidyut Chakraborty,(2004) The Partition of Bengal and Assam, to name a few.
10. Between Memory and History, Representations 26: Spring 1989.
11. Renuka Roy ,*MY REMINISCENCES* p.141
12. Anindita Dasgupta, (2001), Denial and resistance: Sylhet Partition 'Refugees' in Assam, Contemporary South Asia, 10:3, 343-360, at p. 345, p. 252.
13. M. Chakravarti, 'Documentation of the process of Integration of princely Tripura with the Indian Union' in S.Nag, T. Gurung and

A. Choudhury, *Making of The Indian Union*, Akansha Publishing house, new Delhi, 2007, p.316.

14. S.Nag et al., *Ibid*, Making of The Indian Union, p. 317.
15. S.P De, Illegal Migrations and the North East, p. 106 .
16. S.Nag, T. Gurung and A. Choudhury, Making of The Indian Union, p.316
17. M. Chakravarti, 'Documentation of the process of Integration of princely Tripura with the Indian Union' in S.Nag, T. Gurung and A. Choudhury, *Making of The Indian Union*, Akansha Publishing house, New Delhi, 2007, p.319.
18. R.K. De, 'Merger and Princely Tripura's Political Transition:1947-1949' in S.Nag, T. Gurung and A. Choudhury, *Making of The Indian Union*, Akansha Publishing house, New Delhi, 2007, p.348.
19. M. Chakravarti, 'Documentation of the process of Integration of princely Tripura with the Indian Union' in S.Nag, T. Gurung and A. Choudhury, *Making of The Indian Union*, Akansha Publishing house, New Delhi, 2007, p.321.
20. R.K. De, 'Merger and Princely Tripura's Political Transition:1947-1949' in S.Nag, T. Gurung and A. Choudhury, *Making of The Indian Union*, Akansha Publishing house, New Delhi, 2007, p.351.
21. Meghna Guha Thakurta, Meghna Guha Thakurta, *Uprooted and Divided*, Seminar, No.510, February, 2002.
22. Star of India, July 16th & 18th, NAI
23. Diary of Suhasini Das in Jashodhara Bachi, et. al. (ed), Trauma & Triumph, p.169.
24. Suhasini Das, opcit.
25. My interface with Shri. Phani Bhushan Bhattacharjee who now resides in Shillong. Dt. 12.03.05
26. Para 13 of Jogendra Nath Mandal's resignation letter sent to Liaquat Ali Khan, as Appendix IV of the Jurist Commission Enquiry Report, p. 360.
27. Census of India, 1951, Vol.XII, Part I-A, pp. 2-3.
28. Ibid, p. 3.

29. Census of India, 1951, Vol.XII, Part I-A, p.356-57.
30. Binayak Dutta, Violent Parting: Recovering the History of Violence in Sylhet on Partition and After.(1947-50) in *The Heritage*, Vol-IV, Issue-1, 2013, pp20-36.
31. Census of India, 1951, Vol.XII, Part I-A, p.356-57.
32. Ibid.
33. Census of India 1961, Vol III, Assam Part I-A, p.204.
34. Nirode K. Barooah, Gopinath Bordoloi, 'The Assam Problem' and Nehru's Centre, Bhabani Print and Publications, Guwahati, 2010, p.393.
35. B.K.Nehru, Nice Guys Finish Second Memoirs, Penguin Books, Delhi, 1997(2012) Rep.pp.542-43.
36. Chandra Sen, *Tripura in Transition*, Times Press, Agartala, 1970, p. 7.
37. Gayatri Bhattacharyya, Refugee Rehabilitation and its Impact on Tripura's Economy, Omsons Publication, New Delhi, 1988, p.5.
38. Binayak Dutta, Recovering Sylhet, Himal SouthAsian, 22nd November, 2012

(3)
Locating the Khasi and Jaintia people in Partition Scholarship

Faith Elwin Kharbuli

Despite the passage of more than six and a half decades of the scholarship that the Partition of India generates, it still remains diverse and contested. The entire deliberation on Partition has mainly focused and been dominated by the experiences of the Punjab and Bengal. In more recent times, Assam has crept in as a third site of Partition and its unique experience has been brought into the public domain. Against this background, the hill area of northeast India has been one of the most unexplored areas. Although, most of the hill areas of India were never direct participants, the Partition of 1947 has affected and changed the lives of the people. As a whole northeast India has remained largely alienated from the rest of the country and focus on the partition experiences of these people is lacking and can be counted on the fingers of one's hand. Most of these studies have focused on Partition as part of either migration studies or as an event of 1947. However, one needs to go beyond that and view partition as a process also in order to have a better understanding and clearer picture of how the Partition of 1947 changed the lives and still is affecting the lives of the people in northeast India. Though Partition and its consequences including experiences have an overwhelming influence on contemporary times in the field of politics, culture and economy, there is a need to look into the history of Partition in the hill areas of northeast India to understand the significance of East Pakistan for the people of these regions.

The historiography of Partition has undergone a lot of change. In the pre-1947 period debates were carried on by activist who began to polemically engage with the idea of the Partition of the subcontinent. With Partition having taken place on the 15th of August, Partition became integrated with Nationalist assertions of either countries- India or Pakistan. A third party that has engaged with the historical enquiry of Partition were the Imperialist historians and the colonial officials, who were themselves equal participants in the politics and decisions related to the Partition of India. In the late 1950's and 1960's the publication of memoirs, diaries, biographies by political activists added to Partition scholarship and this has spurred historians to ask new questions and look back with a new and fresh perspective on the history of the Partition of India. Of late, historians have been using non-traditional sources such as popular fiction to shed light on the experiences of ordinary people whose lives were thrown into the turmoil by the partition of 1947. Consequently, the historical research on the Partition of India has emerged richer out of this ongoing process.

A major research gap in the study of partition is the lack of engagement with northeast India. Though there are a number of publications which study Partition of India, northeast India has never been a part of the same. Though most of such references are fragmentary, most of these researchers have only attempted to cover the Valleys- Brahmaputra and the Barak-Surma valley in their attempt at writing northeast India into partition histories of India. The hills of northeast India have not received singular focus so far. Some works which make a passing reference to the same, limit their focus to only the economic impact of Partition and huge waves of migration, that accompanied it and not beyond, as such it only points to the fragmentary nature of this investigation. Partition of northeast India and its impact therefore remains a research gap which leaves scope for further debates and justifies a detailed study on it.

The purpose of this paper is to focus and locate the partition experiences of the Khasi and Jaintia people of northeast India, in order to understand the complexity, diversity, mentality, identity and multiple experiences if the lives of the Khasi and Jaintia people, whose voices have for so long been hidden and is striving to be heard. The little research that has been initiated on the Khasi and Jaintia hills have mainly focused on the process of decolonization, the disruption of the economy and inflow of refugees. As such the question on what Partition meant for the people of this region remains to be an enigma.

Northeast India is composed of multifarious communities and tribes, each distinct and different from the other despite their geographical contiguity. Many of them are so small in area and population that they tend to be ignored. The dawn of Independence awakened these diverse minorities from a sleep induced in them by the lullaby of the *Raj*, which kept them isolated, however, 15th August 1947 saw these hill come within India. Partition and Independence for the hill people of northeast India was influenced by the geographical location of the region and its ethnic composition. To their east was Burma, separated from British India in 1935 and promised independence; to their south were the Muslim dominated districts of Bengal which would later become part of East Pakistan, and to their north lay Tibet and China. This setting was also to determine their attitude towards Burma, Pakistan and India within which their future lay.[1] The administrative history of the hill tribes immediately preceding the events of 1947 further determined their response to partition and independence.

In the days of the *Raj* there were twenty-five Khasi states. The British categorized them by the Government of India Act 1935 as either Excluded Area under the executive control of the Assam Governor or Partially Excluded Area under the control of the Governor and subject to ministerial administration, but the governor had an overriding power when it came to exercising his discretion. No act of the Assam or Indian legislatures could apply to these two hill divisions unless the Governor in his discretion so directed. He could make regulations for the hill districts which had the force of law. The administration of these hills was his responsibility. The politics of the Indian National Congress and the Muslim League parties of the Assam Legislature had no effect in these hills. It is interesting to note that on the 21st of June 1945, Mr. MacDonald Kongor, the General Secretary of the Central Organization of the Assam Tribes was requested by the Khasi and Jaintia people to communicate in a letter addressed to lord Wavell, stating that the tribals were gravely concerned as certain ex British officials attempted to convert the hill districts of Assam into a separate political zone. The hill tribes believed that this would bound to weaken the position of the hill tribes and retard their progressive growth.[2]

With independence in the offering in July 1947, as agreement was reached between the first governor of Assam- Akbar Hydari and the Indian Dominion on the one hand and the twenty-five Khasi states(nominally under the administration of their chiefs- *Syiems, Lyngdohs and Sirdars* or *Wahadadars*). The Khasi states legally regained their full sovereignty by virtue of the Indian Independence Act. According to the Standstill Agreement they stipulated with the Dominion of India that only matters relating to Defence, Currency and Foreign Affairs would be looked after on their behalf by the latter[3] for a period of two years or until new or modified would be arrived at. In trying to get the Khasi states to sign the Instrument of Accession proved to be a task for the governor. Initially, twenty chiefs signed the Instrument of Accession at the governor's residence on 15th December 1947, and finally in the early months of 1948 by the use of force and tact, the remaining five chiefs signed the Instrument of Accession.

The Weight of Partition for the Khasi and Jaintia people

When Partition finally took place in 1947, for the Khasi and Jaintia people the immediate result of it was the virtual blockage of the economy. During the pre-colonial and colonial period, the people had frequent and direct trade relations with the people of the Sylhet District. Although, occasional raids and skirmishes took place between the tribes of the hills and the plainsmen, commercial interaction between the two was strong and regular. Before the Partition days, the main market for the produce of the Khasi and Jaintia Hills was in the district of Sylhet skirting their southern border. The presence of road and river networks encouraged and boosted trade relations between the Khasi and Jaintia people and the people of the plains. There were road connections between Shillong and Sylhet since 1933 that passed through Dawki, the main market centre in the *War* border area, connected Sylhet, the centre of the Surma valley at that time, with Shillong. This road also connected Dawki with Sylhet and Shillong, the capital of Assam province, and Guwahati, the key city of the Brahmaputra valley.[4] Thus, through this road, the people could easily transport their goods and other agricultural produce to the markets. The agricultural produce of the people of the hills was in great demand, helping them tremendously find suitable markets in the plains. In exchange the people from the hills bought from the markets in the plains essential commodities such as fish, rice and other items which were not easily available in the hills. Before Partition, these items were in great demand. With Partition, Pakistan embarked on a virtual economic blockage of the Khasi hills. Movement of goods between the Khasi and

Jaintia hills and Sylhet was discouraged and the Khasis and Jaintias found themselves without a market for their produce. The object of the exercise was to put pressure on the Khasis and Jaintias and create among them a feeling that they would be better off in Pakistan. The hills people of the Khasi and Jaintia hills were driven to a state of near panic. As most of their goods were perishable and road communications were blocked, the only means of disposing of their produce would be if it could be airlifted directly from the locality to the Calcutta market.[5] India's Partition altered the social and economic lives of the Khasi and Jaintia people. It crippled the traditional links that the Khasi and Jaintia people had with the East Pakistani district of Sylhet. It also disrupted and isolated the region, sealing both land and river routes for commerce and trade, cutting access to traditional markets. In such situations, the Khasi and Jaintia people faced severe hardships such as starvation due to food-shortage; break down of commerce, lack of resources, high unemployment where many people were compelled to leave their homes in search of new lands for cultivation, which was completely alien to them. The economic life of the Khasi and Jaintia people came to a complete standstill and this proved to be a thorn for the economic growth and progress of the state. It is interesting to note that before the Partition of 1947, road side-stalls started emerging. However, on the 6th of August 1947, Rai Bahadur H. Blah, the Additional Deputy of the Khasi and Jaintia Hills, requested the Secretary of the Government of Assam to levy a tax on road side stalls. According to the Shillong Municipal Board, road side-stalls were defined as any shed which is not a dwelling house but used for sale of sundry goods standing over or along any public drain or any land by the side of any road within fifteen feet from the toe of the road. As a result, the Municipal Board imposed such a fee with the sanction of the Provincial Government under section 59(1)(c) of the Assam Municipal Act, 1923, these stalls were required to pay a tax of Rs six per annum. The Partition's consequences was not only in the disruption of the economy of the state; it was also the huge waves of refugees from East Pakistan. This migration brought about a drastic change in demography and also altered the social and economic life of the people. In Shillong, in the Khasi Hill district where about 66 acres of land was requisitioned by thr Government of Assam in two blocks of Bhagyakul estate and Umpling village for the settlement of 351 families, tribal, non- tribal relations deteriorated as the non-tribals came to be perceived as 'Dkhars' or 'foreigners' for the first time. Inclusion of non-tribals in the District Council under the 6th Schedule of the Indian Constitution led to staging of black flag demonstrations on 27th June, 1952 at Shillong.[6] The influx of refugees in the state reached unprecedented heights during the middle of May 1971. Refugee camps were opened at *Pynursla, Dawki, Balat* and other places in the Khasi and Jaintia hills. Each camp was proposed to accommodate minimum 5,000 and maximum 50,000 people. Relief measures in the shape of transport, building, medicines, food-stuffs and other facilities were accelerated to enable the Government to cope with this complex exigency. However, many were of the opinion that the approach to this problem should be on humanitarian grounds, although the State had already been pressed with many problems like population pressure, employment and others. The Union Government had already committed to extend help to those states which shared in shouldering this difficulty but the State Government was also bisected with problems such as shortage of medical and technical personnel. The situation had also necessitated Meghalaya to raise a special force of Police. The sudden influx of thousands of people into the state where the services were already stretched to their limits was not a welcome event. The Khasi and Jaintia people were unprepared and unequipped to deal with the growing number of migrants. An attempt to prevent continued migrations was made by the Tribal Youth Welfare Association and the *Ka Synjuk lang ki Rangbah Shnong* comprising of elders from the towns of Shillong, Nongthymmai and Mawlai. They organized a *hartal* on the 9th of June, 1971, in order to express their desire to discourage the migration of people from East Pakistan to the State as they felt that the tribal population was comparatively of static growth and too weak to resist large migration inflow. The Government of Assam issued necessary instructions for the proper registration of the refugees from Shillong with the help of the localities and wards in Shillong by organizing teams of volunteers to undertake the responsibility. The migration situation also tightened the Government's position with problems such as the mountain terrain, difficult water supply, absence of proper means of transportation and shortage of funds It was also pointed out that Meghalaya being a sensitive area, that its economy had deteriorated since partition, had not recovered from the strains, was aggravated by these influxes, and the roads were unfavourable to meet transit points. Such measures to accommodate more refugees would jeopardise the conditions of the infant state. Such crowded conditions led to an increased spread of diseases, made worse by the scarcity of water. An extract from the *Statesman* (Calcutta) dated August 2, 1971 revealed that 'The influx of over 2, 50,000 refugees has more than doubled the population of the border area. Prices had risen and destruction of jungle wealth and vegetation had led to local resentment and health hazards'. Towards November 1971, the population of refugees accommodated in the state almost shot up to 7, 00,000.[7] The Partition of 1947, which led to a destabilized economy and extended period of migration ebbed and flowed over several decades, which brought about social and economic repercussions, which faced the average Khasi and Jaintia people.

Reconciling Partition: The Khasi and Jaintia Experience

Towards the end of the twentieth century, the focus of scholars shifted from the national to the regional level and from politics to society and culture. Now more than ever before writers and researchers are questioning the stereo-types which have dominated the study of Partition. This new historiography of Partition that has developed primarily focused on the experiences of Punjab and Bengal. Brendan O' Leary in a paper 'Analysing partition: Definition, classification and explanation',[8] states that the Partition of India is also called the Partition of Punjab and Bengal, as most of Partition historiography concentrated mainly on these areas. The focus on Punjab and the subsequent accommodation of Bengal in Indian Partition historiography is gradually being challenged by new scholarship. There is a steady realization that there are certain other areas which were affected by Partition but which have not been studied seriously as yet.

Many societies have been shaped in significant yet unique ways by the Partition of 1947. For the Khasi and Jaintia people of northeast India, the experience of partition was different as compared to that in the Punjab and Bengal, where violence, riots, mass-killings has been a common occurrence. Their experiences find little reflection in written history. To try and begin to understand what Partition meant for the Khasi and Jaintia people interviews were carried out to reconstruct the different voices of Partition.

The (L) Rani Shullai[9]- a cheerful, friendly and energetic woman, worked as a teacher in a school at Jowai and travelled from Shillong to Jowai and vice-versa almost every weekend as her family lived in Shillong. For her, the Partition was more of a sad affair not because India was being divided but because her European friends had to leave. She recalls that under the British government she was oblivious to what was happening in the Punjab but was aware of the major riots that took place in Calcutta, as her sister was studying there. According to her, British rule, inspite of their strict laws, treated the Khasi and Jaintia people well, in fact she stated that the women were treated with dignity and respect and it was only with the coming of the Indian Government to power that she became aware of terms such as 'rape' or 'molestation'. She states that while the British were still in control there was not much chaos and felt that they understood that the tribals were different in their thinking, way of life, as compared to the rest of India. She feared that their departure and the coming of the Indian government to power would distress and disrupt their way of living.

George Richmond[10], a humorous and energetic man, was about ten years old when the Partition took place. He recalls that there was a big 'tamasha' at Polo Ground, Shillong, where the hoisting of the Indian flag took place. As he was very young when the partition took place, he recounts that his father and his friends were worried as they were not sure what the Indian government's intention was for the tribals. According to him under the British *Raj*, the women were treated with dignity and lived peaceful lives and were not confined to the four walls of the house. He fondly remembers his aunt having a small vegetable shop, where she supplied vegetables to the Indian Army, under the British rule, who took advantage of her by not paying her, her dues. In a similar manner as the (L) Rani Shullai, he too was clueless about what was happening in the Punjab or Bengal. He remembers that as they were under the British influence, they were taught English history and were oblivious about Indian history.

The (L) Ms. Silverine Swer[11]- a cheerful, warm woman, worked as the Assistant Controller of Rationing, under the Assam Government when the Partition took place. When the British had to leave she felt lost for she feared that the Indian government would come down heavily on the tribals and upset and confuse their way of living. As she had got her degree from the Scottish Church College in Calcutta, she was aware of the riots and mass-killings that took place there. When it came to the question on women, she recalls that the Khasi and Jaintia women never felt threatened for their safety as the British treated them well. Most Khasi women had jobs and families, which was their main priority. According to her the people in northeast India were fortunate as they did not have to endure the horrors that accompanied Partition in the Punjab or Bengal. She recollects that the refugees who came to settle in Shillong lived in harmony and blended well with the Khasi and Jaintia people.

Rose Batthew[12]-dynamic, quick-witted women was a student in college when she first heard that India was finally getting her Independence. For her most Khasis got Independence without understanding the concept of it, where they blindly took part in the celebration at Polo Ground for an Independent India. She was of the similar opinion as the (L) Ms. Rani Shullai and Mr. George Richmond, that under the British rule, she was oblivious to what was happening in the Punjab or Bengal. Similarly, she too feared the outcome of their departure on the tribals. She recalls that under the British rule, women were never harassed, and in a similar manner as the (L) Ms. Rani Shullai she stated that it was only with the coming of the Indian government to power that terms such as 'rape' or 'molestation' were heard of. According to her the people who came from Bengal, Bangladesh and other places had nothing to fear from the Khasis, infact, most of them decided to stay on and started their own businesses.

Partition Scholarship has generally fallen somewhat short in its neglect to accommodate the Khasi and Jaintia hills of northeast India. Although, the people of this region were not direct participants, this event continues to leave a mark on their lives. The Partition for them brought with it a mass exodus of refugees who came from East Pakistan and settled here. These refugees drastically changed and affected the demography of the Khasi and Jaintia state. The Partition of 1947 also paralysed their economic progress and growth. Since Meghalaya became a full-fledged state in 1972, steps have been taken to overcome this crisis. The response of the Khasi and Jaintia people of northeast India towards the British *Raj* is perhaps the other side of the coin as compared to the rest of India. Perhaps for the people interviewed, the departure of the British *Raj* seemed to have instilled a fear that the Indian Government might disrupt their way of living, for most of them felt that they were different from the people living in the rest of India. The British rule probably infected them with a sense of 'othernesses'. Even after more than sixty years of Independence, Partition continues to impinge the lives of the Khasi and Jaintia people even today. The question of immigration or the border issue have all contributed to keep the discourse of Partition alive.

Although their experiences are probably on the flip-side as compared to Punjab and Bengal, their history finds little reflection in Partition scholarship. Partition needs to be seen through the eyes of these subjects who have rarely appeared or disappeared from history as active subjects. Thus, there is a growing need to accommodate the Khasi and Jaintia Hills in Partition scholarship in order to gain an insight of how the Partition of 1947 changed their lives.

Notes and References:

1. David R. Syiemlieh, ' RESPONSE OF THE NORTH EAST HILL TRIBES OF INDIA TOWARDS PARTITION, INDEPENDENCE AND INTEGRATION: 1946-1950', in *PRATIBHA DEVI MEMORIAL LECTURES 2003*, Department of History, Gauhati university, 2003, p.2
2. Governor's Secretatiat, File No. GS/ MISC.215/45 G.Sectt. Dept.,Meghalaya State Archives, Shillong.
3. R.T.Rymbai, 'Integration of the Khasi States', in *The Shillong Times,* Shillong, 1997.
4. L.S.Gassah, 'Effects of Partition on the Border Markets of Jaintiya Hills', in *Marketing in North East India(Problems of Rural Markets)*, New Delhi, 1984.
5. Nari Rustomji, *Enchanted Frontiers*, Oxford University Press, Delhi, 1973.
6. Binayak Dutta, 'The Past as Present: Partition in Assam politics during independence and beyond', in *Dialogue, Volume-16 No.1.*
7. Hamlet Bareh, *Meghalaya*, Shillong, 1974.
8. Brendan O' Leary, 'Analysing partition: Definition, classification and explanation', in *Political Geography* xx (2007), pp.1-23.
9. My Interface with the (L) Rani Shullai, dt. 12/06/2013 at Shillong.
10. My Interface with Mr. George Richmond, dt. 13/06/2013 at Shillong.
11. My Interface with the (L) Ms. Silverine Swer dt. 14/06/2013 at Shillong.
12. My Interface with Ms. Rose Batthew dt. 14/06/2013 at Shillong.

(4)
Geopolitics behind the Migration in the Northeast India

Atom Sunil Singh

Introduction

In this globalised world, migration is indiscrete for development and the issues on migration are also augmented. Northeast is situated in the very significant location between the two rising superpower and other three more regional powers. Hence, Northeast India is the "Heartland" of Migration. The region, geopolitically and geostrategically, can be assimilated with the "Heartland" of Halford Mackinder which is locatedin the most inaccessible region by sea power in East Europe where the world's largestconflicts known as the world wars were originated. In such a way, is it becauseof the heartland that there are a variety of identity conflicts in Northeast India? Is Northeast India's geopolitical too significant to develop? Is migration a necessaryissue in Northeast India? Migration in the region took place since antique period inthe form of transhumance to present form of migration. Due to the localizationof heartland, migration is ramped up in the region and again, it conducesvarious forms of conflicts in the region. Neither most of the labours migrated in Northeast are coming for betteropportunity of educational facilities, better job opportunities nor Northeast isso develop to attract the migrants. Rather is migration in Northeast largely"perverse migration?" Large numbersof native people, on the other hand, are migrated out of the region as a result ofjeopardous political situation as political refugee, environmental refugee andalso to find out for better security, better opportunities, etc. in the neighbouringstates and aboard. Migration in Northeast is an accumulation of both local and global issues.Whenever, we talk about migration in Northeast India, generally, it comes up with migration issues in Assam and Bangladeshi Muslim migration. It seems hat migration in Northeast India is Assam centric issue andBangladeshi Muslim is the main actor for illegal migration. It will be wrong tosay that the Bengali Muslim migrants are treated as more problematic than theHindu migrants. Illegal migrants are illegal at all regardless on religion. It needsto study the issues on migration not only across border but also migrationwithin state. Migration across the border is hinged upon geopolitical relation between them.Large Bangladeshis were migrated as a political refugee specially duringBangladesh Liberation War of 1971. Indeed, Bangladesh rejects that there isno illegal migration to Northeast at present but consents that there aredisplacement took place from Bangladesh to India (Northeast). Displacementis happened owing to environment hazards including global warming, sea levelrise, etc. and Bangladesh excuses India for the main creditworthy for theenvironmental hazards. In such a dilemma, the geopolitical relations betweenneighbouring countries are very pertinent to solve the migration problem inNortheast. One of the most vulnerable forms of illegal migration in Northeast is chain migration. Once individuals are migrated and later their families' andrelatives, friends are encouraged to migrate to the "destination." It challengesthe identity of "destination" as well as to the "origin" and they are potentialpermanent migrants which tend to generate conflict in the region. It appears that it is analogous to a hate politicsagainst Bangladesh in general and Muslim in particular. This lopsidedness ofthe issue of migration may complicate the geopolitical relation betweenBangladesh and India rather than solving the issue.

Geopolitical Perspectives

It is high time to look on geopolitics behind migration in Northeast India. Northeast India, bordered with China, Mynamar, Bangladesh, Bhutan and Nepal, is located in a very significant geo-strategic area of India. However, the region becomes an "Exclave" region of India. Northeast India is situated between the rising superpower (China) and the other regional powers (Bangladesh, Mayanmar, Nepal and Bhutan). Apart from China being a superpower, it is time to understand very carefully development programmes initiated by China in the Myanmar, Bhutan and Nepal as well as geopolitical relationship between China and Bangladesh. The construction routes in the border areas of Myanmar are almost completed. The Kunming Initiative is one of their geo-strategy to control the region. In spite of being Northeast India is located in the territory of

India; the nature of being an "Exclave" region is the greatest advantage for China than India. Better transport and communication in the border areas of the Northeast India and problem of connectivity within Northeast India make more advantage for China. That is why some part of Arunachal Pradesh is easily under their control at present.

Such large number of population migrated in the region is due to its nature of exclaveness which are not under the control of the India. There is one means to control the illegal migrations in the region. That is to remove the artificial exclave from the region. The mindset of the people is that Bangladesh, China and Myanmar are the only countries to pull off from the "Exclave." However, geopolitically, it is not.

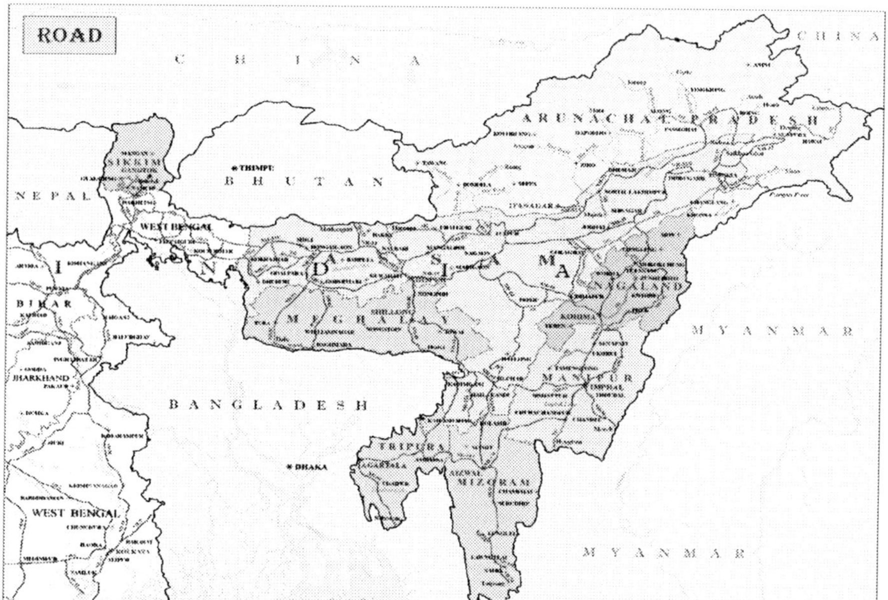

Courtesy: Ministry of Development of North Eastern Region, retrieved from http://www.mdoner.gov.in/node/1260 on 29/01/2015.

Cognitive Distance

Since after India got Independence, there is a paradigm shift in geopolitical scenario in Northeast India and a cognitive distance was formed. Though the Northeast India share same geography with Southeast Asia, the cognitive distance between the regions is very far away.

Similarly, it seems that Delhi is close to Northeast Indian than Dhaka, Bangladesh.

Exclave Region

In general conception, Northeast India is very poor due to many issues, politically, socio-economic condition. One of many issues in the region, the nature of exclaveness is necessary to study because this exclaveness make a heaven for illegal migrations. In short, the movement of illegal migrations is not under the control of the local people. Due to its exclaveness, it becomes under the control by the outside the region. In short, even the economy of the region is not control by India itself but it is under the control of China. Most part of the region is flooded with the Chinese products. Korean wave is also under example. It will be quite surprising the region which is very far from the region, how Korean wave is able to reach in the region, where there is lack of infrastructure and economically every poor. Northeast India is a small region and almost all the region is surrounded by the international boundaries. The region has international bordered with China, Bangladesh, Mayanmar, Nepal and Bhutan. Power control over the region is multiplied within the neighbouring countries rather than controlling by the nation itself. Thus, the external powers are controlling the region and local powers are in dump. In such a way, the region becomes an exclave and the socio-economic as well as political condition of the region becomes worse.

Frontier Zone

Due to the exclaveness and geographical condition of the region, geopolitically, the region becomes a frontier zone between India and Southeast Asia, with India and China, India and Bangladesh, India and Nepal and also India and Bhutan. The geographical condition is one factor for it. The region is dominated by the mountainous terrains. It is one factor advantages for the illegal migration. It is very difficult to control and tract the illegal migrations in the frontier zones. Thus, the illegal migration took various advantages and "perverse migration" is one of the characteristics in Northeast India.

Shatterbelts

Socio-economic and political condition of Northeast India is not so good but in certain conditions the Northeast India is quite better compare to other neighbouring regions. In short, Southeast Asia is located in shatterbelt. Socio-political and economic condition in the neighbouring region of Northeast India is not stable. Myanmar is under the control of military junta for many years as well as poverty are the major factors for the illegal migration in the region. It can be seen both phenomenon of Push and Pull Factors in the region. On the other hand, there are many deprived citizen are inhabited in the border regions. In a 2012 news story, the CSM reported, "The estimated 750,000 Rohingya, one of the most miserable and oppressed minorities in the world, are deeply resentful of their almost complete absence of civil rights in Myanmar. In 1982, the military junta stripped the Rohingya of their Myanmar citizenship, classing them as undocumented immigrants and rendering them stateless." There are evident of illegal migrations to Northeast India. It may be due to better socio-political and economic condition or the close cultural similarity and geographical very close. They are quite happy to stay and mingled with similar culture and tradition in spite of Socio-economic and political of Northeast India is not so good. Such migrations are social migration who are moving somewhere for a better quality of life or to be closer to family or friends or chain migration. Some illegal immigrants seek to live with loved ones, such as a spouse or other family members. Family reunification visas may be applied for by legal residents or naturalized citizens to bring their family members into a destination state legally, but these visas may be limited in number and subject to yearly quotas. This may force their family members to enter illegally to reunify.

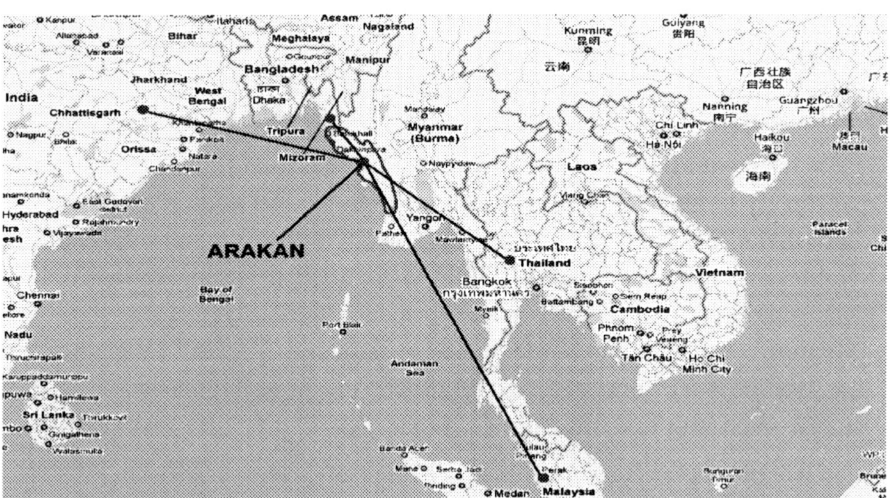

Conclusion

Immigration, including illegal immigration, is overwhelmingly upward, from a poorer to a richer country. Geopolitically, there are many root cause of illegal migrations in Northeast India. For instances, the introduction of free trade agreement between India and Myanmar, India and Bangladesh, India and Nepal, India and Bhutan, India and China etc. Apart from that, Northeast is a big zone of frontier, frontier zone is the heaven for illegal migration. Most illegal migration is happened in the frontier zones. Such illegal migration is also very difficult to check it. In such causes of the illegal migration are due the nature of exclaveness of the region. Exclaveness makes Northeast India, the heartland of migration in India. In another way, the problem of illegal migration is not located to Northeast India. It is problem of whole India. An example can be cited here that a girl from Myanmar who is studying in Bangalore without any valid visa. They are very difficult to distinguish from Northeast India. Many thought that they are from Northeast India. She crossed India from Myanmar through the border of Mizoram and reached Bangalore very easily. She is not only the one who uses the route regularly for studying many metropolitan cities of India. Most of the politicians and academicians seem to be referred to Bangladesh when we talk about illegal migration in India. It will also wrong to highlight that only Bangladeshi migrants are the major problem in Northeast in particular and India in general. The most vulnerable those illegal migrants, who are beyond the control, are very difficult to trace out. All such problems are making due to the formation of the exclaveness in Northeast India and external forces are controlling in the region. The most problem for the illegal migration are not able to be documented. That is why illegal migration is very difficult to check. There is a big discussion on the issues of Bangladeshi illegal migration in Northeast India because the Bangladeshis are clearly visible in Northeast India due to racially and culturally different whereas in others areas such the illegal migrations from China, Nepal, Bhutan and Myanmar are also existed extensively but they are not easily visible because they are very difficult to identify due to similar culturally with the destinations. It can be concluded the geopolitics of migration in Northeast India are due to the unique geopolitical phenomenon of cognitive distance, frontier zone, nature of exclaves and shatterbelts in the neighbouring countries.

Geopolitics of Migration

Cognitive Distance –Exclaves – Frontier – Shatterbelts

References

1. Agnew, John A.; Mamadouh, Virginie; Secor, Anna and Sharp, Joanne (Eds.) (2015), The Wiley Blackwell Companion to Political Geography, Oxford: John Wiley & Sons.
2. Bhaumik, Subir (2007), Insurgencies in India's Northeast: Conflict, Co-option & Change, Working Paper, and East-West Center, Washington.
3. Chapman, Graham P. (2012), The Geopolitics of South Asia: From Early Empires to the Nuclear Age, Burlington: Ashgate Publishing, Ltd.
4. Clad, James and McDonald, Sean M. (Eds.), (2011), The Borderlands of Southeast Asia: Geopolitics, Terrorism, and Globalization, Washington, DC: National Defense University Press.

5. Cohen, Saul Bernard (2003), Geopolitics of the World System, New York: Rowman & Littlefield.
6. Cohen, Saul Bernard (2014), Geopolitics: The Geography of International Relations, New York: Rowman & Littlefield.
7. Dalby, Simon, and Gearóid Ó Tuathail (eds.) (1998), Rethinking Geopolitics, New York: Routledge.
8. Flint, Colin (2012), Introduction to Geopolitics, London: Routledge.
9. Hazarika, Joysankar (1996), Geopolitics of North East India: A Strategical Study, New Delhi: Gyan Publishing House.
10. Jones, Terry-Ann and Mielants, Eric (2015), Mass Migration in the World-system: Past, Present, and Future, Volume 31 of Political economy of the world-system annuals, New York: Routledge.
11. Kumar, Satish (Ed.) (2013), India's National Security: Annual Review 2010, New Delhi: Routledge.
12. O' Hanlon, Michael E. (2015), The Future of Land Warfare, Washington, DC: Brookings Institution Press.
13. Thongkholal Haokip (2010), "India's Northeast Policy: Continuity and Change," Man and Society, Vol. VII, Winter 2010, pp. 86–99.
14. Report (2012), The Other Burma? Conflict, Counter-insurgency and human rights in Northeast India, 11 October 2012.
15. Singh, Atom Sunil (2009), Notorious "Golden Triangle": India's Golden Opportunity? IPCS Artilce, New Delhi: 2806 (11 February 2009).
16. Twentieth Century Population Thinking: A Critical Reader of Primary Sources edited by The Population Knowledge Network (2015), New York: Routledge.

(5)
Non tribe Migration in Tripura during Partition Era

Nirmal Bhadra

Population movement has always been a part of life in South Asia. It has always been a significant phenomenon across south Asia. During British period people of this continent become bonded or contracted labour and the British transported them to several British colonies around the world. Finally at the time of independence and the subsequent partition of the Indian sub continent in 1947 resulted in bloody ethnic, religious and communal conflicts leading to massive movement. Approximately 35 to 40 million people moved across the boundaries of India, Pakistan, Srilanka, Nepal and what is known today Bangladesh[1].

Infect there are some factors which are basically liable for immigration. Mainly the theory of immigration traditionally distinguishes between Push-Factors and Pull-Factors. Push and pull factors are those factors which either forcefully push people into migration or attract them. A push factor is forceful and a factor which results to the country from which a person migrates. It is generally due to some problem which results in migration of the people. A push factor is a flow or distress that drives a person away from a certain place. A pull factor is some-thing concerning the country to which a person migrates. It is generally a benefit that attracts people to a certain place. It can be said that Tripura has witnessed all this types of migration held during the period under discussion. Our ensuing discussion will reveal the fact.

The immigration of non-tribes to the hill state of Tripura, which started in the last phase of the nineteenth century, was gradually increasing from the decade of Partition. There was nothing abnormal in the picture of the non-tribe migration in this State. Table 1 showing population of Tripura, increased in decadal percentage, and sharp decline in the percentage of Tribal population during the period from 1931 to 1951which bear proof of large scale migration of non-tribal people in the state.

Table: 1
Population of Hill Tripura

Year	Total Population	Tribal Population	Non-tribal Population	% of Tribal Growth	% of Non-tribal Growth
1931	3,82,450	2,03,327	1,79,123	18.48	34.85
1941	5,13,010	2,56,991	2,56,019	26.39	42.92
1951	6,39,027	2,37,953	4,01,074	-7.40	59.56
1961	11,42,005	3,60,070	7,81,935	51.39	91.76

Source: Compiled from various Census Reports of India for the relevant years, Department of Census, Government of Tripura

We can clearly understand from the table 1 that the number of non-tribal population was rapidly increased between 1931 and 1951 and this increase was unnatural. It can also be seen from the study of density of population and decadal variation in connection with the State.

Table: 2

Population of Hill Tripura

Year	Total Population	Decadal Variation	%	Density of Population /skm.
1931	3,82,450	78,013	25.63	36
1941	5,13,010	1,30,560	34.14	49
1951	6,39,027	1,26,019	24.56	61
1961	11,42,005	5,02,976	78.71	109

Source: Compiled from various Census Reports of India for the relevant years, Department of Census, Government of Tripura

The table 2 shows that, the decadal variation of Hill Tripura in the year 1931 was 78,013, which through gradual abnormal growth, stood 1,26,019 in 1951 and consecutively 5,02,976 in the year 1961 .Side by side the density of population per square kilometer also too high rather than all Indian %.

Table: 3

Density of population of Hill Tripura

Census Year	All India	Tripura
1931-41	14.2	34.1
1941-51	13.3	25.9
1951-61	21.6	76.9

Source: Compiled from various Census Reports of India for the relevant years, Department of Census, Government of Tripura

Through the different tables given above we can come to one conclusion that the migration of the non-tribal into Hill Tripura and settling down permanently there rapidly increased during the decade under discussion. The factors that were identified as responsible for the non tribal migration into Tripura were.

I). Policies by the British and Communal riots in British Bengal and later on in the East Pakistan.

II). Partition of the country with craterous two independent states – India and Pakistan.

An important and indirect reason behind the immigration of non-tribes in this phase was the dirty hands of the British imperialists. For this they adopted different strategies in different areas of the tribal dominated regions of the North East. In some places they introduced inner-line permit system to isolate a region from the rest of the country. Thus they were able to keep these areas insulated from the surge of National movement. During the extreme part of colonial rule in India the ethnic groups such as *Bodo, Barak, Dimasa*, Garo, *Gurkha, Khasi*, *Manipuri, Mizo, Naga* etc joined the stream of Indian Nationalism. In fact the British wanted to rule over the North East India and exploit the people by keeping them isolated from the rest of the country. Lal Denga described this as rebellion dominated Saga[2].

Hill Tripura was also not an exception to this. The British repeatedly utilized the king of the state for their self interest. During the great recession of the thirties and the initial stage of the Second World War in 1939 some such events took place by the collaboration of the king and the British, as a result of which the British did not slop their economic exploitation even in the days of its sheltered economic condition. The British continued their economic exploitation by keeping the king in good spirit[3]. To get out of this situation the king of Tripura encouraged a lot of non tribal people from the bordering areas of British India to immigrate in to Tripura [4].

Incidentally in 1930, during the year of the great economic recession, the colonial government of India included "The First Bir Company" into the 'A' Class unit of India state force[5]. On the other hand the Maharaja of Tripura was appointed as the honorary colonel of the 5 Bengal Urban Infantry. As a result of this just at the beginning of the Second World War Maharaja Bir Bikram Kishore Manikya declared his support to the British. He also assured to help the British with all the resources of his kingdom in their war effects[6]. Towards the last part of the financial year 1939-40, the king declared the amount of its annual contribution. It was said in this connection:

I). Rs. 30,000 would be given to viceroy's War Fund on behalf of this state.

II). Rs. 15,000 from His Highness to St. John's Ambulance Association

III). Rs. 5000 from the same source to the St, Dunstan's fund.

Besides, a huge fund allocation was announced to increase the strength and capacity of the army of Tripura to help the British in their war effort. Needless to say, this additional fund allocation in the decade of economic recession was not at all good for the economic health of the state. As a measure, the government widely encouraged immigration of the Bengalis from British Bengal, so that they could reclaim un-cultivated land and thereby increase land revenue income.

When India was passing through the period of extreme communal tension the British Government declared its communal award and arranged for reservation of seats in the central and state legislative Assemblies on the basis of caste and religion and this fuelled the fire to the already burning communal flame[7]. Later on, in the new constitutional law of 1935, all communal demands were passed.

Table: 4

The Communal Award in Bengal (1937)

Sl. No.	Constituency	Number of Seats
1.	Muslims	117
2.	Muslim Women	02
3.	General	70
4.	Disperse Class	10
5.	General Women	02
6.	European	11
7.	India Commerce	05
8.	Land Holders	05
9.	Universities	02
10.	European commerce	14
11.	Labor	08
12.	Anglo India	03
13.	Anglo India Women	01

Source: Chatterjee, J., Bengal Divided-Hindu Communalism and Partition, 1932-47, Cambridge University Press, p. 20.

Meanwhile the Hindu Muslim riots which worsened Hindu Muslim relations had their influences on Hill Tripura and near British districts of *Comilla, Noakhali* along with the adjoining districts of Dacca, Mymensingh etc. In fact they influenced the entire East Bengal[8]. As a result the political and other powers of the Hindus naturally decreased. So there was no alternative for the Hindu Bengalis of East Bengal to migrate into the other Hindu populated State of India. Certainly Tripura was a Hindu popularity State during this time and especially the king of Hill Tripura patronized himself for the relief and rehabilitations in fevour of the then displaced Hindus.

The tremendous unrest that was create the communal unrest again resulted a communal riot broke out in Dacca and its neighboring areas during the last part of thirties [9]. In those places the Muslims began to kill minority Hindus in a mass scale and resorted to torture and loot against them. Being placed in such a dangerous situation the Bengali Hindus of the affected areas began to take shelter in Hill Tripura. In the hour of crisis of the Bengali Hindus of East Bengal, Maharaja Bir Bikram Kishore Manikya generously provided relief and rehabilitation. At that time about 15 thousand displaced Hindus were registered. The Maharaja arranged for all possible assistance to these Hindus through his relief and

Rehabilitation programmes[10]. Later on, when arrangements were made for their return to home, no data is available as to how many did actually return. It was written in the District gazetteer of Tripura that this riot of Dacca and Raipur continued up to 1942[11].

Later on with the declaration of Direct Action Day by the Muslim League on 16-08-1946 a widespread riot broke out in the districts of *Tipperah* (now *Comilla*) and in *Noakhali* and *Chandpur* subdivisions. A serious riot broke out in Calcutta in 1942. Leadership of this riot was provided by the non-resident Muslims. But due to a fear of retaliation these non-resident Muslim began to move to East Bengal and made the Hindus and Hindu *Zamindars* their fresh targets. As a result another fresh group of refugees came to Tripura. In this case also the Maharaja, of Tripura undertook relief and rehabilitation work among the refugees. Later on when the riot stopped some of them returned home being assumed by Gandhiji about their safety and security there. But a lot of the Hindus stayed back in Tripura[12]. When a large number of refugees took shelter in the capital, they were being given food, health care etc. by forming a committee.

At that time (1943-46) two things happened simultaneously in British Bengal and hill Tripura to which the push and pull factors for immigration of non-tribes supplemented each other. One of these two matters was the need of the king for huge money for contributing to the war fund of the British, supplying soldiers, war related construction. For this the king needed huge number of agricultural labourers and construction workers[13]. On the other hand severe famine broke out in Bengal in 1943 and there was a tremendous food shortage. The famine took the turn of an epidemic. However there was not much food scarcity in Tripura. The price of chief food item rice was well under control. To utilize this opportunity properly the government of the state adopted the policy of increasing the area of cultivable land and also increased the productivity per unit area of land through its "grow more food" campaign[14]. Needless to say, the huge scheme needed a huge number of plough cultivators for its agricultural component and also a large number of workers for its construction. Both the types of workers were not available in adequate number in Tripura. The penniless people of neighboring British Bengal, who were shattered by famine and epidemic responded to the call of the king of Tripura, started coming to Tripura for a more secure life.

In the meantime, the policy of granting independence to a partitioned India was accepted. This partition of India was done on the theory that the Hindus and Muslims were two separate nations. A commission headed by Sir Radcliff was given the task of demarcating the boundary between the two states. Bengal was divided for second time and the part called West Bengal was made a part of India while the part called East Bengal became a part of Pakistan under the name of East Pakistan. Radcliff Commission was also given the responsibility of determining the fate of *Zamindari* estate of *Chakla Rosanabad* belonging to the king of Tripura. Radcliff gifted *Chakla* to East Pakistan[15]. The decision of Radcliff regarding *Chakla* and partition of Bengal made a radical change in the immigration of the Bengali Hindus. They began to enter into Tripura in a mass scale. The reasons for this were:

i). Before the partition of the country Radcliff identified the nearby districts of Tripura state like Dacca *Chittagong, Noakhali, Tipperah, Maymansingh* etc as Muslim majority districts. As a result of this the Hindus of these districts had to leave East Bengal and take shelter in West Bengal, Tripura and Assam[16].

ii). The British districts, which later on, became a part of East Pakistan had a large number of Hindu population. Although the country was divided in accordance with the pact of partition, the Hindus and Muslims were not transferred on logical basis[17]. The following table shows the percentage of Hindus in the British districts near Tripura.

Table: 5

Percentage of Hindus in the British districts near Tripura

Name of District	% of Hindu
Dacca	24.14
Mymensingh	24.89
Faridpur	35.86
Bakargang	26.42
Tipperah	24.14
Noakhali	21.47
Chittagong Hill Tracts	17.27

Source: Chatterjee, J., Bengal Divided-Hindu Communalism and Partition, 1932-47, Cambridge University Press, p. 245.

iii). Side by side during the partition as per Radcliff commission the total Muslim population of West Bengal was 16%. On the other hand, the Muslim population of East Bengal was 42%[18].

iv). under the provisions of Indian Independence Act of 1947, the *sylhet* district of Assam was awarded to Pakistan. About 50% of the population of this district was non-Muslims[19]. A majority of them had at one time had to migrate to Assam and to Hill Tripura. By 1951, 25,256 people took shelter in Tripura[20].

v). Radcliff commission suggested for the inclusion of *Zamindari* estate of the Maharaja of Tripura, which at one time was a part of the state of hill Tripura, to East Pakistan. As a result the subjects of this area especially the Hindus migrated to Tripura[21].

vi). the only means of communication of Tripura with the rest of the country was through British Bengal. But the birth of East Pakistan encircled the state from three sides. On the other hand, declaration of accession of the state on 9th September, 1949 under the background of Pakistan's conspiracy to grasp Tripura along with other animus signals led to further increase in the rate of immigration of the Hindus from East Pakistan[22].

During the partition about six million Hindus and Sikh refugees took shelter in India. However its rate was not too high in Bengal because. a)-Indian National Congress and Gandhiji advised people not to leave their respective homelands and face the situations by remaining there. b)-Although communal riots broke out in North and North West part of India immediately, after partition of the country Bengal was absolutely calm. Some incidents took place in Calcutta but it adopted the intervention of Gandhiji's. c)-After the constituent Assembly elected Mohammad Ali Jinnah as the President of Pakistan he addressed the people of his country by saying, "You are free, you are free to go to your temples, you are free to go to your mosques or to any other place of worship in this state of Pakistan, you may belong to any religion or caste or creed; that has nothing to do ……we are all citizens and equal citizens of our State[23].

As a result migration of Hindus from Bengal was less due to the partition of the country. Coming to our Hill State of Tripura, among its neighboring districts, the Hindus Muslim relationship was very cordial. This cordial relationship did not suddenly collapse with the partition of the country. But gradually deteriorated in the post independent period and immigration of Hindus continued for a long time.

Yet while searching facts we can notice that due to various factors, such as inclusion of *Chakla* into East Pakistan, separation of the district of *Sylhet* from Assam and making it a part of East Pakistan, partition of Bengal, accession of Tripura with India, communal tension in the various neighboring districts of Tripura a large section of the Hindus entered into Tripura as refugees within the year 1946 to 1951. A related data is given below:

Table: 6

Immigration of Non-Tribal People in Tripura from Bengal and other Places during 1946 to 1951

Year	Bengal	Other Place
1946	3317	
1947	8189	65
1948	9580	26
1949	11612	37
1950	67402	251
1951	184000	03

Source: Dutta, K.P., *Tripurar Itikata*, Kolkata, 1365, (BS), p. 49.

From the table 5 we can see that in 1950-51 a large number of displaced persons suddenly immigrated to Tripura. The most important reason for this was the introduction of Passport-Visa system for traveling across the border of two countries. However the number of immigrations of the Bengali Hindus had been gradually increasing since independence. The communal riots were basically responsible for this. At first after the *Raipur* riot of Dacca in 1946 some people came to Tripura. But later on this rate of refugee influx in Tripura rapidly increased, when widespread riot broke out in *Vairab* and other nearly areas close to the border of Tripura in 1950[24].

Another reason for the rapid increase in the rate of arrival of the refugees was the coming of Pakistani labourers in large numbers into this state. In 1949 when the construction of Assam-Agartala Road started there was a need for a huge number of construction workers in the state. Accordingly a large number of non-tribal labourers were brought from East Pakistan because there were almost no general and construction labourers among the tribal and non tribal population of the state. It was natural that a majority of these labourers settled here permanently[25].

Consequently in ten years between 1941 and 51 large scale immigration of non-tribal people got recorded; while the population of Tripura was 5, 13, 000, it rose to 6, 39, 029. This implies decadal variation of 1, 26,019 representing a growth of 25.02%. This huge growth was a sharp contrast to the all India figure of 13.3%. During this decade a sizeable portion of Hindus of East Bengal came to this state. On the other hand, a large number of Bengali Muslims migrated from this state to East Pakistan.

In the decade following 1950 the immigration of non tribes, i.e. Bengali Hindus increased rapidly. There was a record number of immigration of non-tribal refugees to the hill States of Tripura, whereas the Sikhs and Hindu refugees from West Pakistan migrated to India in almost one flash immediately after the partition of the country. But in case of East Pakistan for various reason the Hindus did not come all at one time immediately after partition. In this phase due to rapid deterioration of communal situation, large number of Bengali Hindus migrated to Assam, Tripura and West Bengal[26].

Accession of Tripura to India in 1949 encouraged the Bengali Hindus of East Pakistan to migrate to Tripura. Besides, at that time the Government of India adopted the policy of all round help and rehabilitation facility to the refugees from Pakisan. The migration of the Bengali Hindus continued to take place due to the expectation of getting relief and rehabilitation facilities. The government stopped refugee registration in India from 1958. Till the end of 1957, as many as 3, 65, 000 displaced persons settled down in Tripura. At that time the Total population of the state was 6, 40 lakhs (1951 census) But including the displaced persons in 1958 the total population of the state was 9, 05, 000, out of which 40% were non-tribe immigrant[27]. The total number of displaced persons that were registered since 1951 was 1, 89, 300. This registration was done up to 1957 and this effort has been made as a part of the partition programme of India.

Table: 7

Migration of non-tribes in Tripura from Bengal and other places during 1951 to 1957.

Year	Number of Families	Number of Persons
1951	6000	23000
1952	16800	80000
1953	800	3200
1954	1500	4700
1955	5100	17500
1956	15600	57700
1957	1000	3600

Source: Statistical Abstract, Govt. of Tripua, 1978, p. 243.

It may be concluded that even after partition, communal peace was not restored in East Pakistan. The Hindus of that country were still nurturing the hope in their hearts that they would not have to leave their *Sonar Bangla*. But by torture, rape, plunder, murder, the Muslims forced the people of the minor community of Hindus to leave their native land. It was seen after the Noakhali riot that many Bengali Hindus wanted to continue to live in their camps. But unfortunately the extremist Muslims always worked against their homeland, for which the distressed and helpless Hindus were not even given the opportunity to lodge complaint with the police. Rather they were repeatedly threatened to be murdered. Consequently the Hindus of East Pakistan had to migrate to India much against the will of their heart.

References:

1. Haque, Md. S., *Migration Trends and Patterns in South Asia and Management Approaches and Initiatives. Bangkok,* 2005. http://www.unescap.org/esid/psis/psis/mulings/s11m/No3/Trends.patterns.pdf, Dated; 6.2.2010
2. Dena, L., Presidential Address, NEIHA 23rd Session, 26th November 2002, pp. 10-13.
3. Sur, H.K., *British Relations with the State Of Tripura 1763-1947,* Agartala, 1986. pp. 166, 167.

4. Gangoli, J.B., *An Economic History of North East India, New Delhi,* 2006.p. 456
5. Chakraborty, M., (Ed), Administration Report of Tripura State, Vol.-III, p. 1399.
6. Chakraborty, M., Vol.-IV, p. 2009.
7. Pahari, G.K., *Bharater Itibritya*, Vol.-II, pp. 408-10
8. Dey, A., *Bangali Boddhijibi O Bichinnatabad*, Kolkata, pp. 333-335.
9. Battacharjee, G., *Op. cit.* p. 12.
10. Chakraborty, M., Vol.-IV, p. 2086.
11. Menon, K.D., Tripura District Gazetteers, 1975. p. 137
12. Menon, K.D., *Op. cit.* p. 137.
13. De, R.K.,(ed) *Report On The Administration Of Tripura State, (1898-99, 1899-1900, 1943-46*), Varanasi, 1997. pp. 61, 63, 64.
14. De, R.K.,*Op. cit.* pp. 119-121
15. Sur, H.K., *Op. cit.* pp. 188, 189.
16. Menon, V.P., *Transfer of Power,* New Delhi, 1967, Re-Print 1998, p. 402.
17. Menon, V.P., *Op. cit.* pp. 435, 402.
18. *Ibid.* p. 402.
19. Deb, R., *Srihatta Parichoy*, Kallayni, 1997, p. 26.
20. Gangoli, J.B., *Economic Problems of the Jhumia of Tripura,* p. 69
21. Sur, H.K., *Op. cit.* pp. 188, 189.
22. Debroy, A., Unpublished pp. 70, 71.
23. Menon, V.P., *Op. cit.* p. 418, 434,440
24. Debroy, A., *Op. cit.* p. 66.
25. *Ibid.* p. 183.
26. Bipan Chandra, (others), *Op. cit.* pp. 101, 102.
27. Gangoli, J.B., *Economic Problems of the Jhumia of Tripura, Op. cit.* p. 69.

(6)
The Impact of Partition of India on Tripura

Pradeep Kumar Deepak

Abstract

This paper makes an attempt to justify the over-all impact of Partition of India on Tripura. The Partition of India had not only changed the geographical landscape of this tiny Princely state, but also changed its political landscape. Due to the British policy of 'Divide and Rule' India attained independence on 15th August, 1947 in the wake of Partition. Really, the partition of India on the basis of religious parameter produced abundant problems of migration in the Princely state of Tripura.

It is observed that like other parts of India, Tripura also witnessed the worst effects of Partition in the form of mass butchery of common people due to common riots, which ultimately led to the outcome of the problem of the refugees. After independence, within a decade or so, a great change came in the demography of Tripura as a result of heavy influx of migrants from East Pakistan due to common violence. The partition of India disrupted the chain of socio- economic relationship that Tripura built up with Colonial Bengal. Thus, it was the worst impact of the Partition that the people of West Pakistan as well as East Pakistan were compelled to be migrated into India in quest for peace and settlement to leave their place of origin and to move towards their 'uncertain home' leaving behind them their all ancestral property and even their personal identity. Before the Partition of India the tribal population of the state formed the majority, but the Partition made them to the level of minority.

This paper also explains in detail about the social, cultural and economic impacts of the Partition of India on Tripura. The Partition of India deprived the state of its chief railheads in East Pakistan so that the state was cut off from the rest of the country and resulted in a huge infrastructural and economic setback for Tripura. As a matter of fact, the Partition of India was a disaster for Tripura.

Keywords: - Partition, Migration, Common riots, Disaster.

Introduction

The Partition of India in 1947 A.D. was one of the most cataclysmic events in the history of the modern world. It was one of several partitions that were carried out in Europe, Asia, Africa and the Middle East since the eighteenth century. Actually, the Partition of India was one of four partitions by Imperial Britain. The British also partitioned Ireland, Palestine and Cyprus on the grounds that different communities could not live together. Religious and ethnic division was not the only reason for the partitions by Britain: the military interests of the United Kingdom partly determined its strategies and tactics during the negotiations that led to all four partitions. We know that the joy of our country's independence from colonial rule in 1947 was tarnished by the violence and brutality of partition. The Partition of British India into the sovereign states of India and Pakistan (with its western and eastern wings) led to many sudden developments. India was ruled by the British on the principle of 'Divide and Rule' and the British India was also partitioned because of the British policy of 'Divide and Rule'. Thousands of precious lives were snuffed out, many others changed dramatically, cities changed, India changed, a new country was born and there was unprecedented genocidal violence and migration.

As a matter of fact, the great upheaval which shook India from one end to the other during a period of about fifteen months commencing with 16 August 1946, was an event of unprecedented magnitude and horror. History has not known a fratricidal war of such dimensions in which human hatred and bestial passion were degraded to the levels witnessed during this dark epoch when religious frenzy, taking the shape of a hideous monster, stalked through cities, towns and villages, taking a toll of half a million innocent lives. History is the evidence of the fact that for over a thousand years, the various communities had lived together in peace and amity. Peace and communal harmony persisted everywhere. Either be the Hindus or Muslims, either be the Sikhs or the people of other communities- all lived in friendly atmosphere and enjoyed the happiness and sorrows of their fellow- beings equally. As per the census of 1941 A.D., United India (British India) had a population of 389 million comprising 255 million Hindus, 92 million Muslims, 6.3 million Christians, 5.6 million Sikhs and a number of smaller communities. There were Muslim majority areas (in the north-east and north-west) and Hindu majority areas, but no part of India was exclusively inhabited by any one community. Everywhere Hindus, Muslims and Sikhs lived together as neighbours.

The impact of Partition on Violence & atrocities

It was the tragic impact of the partition of India that several hundred thousand people were killed and innumerable women raped and abducted. Millions were uprooted, transformed into refugees in alien lands. It is just impossible to arrive at any accurate estimate of casualties: informed and scholarly guesses vary from 200,000 to 500,000 people. Between 1946 and 1951, some 09 million Hindus and Sikhs crossed over India into from Pakistan and about 06 million Muslims went to Pakistan from India. (Anita Inder Singh, 'The Partition of India', N.B.T., New Delhi, 2006, page No-1). In all probability, some 15 million had to move across hastily constructed frontiers separating India and Pakistan. As they stumbled across these 'shadow lines'- the boundaries between the two new states were not officially known until two days after formal independence. They were rendered homeless, having suddenly lost all their immovable property and most of their movable assets, separated from many of their relatives and friends as well, from their houses, fields and fortunes and also from their childhood memories. In this manner, they were stripped of their local and regional cultures and they were forced to begin picking up their life from scratch.

The Impact of Partition in Communal Holocaust

Was this simply a Partition, a more or less orderly constitutional arrangement, an agreed upon division of territories and assets, a sixteen month civil war or a 'Holocaust'? Speaking of the killings, rape, molestation, arson and loot that constituted partition, Contemporary observers and scholars have sometimes used the expression "Holocaust' as well, primarily meaning destruction or slaughter on a mass scale. In a true sense, the term 'Holocaust' captures the gravity of what happened in the sub-continent in 1947, something that the mild term 'Partition' hides. It also helps to focus on why partition, like the Holocaust in Germany, is remembered and referred to in our contemporary concerns so much. Yet, differences between the two events should not be overlooked. In 1947-48, the sub-continent did not witness any state-driven extermination as the case with Nazi Germany where various modern techniques of control and organisation had been used. The 'ethnic cleansing' that characterised the partition of India was carried out by self-styled representatives of religious communities rather than by state agencies.

We have seen how a hundred years of revivalist tendencies, sixty years of economic rivalry, fostered and promoted by the insidious British policy of 'divide and rule', and a generation of separate electorates created and steadily widened the gulf between the Muslims and non-Muslims of India. The efforts of the Congress to bridge this gulf had some measure of success and a final break was avoided for a considerable time. Failure, however, was inevitable and came partly because the British rulers always had the whip-hand and partly because the remedies applied were inadequate and not indicated by a correct diagnosis of the malady. It is in this context that the more recent events of the period 1937-46 must be studied.

The Impact of the Partition on the Infrastructure of Tripura

The partition of India in 1947 had an enormous effect on the process of social and economic development of the State. The partition deprived the state of its chef railheads in the west, south and north which fell in East Pakistan so that the state was effectively cut off from the rest of the country but for a tenuous road link. This resulted in a huge infrastructural and economic setback for Tripura. The state's resources came under severe strain due to a heavy influx of refugees into the state from East Pakistan right from the early fifties. This created tremendous pressure on an already over-burdened land with little infrastructural facilities and insignificant supporting industries. Even after the upheaval of partition, migration from East Pakistan tended to swell the populations of Tripura, especially during and immediately after the Bangladesh War. This tended to add to the population pressure on the State.

The power of stereotypes in the minds of Hindus and Muslims

India haters in Pakistan and Pakistan-haters in India are both products of Partition. At times, some people mistakenly believe that the localities of Indian Muslims lie with Pakistan. The stereotype of extra-territorial, pan-Islamic loyalties comes fused with other highly objectionable ideas: Muslims are cruel, bigoted, unclean, descendants of invaders, while Hindus are kind, liberal, pure, children of the invaded. The journalist R.M. Murphy has shown that similar stereotypes proliferate in Pakistan. According to him, some Pakistanis feel that Muslims are fair, brave, monotheists and meat-eaters, while Hindus are dark, cowardly, polytheists and vegetarian. Some of these stereotypes pre-date Partition but there is no doubt that they were immensely strengthened because of 1947. Every myth in these constructions has been systematically critiqued by historians. But in both countries voices of hatred do not mellow.

Partition generated memories, hatreds, stereotypes and identities that still continue to shape the history of the people on both sides of the border. These hatreds have manifested themselves during inter-community conflicts, and communal clashes in turn have kept alive the memories of past violence. Stories of Partition violence are recounted by communal groups to deepen the divide between communities: creating in people's minds feelings of suspicion and distrust, consolidating the power of communal stereotypes, creating the deeply problematic notion that Hindus, Sikhs and Muslims are communities with sharply defined boundaries, and fundamentally opposed interests. The relationship between Pakistan and India has been profoundly shaped by this legacy of Partition. Perceptions of communities on both sides have been structured by the conflicting memories of those momentous times.

The impact of Partition on migration

After independence, the demographic picture of the state has changed. Since 1947 successive waves of influx of refugees from erstwhile East Pakistan gave a phenomenal rise in population in Tripura which reversed the tribal-non-tribal ratio of population in the State. The following table shows the changes in tribal population figures in relation to total population in the State since 1931.

Table-

Census year	Total population	Tribal population	Percentage of Tribal population
1931	3,82,450	1,92,249	50.26
1941	5,13,010	2,56,991	50.09
1951	6,45,707	2,37,953	36.85
1961	11,42,005	3,60,070	31.53
1971	15,56,342	4,50,544	28.95
1981	20,53,058	5,83,920	28.44
1991	27,57,205	8,53,345	30.95

From the above table, it is seen that the number of tribal population in the State decreased in 1951 from what it was in 1941. The reason may be the migration of many Reang families from Tripura to the Mizo Hills due to tremendous repressions of the ruling authority in the wake of the Reang-uprising in 1942-43. It is also further seen that the tribals were the majority in the State up to 1941. Thereafter, the percentage of tribal population registered a gradual down-ward trend from the census year of 1951.

The tribals are known for their catholicity of temperament and hospitality by nature. They, in fact, received the outsiders all along ungrudgingly. Tripura had, thus, emerged with a new socio-economic and political structure with people of motley character.

Among the people of Tripura, the tribals and the Bengalees are the two dominant communities living together from time immemorial. Tripura is closely related to Bengal. The contact between the two lands had been established long ago. The Zamindari Estate of the Tripura Maharajas, inhabited by the Bengalees-Hindus and Muslims, was just close to Tripura State. The people of the Zamindari Estate frequented Tripura State regularly.

It is also historically inaccurate to suggest that the decision to partition the province of Bengal along religious-demographic lines actually involved the participation of masses of people. As far as opinion within Bengal was concerned, the relevant decisions were made by members of the Bengal Assembly, elected on the basis of a very restricted suffrage. There was some campaigning on the issue of partition in 1947, both in favour and against, but by the standards of mass agitation of the time they involved small numbers of people. In fact, the evidence from the period suggests that the incidents that most strongly framed all discussion on the subject were in fact the communal killings in Calcutta in august 1946 and those in Noakhali a few weeks later.

These were perhaps the most powerful 'mass actions', organised by Hindu and Muslim communalists, contributing to partition. Some people understood the unprecedented communal violence of 1946 as the cataclysmic sign of a general transition of power, with its associated feelings of anxiety as well as of anticipation. Others took it to mean that Pakistan, whatever its precise legal or communal form, was inevitable.

Reading through the political debates that took place in Bengal from August 1946 to August 1947, one cannot but sense that positions were being taken on the assumption that Pakistan was in the offing, that there was nothing left to be done to change that eventuality and that all that remained was to strike the best bargain for each sectional interests, be it the majority community, minority community.

Tripura and the Partition of India

History of Tripura witnessed several changes in the first half of the nineteenth century. The sudden and untimely demise of Maharaja Bir Bikram Kishore Manikya on 17 May 1947 at the age of thirty-nine was followed by appointed of the minor Maharaja Kirit Bikram Kishore Deb Barman as the ruler of the State and the zamindari according to the conventions of the royal family. Later, as per decision of Government of India a Council of Regency headed by Maharani Kanchan Prabha Debi (widow of the late Maharaja) was formed to run administration of the state. On 8 August 1947, the council took over the administration and just after seven days, the British rulers transferred powers to India on august, 1947, after partitioning the country into India and Pakistan. The administration of the Regent Maharani was confronted with three problems of :(1) protecting the frontier territory (chaklaroshnabad); (2) refugee rehabilitation and (3) tribal land protection.

Efforts to save Tripura from isolation

Even before independence of India, the Maharani, as astute lady could realise what a troublesome situation was in store for her if India was partitioned. Therefore, before partition she put her claim over those areas which were once within the principality of Tripura's Maharaja in order to maintain Tripura's bigger entity and save it from isolation.
B. K. Deb Burman, Chief Minister of the State, was sent to Delhi to place the demand before the Central authority. The Chief Minister held parleys with the high dignitaries including Sardar Patel.

The central government appointed the 'Bengal Boundary Commission'(Red Cliff Commission) to demarcate the boundary of East Pakistan with India. The Award of the Boundary Commission put Tripura State into troubles. It cut off the state from the mainland of the country. Even before India's Independence the Maharani could have realized what a troublesome situation was in store for her, if India was partitioned. Therefore, before partition she put her claim over those areas which were once within the principality of Tripura's Maharaja in order to maintain Tripura's bigger entity and save it from isolation.

In a telegram from Tripura durbar to Sardar Patel on 11july 1947 it was stated, "A compact area comprising Tripura state, Chittagong Hill Tracts, Lushai and Khasi hills together with Hindu majority areas in Noakhali, Tippera and Sylhet districts contiguous to Tripura state under the Indian union absolutely needed to be formed on political strategical and economic grounds to save from isolation Tripura state which has already joined Indian union. We are represented to Bengal boundary commission. Earnestly soliciting your help."

The maharani also personally called on Sardar Patel in July, 1947 to make him acquainted with the precarious position of her State and requested him to take necessary steps to save Tripura from isolation. Unfortunately the central leadership did not see to the just demands of the state which had lost its ruler a few months back. They only looked into the matter of finding out a corridor so as to establish a communication link between Tripura and the territory of the Indian union. The Central leadership did not consider the legitimate demands of the Regent

Maharani for getting back Chittagong Hill Tracts and Chaklaroshanabad which were once parts of Tripura.

The Impact of Partition on Demography of Tripura

Bu unfortunately it was not done and the state had to sustain a great loss as Tripura is bordered with Chittagong, Noakhali, Comilla & Sylhet. The communal riots at these places resulted in huge influx of migrants from these places to Tripura. As a result, the demography of the state changed completely, which was noticeable in growing percentage of non-tribals with the passage of time. In 1951 A.D., the population of Tripura was 6, 45,707 whereas it increased to 11, 42,005 in 1961 A.D. This abnormal growth of 78.71% was because of vthe forceful Immigration of Bengali Hindus from Chaklaroshabad and Chittagong Hill Tracts.

We observe that after getting independence, a massive change in the demography of Tripura can be witnessed as result of heavy influx of migrants from East Pakistan due to communal violence. It is a universal fact that since independence the tribal people in Tripura were confronted with a new challenge of safeguarding their tribal identity in the state and a great fear of the level of the minority community. As a result, some ethno-centric tribal organisation had been formed for protecting tribal population and their interests in the region.

Conclusion

In the light of above- statements, we can say with surety that the Partition of India led a lot of communal problems in the peaceful co-existence of the people of India and Pakistan. The British India felt easy prey to the communal violence and a lot of atrocities were faced by the people of India and Pakistan. The tiny state Tripura faced multi-faceted problems leading to the Partition of India in 1947 A.D. The problem of migration and the shelter of the refugees became one of the burning questions for the people of Tripura. The impact of the Partition of India on Tripura can also be witnessed in the aspects of social, economic and cultural aspects as well. The tribal population of the state declined from majority to minority. They suffered a lot and their identity is also at risk. Though Tripura became one of the states of Independent India, but still the actual inhabitants of the state are deprived of their basic rights. This is why, it is imperative to take care of their problems for the all-round development of the state. Let us take a solemn vow to avoid any type of communal feelings and march on the path of development and success. The tribal and non- tribal population of this state must join together to solve their mutual problems in an amicable way.

References

1. Zakaria, Rafiq.2004.*The man who divided India.Mumbai* :Popular Prakashan Pvt.Ltd.
2. Guha Thakurta, S.N.1999. *Tripura*. New Delhi: National Book Trust.
3. Roy, Kaushik (ed.). 2012. *Partition of India Why 1947?*.New Delhi: Oxford University Press.
4. Saha, Palash(ed.). 2013. *Tripura* Year Book. Agartala: Tripura Info.com
5. Anita Inder Singh.2006.*The Partition of India*. New Delhi : National Book Trust.
6. Chakravarti, Mahadev.1994.*Administration Reports of Tripura State (In 4 Volumes)*. New Delhi: Gyan Publishing House.
7. Bhattacharya, Ruma & Deepak, Pradeep Kumar.2014. *Tripura* .Noida :Vikas Publishing House Pvt. Ltd.
8. Chandra, Bipan, Mukherjee, Mridula & Mukherjee, Aditya.2008. *India Since Independence*. New Delhi: Penguin Books.
9. Sankarnarayanan, Vijayan(ed.). 2007. *Themes in Indian History Pt III*. New Delhi: N.C.E.R.T.

(7)
Partition, Islamization and the Rise of Islamic Fanaticism in East Pakistan and Bangladesh: Its Implications on India's Security in the Northeast India

Bindu Ranjan Chakma

Key words: Islamization, Islamic fanaticism, secularism, multiculturalism, ethnic nationalism, ethnic insurgencies, ethnic minorities, regional super power, extra regional power, hostile neibhours.

Introduction:

India is a liberal democratic country with strong foundation of constitutionalism, secularism and multiculturalism. India perceives itself as the most powerful nation in South Asia with its strong democratic institutions, powerful economy and military might with nuclear capability and geo strategic location. However, India had to face many internal and external challenges in preserving and promoting its institutional values as envisioned in the constitution. Similarly India's position as the undisputed regional super power in South Asia has not gone unchallenged. Religious fundamentalism and religious intolerance are antithetical to the values of secularism, multiculturalism and democracy. India being a liberal, secular, democratic and multicultural country, it perceives religious fundamentalism and Islamic fanaticism as threat to its long cherished political institutions and political integrity.

Objectives of the study are:

(1) To analyse how Islamic nationalism and religious intolerance in East Pakistan and Bangladesh after its emergence as an independent entity constrained India's position and geo political and strategic and economic interests in South Asia.

(2) To explain how Islamization in East Pakistan and Bangladesh remained antithetical to preservation and promotion of India's values of secularism, multiculturalism and political pluralism in India and South Asia.

(3) To explore the possibility on how India can contain and neutralize these challenges by giving some useful suggestions in this regard.

Methodology of the study

The study is purely explanatory. Books, documents and researched papers are evaluated, interpreted and examined through content analysis method for gathering useful information. The study is primarily carried out in two principal chapters. The first part explains how the British colonial administration fomented religious communalism in British India and how it led to territorial disintegration of India in 1947 with emergence of two independent countries and how such policy of British colonial India factored in post colonial reconstruction of nation state and in determining bilateral relations between India and Pakistan in post colonial South Asia. The second part locates the areas where and how Islamic nationalism in Pakistan (East Pakistan) and present Bangladesh stood as irritant in the nature of bilateral relations and how it impinged on India's national security in the Northeast in particular and the South Asia as whole.

"Partition, Process of Islamization and the Rise of Islamic Fanaticism in East Pakistan/Bangladesh"

Secularism is an important feature of modern democratic countries. Despite predominance of Christian population, countries like the USA, the UK and Australia adopted secular character and provided religious freedom to all religious groups. India is also no exception to this. The Preamble to the constitution of India defined India as a secular country despite predominance of Hindu communities within the demographic character of the India's population.

The British colonial administration had sown the seeds of religious communalism, particularly between the Hindus and Muslims in British India to suit their colonial interests. Bengal was the epicentre in strong anti British agitation in the beginning of 19th century. The British rulers divided Bengal on religious communal line in 1905 into East Bengal and West Bengal to create communal disharmony and enmity between the

Hindu and Muslim Bengalis. Since 1905, the British colonial administration continuously played the religious card to weaken the freedom struggle injecting communal ideas. The British rulers concluded their prolonged colonial administration in 1947 but their policy of 'divide and rule' on communal line led to territorial disintegration of India. While India was born with the motto of 'unity in diversity', Pakistan was formed with communal ideas. Pakistan (with East and West Pakistan) was proclaimed as Islamic Republic with Pakistani Islamic nationalism. It adopted a constitution that did not retain any provision for providing religious freedom on other religious minorities who accounted about 24 percent of the Pakistan's population in 1947 (Dastidar, 2008). The Hindus, the Buddhist and Christian minorities have been converted into unwanted citizens in the wave of strong Pakistani Islamic nationalism. According to Clause 15 (1) of Pakistani constitution, only a Muslim could hold the position of the Head of the state in the Islamic Republic of Pakistan (Choudhury, 1959: 89-90, Mohsin, 1997:45). State sponsored policy of religious communalism unleashing regular anti Hindu programs fomented Islamic radicalism within Pakistan.

Bangladesh emerged as a sovereign country through a long drawn bloody liberation war against the Pakistan on 16 December 1971. Bangladesh is predominantly a Muslim country. However, considering the presence of sizable number of non Muslim population in independent Bangladesh and to provide a strong basis for democratic institutions, the 1972 constitution of Bangladesh under the leadership of Sheikh Mujibur Rahman adopted secular and socialist character. The constitution in its Preamble of Para 2 accepted 'nationalism', 'socialism' 'democracy' and 'secularism' as state principles (Mohsin, 1997: 60). But, Mujib's Bangladesh adopted an assimilitionist approach of ethnic integration with total disregard to the non Bengali minorities. Article 6 of Part I of the 1972's constitution of Bangladesh defined all citizens of Bangladesh as Bengali (Mohsin: 1997, 59, Chakma: 2013, 231). The assassination of Sheikh Mujibur Rahman in 15th August in 1975 brought a dramatic change in the secular character of Bangladesh. Islam was declared as the state religion by discarding 'socialism' and 'secularism'. The state policy declared to have absolute trust and faith in the Almighty Allah for all actions. Therefore, Sheikh Mujibur Rahman's assassination paved the way of Islamization process in institutional manner. The situation strengthened the position of the radical Islamic forces within the politics of Bangladesh.

Now let us look at the ideology and objectives of the major political parties of Bangladesh to understand the institutional structures of present Bangladesh. The major political parties of Bangladesh are Awami League, Bangladesh Nationalist Party (BNP), Jatiyo Party (Ershad), Islamic Okyo Jhote (Islamic United Front) and the Left Parties (Bangladesh Communist Party, Workers Party).Among these political parties, Awami League and Left parties are socialist oriented and have faith in politics of secularism and representative democracy. Awami League as a political party has nationwide influence and ruled the country for many years. However, the Left parties are marginalized within the politics as they have little influence. The BNP believes in representative democracy. But it maintained closer proximity with Islam. It preferred to play the card of Islamic nationalism to suit its political objectives. Therefore, the BNP maintained cordial relations with the radical Islamic forces and entered into electoral alliance with such forces in 2001. Its alliance with these forces is still continuing. The Jatiyo Party headed by General Hossain Mohmad Ershad has also leaning towards Islam. When General Ershad ruled the country as a military dictator, he amended the constitution in June 1988 and introduced 'Islam' as the 'State religion' by discarding 'secularism'. Such move of General Ershad proved his strong assertion towards Islam and Islamic nationalism.

The Army in Bangladesh also plays an influential role in the politics in Bangladesh. The powerful military perceives itself as the only force that can hold Bangladesh together. Therefore, without inclusion of the Bangladesh military within this study, our understanding about the institutional structure of Bangladesh shall remain incomplete. According to Dr. Subhas Kalita, in term of socio-economic composition, the bulk of the regular armed forces of Bangladesh are drawn from the poor and economically backward rural areas. They are more susceptible to Islamic influences and current day trends of pan Islamism in the Muslim world (Jena and Chakma: 2008, 92). Moreover, initially bulks of the Bangladesh's Armed forces were drawn from the repatriated Bengali personals of the Pakistani Army (East Bengal regiment). They were brought up as army personal under military rule and Islamic culture in Pakistan. Therefore, their inclination towards Islamic culture and military ruled state has been reflected when military ruler ruled the country for several years with strong disregard to secular values. The anti secularist and pro Islamic forces in Bangladesh always reiterated and harbored anti

Indianism in their politics of national consolidation. They perceive India as inimical and a great threat to realization of their political objectives and their existence and position within the politics of Bangladesh. They also project India as a threat to the security and territorial integrity of Bangladesh. It is only Awami League that emphasizes on friendly relations with India for securing national interests of Bangladesh and better political environment in South Asia. However, it appears that the forces having faith Islamic state structure and Islamic nationalism are more effective and influential than the socialist and secular forces within the politics of Bangladesh. The predominance of Islamic forces, Islam as an important determining factor in the politics of Bangladesh led to religious polarization in the Bangladesh's politics. Along with this religious polarization, continuous political instability and absence of strong foundation of the democratic forces strengthened the position of the fundamentalist forces. There are many who believe that Bangladesh is emerging as a major sanctuary for various radical Islamic militant organizations. For example, according to Bertil Lintner, a revolution is taking place in Bangladesh that threatens the region and beyond if left unchallenged. (Jena and Chakma: 2008: 93).

"Security Implications of India in the Northeast"

The bilateral relations between India and Pakistan did not begin in friendly atmosphere due to stiff ideological differences in the process of formation of nation state and in the approach of nation building process. Hostility based on Islamic nationalism (Pakistan) and multicultural nationalism (India) created strained bilateral ties between the two nations. Pakistan did not accept the British's decision of conferring Kashmir with power of deciding its political future. According to the Pakistani leadership, the religious theory of creation of Pakistani state justified natural merger of Kashmir because of its Muslim majority demographic character. But, Pakistan failed to do so even after waging a war against Pakistan in 1947 in the Kashmir valley. Instead, Kashmir was integrated with the Union of India. The merger of Kashmir with India was a big jot to the theory of creation of Pakistani state. This humiliation of Pakistan emboldened Pakistan's anti Indian position. It instigated violent anti Indian activities in many parts of India including the Northeast. Islamic Republic of Pakistan joined hands with India's hostile countries like the USA and the Peoples' Republic of China (PRC) during the peak of Cold war period. It became member of the US led strategic military alliances in South East Asia (SEATO) and West Asia (CENTO). It concluded military and strategic agreements with the PRC in its attempt to create strategic and military balance with India. The objective was to contain India's emergence as undisputed regional super power in South Asia. Islamic nationalism in Pakistan also instigated religious communism in India. It argued that Muslims were not safe in India (Hindustan). At the same time, Pakistani State with Islamic radicalism invited discrimination against the Hindus and other Muslim minority communities on religious grounds. The State sponsored policy of religious persecution and forceful conversion of religious minority groups created the problem of forced migration among the religious minority communities into India. As a result, the Hindus, as noted earlier, who constituted about 24 percent of Pakistan population during 1947 came down to less than 2 percent now (Dastidar, 2007). It created great exodus among the Hindus, Sikh, Buddhist and Christian population into India including many of the India's Northeastern states like Tripura, Assam and Arunachal Pradesh. The change of demographic character with the majority becoming minority and the fear of being overtaken by the forced migrants from East Pakistan fomented ethnic tensions unleashing ethnic violence in many parts of Northeast India. The ethnic tension between the Chakmas and other Arunachalese tribes, between the Bengalis and tribal groups in Tripura, between Assamese and Bengalis, between Bodos and Bengalis (mostly Muslims) in Assam have their origin in population migration from East Pakistan. This ethnic polarization fomented ethnic nationalism which subsequently resulted into the rise the rise many problems including the rise of ethnic insurgencies in the Northeast India. Ethnic insurgencies with modern sophisticated arms and weapons crippled security environment and disturbed the process of initiating good governance, halted the growth and development in the region. Pakistani establishment established political and military nexus with the leaders of different insurgent groups of Northeast with a view to disintegrate India. It backed Mizo and Naga insurgencies against India and allowed its soils, particularly, the Chittagong Hill Tracts (CHT) to use against India. Pakistani establishment also facilitated the leaders of Mizo and Naga insurgencies to establish liaison with the PRC and their European sympathizer (Bhaumik, 1996: 147-163). The silent war by Pakistan against India in the Northeast had two immediate objectives. First, it wanted to use cross border insurgency in the Northeast India as diplomatic tool to exert political pressure on India to change its policy in the Kashmir. Secondly, it wanted to use as a political deterrence against pro India leaning among the Chakmas and other tribes in the CHT by using the historical animosity between the Mizos and the Chakmas.

Looking at the national security challenges emanating from the anti Indian activities of Pakistani establishment in overt or covert collision with extra regional powers like the USA and the PRC, India also exploited the anti West Pakistani sentiment of the Bengalis of East Pakistan. It backed and supported with arms and ammunition supply to the liberation forces and finally involved into a war against Pakistan by extending full fledged military support to the liberation forces. East Pakistan was disintegrated from West Pakistan giving birth to new sovereign independent country in the name of Bangladesh on 16 December 1971. Relations between India and Bangladesh began with friendly ties. A 20 years treaty of peace, friendship and cooperation was signed between India and Bangladesh in 1972. The new Bangladesh under the leadership of Sheikh Mujibur Rahman did not allow the anti Indian forces to use its soils against India. However, the situation in Bangladesh in aftermath of Sheikh Mujibur Rahman' assassination became hostile to India as it was during the Pakistan period in East Pakistan. Like Pakistan, post Mujib Bangladesh proclaimed as an Islamic Republic with strong Islamic nationalism. How did Islamic Republic of Bangladesh with Islamic nationalism impinge on India's national security in the Northeast? There are many areas where India's national security remained at stake when radical Islamic nationalism had formed the basis of national building process in post Mujib's era of Bangladesh. First, their targets were secular intellectuals and religious minority groups. Attacks on secular values in post Mujib's Bangladesh was equally perceived as threat to secular credentials of Indian politics and India's economic, geo political and geo strategic interests in South Asia as a whole. Like the Pakistani regime, the leaders of post Mujib's Bangladesh developed the view that India was an unsafe country for the Muslims and it was their responsibility to help them getting justice. Similarly, like the Pakistani regimes, indiscriminate attacks on the minority communities supported by the State establishment generated the problem of forced migration (official and unofficial) into West Bengal, Assam, Tripura and Meghyalaya. The Hindu population that accounted 31 percent in East Pakistan in 1947 came to nine percent in present Bangladesh. Such forced migration exacerbated the existing communal disharmony between different ethnic groups leading to the occurrence of ethnic backlashes in Assam, Tripura, Meghalaya and many other parts of Northeast India. The leaders of Bangladesh having faith in radical Islamic nationalism when ruled the country, they followed the footsteps and policies of Pakistani rulers against India. They scrapped down the 20 years treaty of peace, friendship and cooperation singed between India and Bangladesh when Sheikh Mujibur Rahman was in power. They established closer diplomatic ties with India's hostile neibhours like Pakistan, and the PRC, and extra regional power, the USA, which opposed Bangladesh's liberation war and the birth of independent Bangladesh. Since Pakistan and the PRC backed and encouraged insurgencies in the Northeast during Pakistan's period, they wanted to reestablish their contact with such India's rebel groups through Bangladesh. They instigated the Bangladeshi security establishment to back cross border insurgency in the Northeast India. Insurgent groups such All Tripura Tiger Force (ATTF), National Liberation Force of Twipra (NLFT), Mizo National Front (MNF), Nationalist Socialist Council of Nagalim (NSCN-IM), United Liberation Force of Assam (ULFA) etc were allowed to use the CHT and Khasiapunji, Srimangal, Chunarughat etc as bases to carry out anti Indian activities in the Northeast India. (Jena and Chakma, 2008: 78-81, Debnath, 2001: 304). During this period, insurgency in the Northeast backed by Bangladesh with overt and covert support of Pakistan and the PRC threatened India's territorial sovereignty in the region and India's security in the remained very much volatile in the region. Besides, religious persecution against the Hindus and other religious minority groups in Bangladesh encourages the Hindu nationalist forces in India to intensify their Hindu nationalist campaign creating communal disharmony between the Hindus and Muslims. Such Hindu nationalist communal politics are also equally threat to India's democracy, secular ideas and national integrity. The situation has now improved to a greater extent with Awami League, the secular force coming to power. The Awami League led government of Bangladesh initiated drastic action against various insurgent groups of Northeast India in Bangladesh dismantling their infrastructures. The insurgent groups losing their external base camps and support became very much cornered and marginalized. This helped to greater extent in bringing down the problem of insurgency in the Northeast India. But, unless Bangladesh becomes a vibrant democracy with respect to secular and multicultural values, India's long term national security interests shall remain at stake in the future.

Conclusion:

The above study tells us that Islamic nationalism in Pakistan and Bangladesh is a legacy of the British colonial rule in the Indian subcontinent. They concluded their prolonged colonial administration in 1947. But their policy of 'divide and rule' on the basis of religious communalism disintegrated India into dominions-India and Pakistan. As Pakistan was created out of the British's policy of religious communalism, its State's policy turned inimical to India. Islam was declared as the State's religion leading to Islamization of entire institutional structures and giving no religious freedom to other religious minority groups. Bangladesh became independent with India's military intervention against Pakistan on 16 December 1971. Although Bangladesh under Sheikh Mujibur Rahman adopted representative democracy with socialist and secular credentials but it lost its secular credentials after assassination of Sheikh Mujibur Rahaman on 15 August 1975. Like Pakistan, Bangladesh turned to be Islamic nation with strong Islamic nationalism which was inimical to India's security interests both at home and in the South Asia. In order to overcome this national security challenge, India needs to play a more proactive role in Bangladesh. It must encourage and provide support to Bangladesh moving towards a vibrant and stable democracy by engaging the major political parties especially Awami League, BNP and Jatiyo Party (Ershad) without any party biasness. India's policy must take into confidence the political parties like BNP and Jatiyo Party (Ershad) that it does not stand for only Awami League. Such policy may act as a catalyst in disassociating the BNP with radical Islamic forces. At the same time, the government of India also needs to have a proactive diplomacy in securing security and rights of the religious minorities in Bangladesh. If it is not done, the population of Hindu and other religious minority communities in Bangladesh will come to zero percent in near future. Such a situation will aggravate the situation in the Northeast India. Similarly communalism on ground of religion at home needs to be contained because it invites similar developments in Bangladesh.

References:

1. Bhowmik, Subhir, (1996), *Insurgent Crossfire: Northeast India*, New Delhi: Lancer Publishers.
2. Chakma, Bindu Ranjan, (2013), *Stateless people in the New Global Order: The Experience of the Chakmas,* New Delhi: Lakshi Publishers and Distributors.
3. Dastidar, Sachi Ghosh, (2008), *Empire Last Casuality: Indian Subcontinent's Vanishing Hindu and other Minorities,* Kolkata:
4. Debnath, Jayanta, (2001), *Santrasklanta Tripura,* Agartala: Dainik Sambad Publishers.
5. Jena, Kashinath and Chakma, Bindu Ranjan, (2008), *Ethnic Unrests and India's Security Concerns,* New Delhi: Abhijeet Publications.
6. Mohsin, Amena, (1997), *The Politics of Nationalism: The Case of Chittagong Hill Tracts, Bangladesh,* Dhaka: The University Press Limited.

(8)
Party System and Ability of Party Support in Northeast India, 1952-2014

Rajshree Dutta

Abstract

Party system has undergone tremendous changes in India since the country began its life as a democratic republic. India today has several vibrant political parties at national and state levels. What began as a one-dominant party system has evolved over the years into a full-fledged multi-party system. The effective number of parties and the variations of party system in different states made political scientists wonder whether India fits into any one type of party system traditionally known in the literature of party politics. Similar trajectory is found in case of the states termed as North-East.

After independence, we find that the party system is not uniform for all the states of the North-East. Indicators such as 'Effective Number of Parties' as developed by the western scholars Markku Laakso and Rein Taagepera and 'Volatility Index' as developed by Mogens N. Pedersen in 1979 will be used in this paper to find out the effective number of parties in case of states belonging to North East since the first general elections of 1952 to the recent general elections of 2014. Thus, the objective of this paper is to find out how many parties are playing an effective role in different North-Eastern states, whether there has been any change in the party system of these states since independence and if there has been changes in the party system, then how many parties are responsible for causing such change and shifts in electoral support for the parties over the span of 16 general elections i.e.1952-2014.

Key Words: Party system, Effective number of parties, Party system change, Stability of Party Support

Introduction

Party systems have been a key factor in the study of political parties and more broadly in comparative political analysis. Political parties competing with each other for elective office and control of government form a party system. Political scientists have sought not only to characterize them, but also to understand their causes and consequences, particularly their sources in electoral laws and cleavage structures and their effects on government and system stability, and more broadly, the quality of democracy (Wolinetz, 2006:51).

Democracies in the modern times have evolved around party systems in which two or more than two political parties compete for political power (Diego and Gonzalez, 2004: 28). While we see stable party systems in the developed western democracies, we see considerable instability in the party systems of the developing countries. This is often characterized by extensive shifts in voter support to political parties, different degrees of ideological polarization or convergence. So the question of party system and stability of electoral support acquires greater importance in developing democracies than the developed ones.

In India, we find frequent party splits and mergers as well formation of new parties, leading to a significant increase in the number of parties at national and state levels. This increase in the number of parties may lead to increase in instability in the party support. This may further result in increase in voter turnout, closeness of party competition, party turnover and formation of party coalitions. However, the increase in the number of parties should not be always looked upon with alarm or as a threat to the stability of democracy. Viewed positively, the entry of more parties introduces vibrancy as well as fluidity in the party system (Suri, 2007:54). This also holds true for the states belonging to north-east.

Much of the work relating to the area on party system change and stability of party support has been done by the scholars in Western democracies (Duverger, 1954; Sartori, 1976; Pedersen, 1979; Gallagher, 1991; Lijphart, 1999; Taagepera, 2003; Grofman, 2003; Mainwaring, 2007; and Zoco, 2007). There has been considerable work on the nature of and changes in India's party system since independence (Weiner, 1957; Kothari, 1964; Arora, 2002; Manor, 2002; Hasan, 2002; Yadav, 2003; Palshikar, 2003; Sarangi, 2005; and Suri, 2007). While the works on Indian party politics analyze the factors for party system change, there are hardly any studies that measure the extent, direction and nature of party system change. Most of the studies done in India are either in the form of political commentary, descriptive accounts and critical interpretation based on the field research.

To know the changes or in order to exactly know how many effective parties are there in a party system, or how many parties cause changes in party system from one form to another, it is necessary to take a look at the index of Effective Number of Parties (hereafter, it will be referred by its acronym, i.e. ENP). The index tells us how many parties play an effective role in the party systems.

ENP can be calculated by the proliferation of votes secured in an election or seats secured by parties in the legislature. The index was developed by Markku Laakso and Rein Taagepera (1979) taking into account the relative size of the parties in the party system. This is now used widely by comparativists in political science. It is calculated as:

$$N=1/\sum pi^2$$

Where, 'N' is the effective number of parties which can be calculated in terms of either votes or seats; 'p' is the proportion of seats/votes secured by 'ith' party in an election; '$\sum$' stands for the summation of components.

The problem of how to count parties of different sizes is solved to some extent by using the effective number measure. It can be easily seen that if one-party secures all votes or almost all votes, the ENP would be 1 or close to 1. Thus, in a one-party dominant system, ENP will be always less than 2. In a two-party system with two equally strong parties, the effective number of parties is exactly 2.0. Similarly, with 3 exactly equal parties, the ENP yields a value of 3.0. If one of these parties is weaker than the other two, the ENP will be somewhere between 2.0 and 3.0 depending on the relative size of the third party. Thus, if the ENP value is between 2.5 and 5, the party system is moderately pluralized or a two-plus party system. If the ENP value is 5 or greater, it is highly pluralized or there is the existence of multipartism.

The stability or regularity of patterns of inter-party competition can be measured through the index of electoral volatility or the Pedersen index as proposed by Mogens N. Pedersen in 1979. It provides one single quantitative index of the changes in electoral support received by parties from one election to the next (Suri, 2007: 54). It is computed by adding the absolute value of change in percentage of votes/seats gained or lost by each party from one election to the next, then dividing the sum by two (Pedersen 1979; and Przeworski, 1975). Thus in a party system with 'n' parties:

$$EV = TNC/2$$

Where 'TNC' is the total net change in party support. Similarly, it can be calculated in terms of seat share. The electoral volatility thus has a range of '0' or perfect stability when there is no change at all in party preferences of voters, to '100' or perfect instability, where there is total shift of voters from one party to the other.

The present study uses quantitative data on general elections in India and takes the help of the two indices mentioned above to find out the relationship between stability of party support and party system change. The objective of the study, therefore, is to understand stability and shifts in party support in India and how it is related to the party system change in case of north-eastern states. The stability model of competition refers to the parties' ability to maintain relatively stable electoral support from one election to the next. The greater the variations, within each party and overall, the less stable the party system. It is generally believed that when there is an increase in the effective number of parties, the party system becomes unstable.

Party System Change in North-East

Ever since the decline of Congress became apparent, two features of Indian politics have attracted the attention of students of Indian political process. One is the coalition-based structure of party politics and the other is the rise of many smaller and regional parties to prominence in national as well as state level politics. What is remarkable about these features is that INC was not being replaced by any single party. A wide range of regional formations at the state level has become the centrepiece of the emerging party system. Given their size and socio-cultural and ethnic specificity, states in India have become the sites of political action and political competition. For a majority of politicians and people, what seems to be important is what happens at the state level or who controls the state governments.

Keeping these studies in mind, change in party system at the state level can be analyzed by calculating ENP for eight north-eastern states for sixteen general elections to find out the change in party system experienced by each state in contemporary times. Table 1 shows ENP in terms of votes. The states are categorised into three groups taking into account the majority of instances of ENP values. Appendix 1 provides an illustration of how ENP is calculated for example in case of Tripura for 2014 elections. The following paragraphs deals with few examples of states from north-east in order to have an idea about party system change in north-east India.

Tripura is what scholars describe as the state of two plus competitive format, with the two main political formations i.e. the Indian National Congress (INC) and the Left front (Communist Party of India-Marxist (CPM), Communist Party of India (CPI) and Forward Bloc). Political competition in the state has often been between the CPM-led Left front and the INC, which had provisional alignments with tribal regional parties, being organisationally weak in the tribal belts. The communists retain significant support in rural areas. The crushing of the tribal insurgency is supported by a governance model that emphasises

Table 1

Effective Number of Parties in Terms of Votes, 1952-2014

States	Year of Elections															
	1952	1957	1962	1967	1971	1977	1980	1984	1989	1991	1996	1998	1999	2004	2009	2014
States with two-party system																
Arunachal Pradesh	--	--	--	--	--	5.9	2.7	3.2	2.7	1.9	8.8	2.6	2.6	2.9	2.4	2.6
Nagaland	--	--	--	1.0	1.9	2.0	4.2	2.0	2.0	2.1	2.6	1.3	2.0	1.7	1.7	1.8
Sikkim	--	--	--	--	--	1.0	2.3	14.9	2.1	1.2	1.7	1.8	2.2	1.8	2.0	2.2
Tripura	2.2	2.4	2.2	1.9	3.1	3.2	3.4	2.2	2.1	1.4	2.5	2.4	2.7	2.0	2.1	2.2
States with moderately pluralised party system																
Assam	3.9	3.1	4.0	4.2	3.0	2.6	--	5.1	--	6.6	4.9	4.3	3.9	4.6	5.0	4.1
Meghalaya	--	--	--	--	--	7.8	--	2.6	3.2	3.1	3.4	3.2	4.2	3.4	2.9	4.7
Mizoram	--	--	--	--	--	7.3	5.7	1.0	2.7	3.2	3.1	5.1	0.0	3.6	2.3	4.2

States with highly pluralised party system																
Manipur	6.4	10.4	5.8	5.2	7.3	3.6	8.0	5.9	4.0	4.2	5.3	5.4	5.2	10.0	4.0	4.0

Source: Election Commission of India, *http://eci.nic.in/eci_main1/ElectionStatistics.aspx*, retrieved on 1st October, 2013.

Notes: 1. The Effective Number of Parties for each election year for different states is calculated based on the data collected from the website of Election Commission of India.

2. Arunachal Pradesh (First General Elections in 1977); Meghalaya, Mizoram, Sikkim (First General Elections in 1977); Nagaland (First General Elections in 1967).

3. In Assam, elections were not held in 12 Parliamentary constituencies in 1980 and 14 Parliamentary Constituencies in 1989, therefore ENP cannot be calculated for 1980 and 1989. In Meghalaya, election was not held in 1 Parliamentary constituency in 1980, therefore ENP cannot be calculated for 1980.

4. In North-Eastern states, the ENP in some elections is very high because no party secured majority of votes. In these elections, the Independents secured the majority of vot development, improvement in the quality of life and grassroots democracy. The Left has been aided by factionalism and organisational disorder in the INC (Roy, 2005:2178). The state of Tripura experienced two-party system till 1967 general elections. The competition was mainly between two largest party of the state at that time i.e. INC and CPI till 1962 and then between INC and CPM till 1967. For the next three election years i.e. 1971 and 1980, the party system was moderately pluralized with ENP above 3.0. The contest was between INC, CPM, CPI in 1971; INC, CPM, Bharatiya Lok Dal (BLD) in 1977; and INC, CPM, Tripura Upajati Juba Samiti (TUS), JNP in 1980. Between 1984-89, the state reverted to two party system competition till 1989. The contest regained between INC and CPM. In 1991, the INC won the majority of votes and seats making

the party system to be a single-party type. From 1996 onwards Tripura has two-party system. The contest is now mainly between CPM and INC.

The party system change is also not uniform in terms of votes and seats. Due to the first-past-the-post system, there has been no direct relation between the vote cast and seats won. There exists a discrepancy in ENP values when calculated in terms of votes and seats. Table 2 shows ENP in terms of seats. The nature of party competition looks different if we take ENP in terms of votes and ENP in terms of seats.

Source: Election Commission of India, *http://eci.nic.in/eci_main1/ElectionStatistics.aspx*, retrieved on 1st October, 2013.

Note: The Effective Number of Parties for each election year for different states is calculated based on the data collected from the website of Election Commission of India.

Table 2

Effective Number of Parties in Terms of Seats, 1952-2014

States	Year of Elections															
	1952	1957	1962	1967	1971	1977	1980	1984	1989	1991	1996	1998	1999	2004	2009	2014
Arunachal Pradesh	--	--	--	--	--	4.0	1.0	1.0	1.0	1.0	1.0	1.0	1.0	1.0	1.0	2.0
Assam	1.2	1.7	1.7	1.8	1.2	1.8	--	2.8	--	2.8	3.7	1.9	1.9	2.2	2.9	2.9
Manipur	2.0	4.0	2.0	4.0	1.0	1.0	2.0	1.0	1.0	2.0	1.0	2.0	2.0	4.0	1.0	1.0

Meghalaya	--	--	--	--	--	4.0	--	1.0	1.0	1.0	4.0	1.0	2.0	2.0	2.0	2.0
Mizoram	--	--	--	--	--	0.0	0.0	1.0	1.0	1.0	1.0	0.0	0.0	1.0	1.0	1.0
Nagaland	--	--	--	1.0	1.0	1.0	0.0	1.0	1.0	1.0	1.0	1.0	1.0	1.0	1.0	1.0
Sikkim	--	--	--	--	--	1.0	1.0	0.0	1.0	1.0	1.0	1.0	1.0	1.0	1.0	1.0
Tripura	1.0	2.0	1.0	1.0	1.0	2.0	1.0	1.0	1.0	1.0	1.0	1.0	1.0	1.0	1.0	1.0

For example: Voting behaviour is usually explained in terms of party loyalty, and this loyalty in turn is decided by multiple factors like caste, social class, religion and regionalism. The base of caste and religion like other parts of India, have not much of significance in the north-eastern state of Manipur. But the concept of social class in terms of occupation, income, education, ethnic factor, hill-valley dichotomy and division into indigenous and migrant's population have influenced the voting behaviour in the small state of Manipur. In terms of ENP by votes, between 1952-2004, the state experienced highly pluralized party system with ENP as high as 10 in 1957 and 2004 respectively. This draws our attention to the Sartori's categorization of party system. According to Sartori (1976), when the number of parties is more than 10, the party system is categorized as atomized pluralized type. No single party won absolute majority of votes. The important role was played by the Independents which resulted in greater ENP for some election years. Out of 16 elections, if we go by the ENP in terms of votes, only in 1977, 1989, 1991, 2009 and 2014 elections, the party system was moderately pluralized.

From 1952 to 1971, the party system was extremely pluralized, with INC being the ruling party, followed by CPI, Praja Socialist Party (PSP) (in 1957); CPI, PSP, Socialist Party (SOP) (in 1962); CPI, Samyukta Socialist Party (SSP) (in 1967); and CPI, Manipur Revolutionary Party (MRP), Nationalist Congress (NCO), SSP (in 1971) along with the Independents in all respective elections. In 1977, the ENP came down to 3.6 making the party system to be moderately pluralized type. This is because the percentage of votes won by INC was 15% higher (i.e. 45.3%) in comparison to what it won in the earlier elections (i.e. nearly 30%). The other main parties in terms of votes in 1977 elections were BLD, CPI and MRP.

In 1980 and 1984 elections, the competition was highly pluralized due to the presence of parties like INC, Indian National Congress-Urs (INCU), Janata Party (JNP), CPI, MRP and Independents in 1980 and between INC, BJP, CPI, Lok Dal (LKD), MRP and ICS (Indian Congress Socialist) in 1984. The moderately pluralized party system regained in 1989 and 1991, with INC being the leading party with highest percentage of votes. However, the INC did not remain in majority position after 1996 elections, as a result of which many other parties in the state gained importance. The party system became extremely pluralized. The ENP in 2004 was as high as i.e. 10 in 1957. But in 2009 and 2014 elections with

INC regaining its position and securing the highest percentage of vote i.e. 42.96% in 2009 and 41.7% in 2014 respectively, the party system became moderately pluralized. Apart from INC, the other parties present in the electoral scenario were CPI and People's Democratic Alliance (PDA) in 2009 and CPI and Bharatiya Janata Party (BJP) in 2014.

In terms of seats, Manipur had two-party system in 1952 and 1962 with ENP 2.0. The contest was mainly between INC and Socialist Party in 1952 and 1962 respectively. As the independents are not taken into consideration in the calculation, the ENP in 1957, 1967 and 2004 becomes 4.0. The contest was mainly between INC and Independents in 1957, 1967 and 2004 elections respectively. For 1971 and 1977 elections, the state had one-party system, with INC ruling the state. With the coming up of CPI into existence in 1980, the party system was two-party type. INC regaining its position in 1984 and 1989, once again there prevailed one-party system. In 1991, with INC and MRP capturing one seat each, the state underwent a two-party system. In 1996, INC was the dominant party with two seats. For 1998-1999, the state experienced two-party contest between CPI and Manipur State Congress Party (MSCP) in 1998; and MSCP and Nationalist Congress Party (NCP) in 1999. In 2009 and 2014, INC was able to regain power capturing both the Lok Sabha seats. The ENP since 2009 is 1.0 seat wise.

Stability of Party Support in North-East

According to Yadav (2003), the sudden demise of the Congress system created a room in different states for the entry of new political forces or for rearranging the format of party competition. It created an opportunity for new issues and demands to be articulated effectively within the party political arena. New opportunities of political bargaining were created for various communities and groups that were traditionally affiliated to the INC. In particular it left INC vulnerable to aggressive sectional mobilization of these groups. This had implications for the political strategy of the INC and its rivals. As the opponents of the INC pursued successfully the path of sectional mobilization, the INC found that its catch-all strategy was increasingly not viable. In response to the sectional mobilization by its rivals, the INC too became more of a sectional party than it was ever before. This affected the stability of the party support in different states in north-east.

The stability of party support can be measured by using volatility index. Electoral volatility can be calculated both by votes and seats. The general understanding of pattern of electoral support is made by taking into consideration electoral volatility by votes. Tables 3 shows electoral volatility by votes. When we calculate the volatility rate, it is necessary to have an idea as to how we treat a particular level of volatility as low and as high. Following scholars like Pedersen (1983); Payne, Zovotto, Florez and Zavala (2002) who have talked about the cut-off values of volatility rate, it can be said in case of India because of its diversity, heterogeneity and party pluralism, that the party system is stable, if the volatility rate (VR) is less than 20 percent; it is moderately stable/volatile if the volatility rate is between 21-30 percent; if the rate is between 31-50 percent, then the party support is highly volatile; and if the volatility rate is above 50 percent, we can term it as very high volatility at that point of time. The states of north-east are grouped into different categories taking into account the majority of instances of volatility index values. Appendix 2 provides an illustration of how volatility index is calculated for example in case of Assam for 2014 elections. The following paragraphs provide a few examples from north-eastern states in order to have an idea about stability of party support in case of north-east India.

Table 3
Electoral Volatility by Votes, 1952-2014

States	1957	1962	1967	1971	1977	1980	1984	1989	1991	1996	1998	1999	2004	2009	2014
States which appear to be stable	Nil														
States which appear to be moderately stable/volatile															
Assam	38.5	9.2	11.4	18.6	33.9	--	--	--	--	21.4	22.1	7.8	16.4	20.8	22.4
Nagaland	--	--	--	60.5	100	25.5	71.5	36.7	16.0	36.9	18.9	16.6	62.5	4.0	1.8
Tripura	21.4	7.7	57.2	15.5	20.9	29.8	21.0	10.0	33.8	52.7	9.5	27.8	14.5	18.4	16.6
States which appear to be volatile															

Arunachal Pradesh	--	--	--	--	--	27.0	10.8	5.8	42.5	38.1	31.8	43.2	51.1	46.5	20.4
Manipur	36.3	17.7	29.4	19.2	26.4	41.7	34.6	21.0	32.9	41.2	51.2	41.4	52.0	40.0	27.3
Meghalaya	--	--	--	--	--	--	--	4.1	2.3	8.1	24.1	30.2	49.4	45.1	39.6
Mizoram	--	--	--	--	--	39.6	71.0	51.1	28.0	15.7	10.8	34.4	29.4	60.5	7.6
Sikkim	--	--	--	--	--	98.0	61.8	52.8	17.1	70.3	32.0	41.8	40.9	8.5	37.6

Source: Election Commission of India, *http://eci.nic.in/eci_main1/ElectionStatistics.aspx*, retrieved on 1st October, 2013.

Notes: 1.The volatility rates for each election period in different states is calculated based on the data collected from the website of Election Commission of India.

2. In Assam, elections were not held in 12 Parliamentary constituencies in 1980 and 14 Parliamentary Constituencies in 1989, therefore EV cannot be calculated for 1980-1991 election periods. In Meghalaya, elections were not held in 1 Parliamentary constituency in 1980, so EV cannot be calculated for 1980 and 1984 election years.

Assam experienced a high electoral volatility since its first general elections i.e. 38.5%. This is because though INC was the dominant party but there were many other minor parties like BJS, SOP, Kisan Mazdoor Praja Party (KMPP), PSP etc which secured certain percentage of votes in 1957. However the volatility dropped in 1962 with the situation remaining the same i.e. INC remaining the majority party. The state continued to have low volatility rate till 1971. But in 1977, the electoral volatility increased because of BLD coming to the scenario. Although INC secured highest percentage of votes and seats but BLD became the second largest party in the state with 3 seats and 35.8% of votes. In 1984, for the first time a regional party i.e. Asom Gana Parishad (AGP) marked its presence in the state's politics with 7 out of 14 seats and 33.4% of votes.

The AGP owes its political existence to the regional issues of the state. Many even thought the end to the one-party dominance by the INC, made way for a bi-polar competition between the INC and the AGP. In parliamentary elections held in 1991, the INC staged a remarkable comeback, remarkable not for the size of its majority, but the recovery staged in the aftermath of the Assam movement[1]. This however, did not actually reflect a resurgence of support for the INC. The main reasons for its victory, despite a poor vote share, were the division of the pro-Assamese nationalist votes between the AGP and Natun Asom Gana Parishad (NAGP), a breakaway faction of the AGP, and the unprecedented performance of the BJP. It could be argued that these three formations put together polled more votes than the INC. The debacle of the AGP in this election was predictable. Rampant factionalism had culminated in a split in the party. Another factor that contributed to eroding the regional image of the AGP was the sudden upsurge in the activities of the United Liberation Front of Assam (ULFA). In 1996, the INC found itself in a difficult situation, facing charges of unprecedented corruption and an indiscriminate use of the repressive machinery of the state. Meanwhile, the AGP and NAGP united. The other opposition parties, including the Left parties and even the United Minority Front (UMF), a party claiming to represent the interests of the religious and linguistic minorities joined hands with other regional forces. The alliance ensured a strong presence for the AGP in all the regions of the state since it had forged a rainbow coalition cutting across ethnic lines (Goswami, 2012).

The INC recovery in the state began in the late 1990s. This is evident from the performance of the INC since the 1998 elections. But it was no longer an umbrella organization that accommodates the various ethnicities and communities of the state. The decline of INC dominance was caused by the emergence of multipolar party competition and the assertion and realignment of ethnic identities. Even as the INC appeared to have consolidated its position, the more significant development was the emergence of the BJP as an important electoral force. On the whole, the mandate was against the AGP led alliance, clearly indicative of its declining support base among the Muslim, SCs and STs communities.

The BJP failed to make any significant breakthrough in terms of seats as its organizational base was relatively weak and the party was devoid of capable leaders. The regional party, AGP, managed to regain its recognition at the national level by winning two seats after its debacle in the 1998 and 1999 elections, when it won no seats. The split in the AGP led to a major break-up in its traditional vote bank, which undoubtedly benefited both the INC and the BJP. The electoral volatility reached its lowest in 1999 because the party support was almost same as compared to 1998, when there were two main national party i.e. INC and BJP sharing the political space and gaining certain amount of strength from the regional party i.e. AGP. However the party system in Assam is acquiring some stability since 1999. There exists a three-cornered contest between INC, BJP and AGP.

In the 2009 election, the INC got away with a minor loss of 2 seats from its tally of 9 in the 2004 elections. Moreover, the party managed to retain more or less retain its vote share. The decline of INC vote share was due to the presence of the All India United Democratic Front (AIUDF earlier AUDF), which contested the Lok Sabha election for the first time and strengthened the process of polarization among Muslims, both domiciled and immigrants. It posed a challenge to the INC base among religious minorities. In 2009 and 2014 elections, the electoral volatility increased to 20.8% in 2009 and further to 22.4% in 2014. This was because BJP was able to increase its support base in 2009 and further it improved its seat and vote tally in 2014 elections.

In Manipur, since 1957, for most of the elections, the electoral volatility is quite high with few exceptions of 1962, 1971 and 1989 elections. The INC was not able to secure the majority of votes. The other parties like CPI, SOP, CPI, PSP, SSP, BLD, CPI, MRP, BJP, Janata Dal (JD), MPP, NCP and Independents also played a prominent role in the state politics at one or the other election years. One of the former governors of Manipur wrote that in Manipur some politicians changed parties as many as six times a year. A Chief Minister changes his party three times in one month and his coalition partners three times in 48 hours (Marwah, 2003:508). This obviously implies grave political instability leading to indifference of the electorate. Change in party loyalty, shifting alliances both in the individual and collective levels are so frequent and ruthless that the state has witnessed frequent change in government, ever since it became full-fledged state in 1972.

Electoral politics in Nagaland has been historically shaped by the Naga national question. An important feature of the state's electoral politics has been the relationship between the legal and ideological forces representing the Naga people. If regional parties like the Naga People's Front (NPF) have willingly displayed their nationalist aspirations and sympathy for the ideological representatives, national parties like the INC shared a distant cordiality with them. Even as electoral politics is restrained by a violent social web that has limited the capacity of the electorate, competitive politics has assisted in formalising a promising institutional political culture. The maturing of a democratic political process is evident from the fact that today the electoral agenda in Nagaland is no longer dominated by competitive expression over the Naga national question. It is now shaped by questions of development and governance. The electorate seems to have genuine expectations from democratic politics. This is evident in popular discourse and the political agenda of leading political parties like the NPF and the INC (Dev, 2013:2).

Nagaland had its first general elections in 1967, since then the state is experiencing high electoral volatility. The party system is perfectly unstable during 1977 elections, when there was a total shift in party loyalties from United Front of Nagaland (UFN) and Naga National Organisation (NNO) to INC and United Democratic Front (UDF). Even for the rest elections, the state has witnessed a greater electoral volatility. Only for 1991, 1998 and 1999 elections, the party system appears to be somewhat stable. In 1991, the state had two party contests between INC and Nagaland People's Council (NPC); in 1998 and 1999, the INC was able to secure absolute majority of votes. In 2004 elections, the volatility increased to 62.5% with the coming up of the regional party NPF and the defeat of the INC. The regional party, NPF is able to continue in power securing about 70% votes between 2004-2014 elections. From 2009 onwards, the electoral volatility is below 5%.

Thus, as stated in earlier sections, we find in several states of north-east, the ENP has increased after 1980s. Four states have nearly two-party system, three states falls under moderately pluralised party system category and one state comes under highly pularlized party system category. On the other hand, as observed from the Table 3, the electoral volatility appears to be high in about five states which have two-party system like Arunachal Pradesh or moderately pluralized party system like Meghalaya or a highly pluralized party system like Manipur. In three states the electoral support for the parties appears to be moderately stable/volatile. No state belonging to north-east appears to be stable. In Table 4, we can see the categorisation of north-eastern states taking into account both party system change as measured with the index of Effective Number of Parties and stability of party support ad measured with the help of Volatility Index over the period of 16 general elections i.e. from 1952 to 2014.

Table: 4

Nature of Party System and Pattern of Electoral Support, 1952-2014

	Stable	**Moderately stable/volatile**	**Volatile**
Two-party system	--	Nagaland and Tripura	Arunachal Pradesh and Sikkim
Moderately pluralised party system	--	Assam	Meghalaya and Mizoram
Highly pluralised party system	--	--	Manipur

Conclusion

A proper understanding of Indian party system[2] need to be centered around states and its party systems. The evolution of party system at the state level represents one of continuing transformation. On the one hand there is a trend towards opening of the competitive format, i.e. single party dominance is now an exception rather than a rule, all the north-eastern states states have shifted to a two-party or two-plus or multi-party competition. On the other hand, the states are undergoing a greater electoral volatility which results in unstable party system. We also find that the pattern of electoral volatility differs across states. The states belonging to north-east which experienced greater stability for a longer time have gone through a period of greater instability in recent times. It may be because of the emergence of small parties, frequent alteration of power and/or active role of Independents demanding for more political space.

Endnotes

1. The Assam Movement led by All Assam Students Union (AASU) and the All Assam Gana Sangram Parishad (AAGSP) was a popular movement against undocumented immigrants in Assam. Later on the agitated leaders of the movements formed Asom Gana Parishad (AGP), which came to power in the state in the Assembly elections of 1985.

2. The main features of the present party system seem to be the following: (a) The INC no longer is the centre of the system; (b) Two national parties (INC and BJP) now contest for alliance leadership; (c) A third front functionally equivalent to a third major party no longer exists. Efforts are made by parties to reconstitute the third alternative to the BJP and the INC. But it is unlikely that they will succeed in the foreseeable future; (d) Regional parties now hold the balance of power necessary for the formation of a ruling coalition; (e) Niche parties representing small segments of the electorate continue to split off from existing political parties; and (f) Leadership, rather than the institutionalization of parties, appears to be of increasing importance (Wallace, 2003:8).

References

1. Arora, Balveer. (2002) "The Political Parties and the Party System: The Emergence of New Coalitions", in Zoya Hasan (ed.) *Parties and Party Politics in India*. New Delhi: Oxford University Press, pp.504-532.
2. Dev, Rajesh. (2013) "The Northeasts of India", *http://m.indianexpress.com/news/the-northeasts-of-india/1076578/*, retrieved on 04th August, 2014.
3. Diego, Archard, and Luis E. Gonzalez. (2004) *A Challenge for Democracy: Political Parties in Central America, Panama and the Dominion Republic*. Washington DC: Inter-American Development Bank (IDB).
4. Duverger, Maurice. (1954) *Political Parties: Their Organization and Activity in the Modern State*. Cambridge: University Printing House.
5. Election Commission of India, *http://eci.nic.in/eci_main1 /ElectionStatistics.aspx*, retrieved on 1st October, 2013.
6. Goswami, Sandhya. (2012) "Changing Trends of Electoral Politics", *Seminar Issue 640*, *www.india-seminar.com/2012/640/640-sandhya-goswami.htm*, retrieved on 30th October, 2014.
7. Hasan, Zoya. (2002) "Introduction: Conflict Pluralism and the Competitive Party System in India", in Zoya Hasan (ed.) *Parties and Party Politics in India*. New Delhi: Oxford University Press, pp.1-36.
8. Kothari, Rajni. (1964) "The Congress System in India", *Asian Survey*, Vol.4, No.12, pp.1161-1173.
9. Laakso, Markku, and Rein Taagepera. (1979) "Effective Number of Parties: A Measure with Application to West Europe", *Comparative Political Studies*, Vol.12, No.1, pp.3-27.
10. Lijphart, Arend. (1999) *Patterns of Democracy: Government Forms and Performance in Thirty-Six Countries*. London: Yale University Press.
11. Mainwaring, Scott, and Edurne Zoco. (2007) "Political Sequences and the Stabilization of Inter-Party Competition: Electoral Volatility in Old and New Democracies", *Party Politics*, Vol.13, No.2, pp.155-178.

12 Manor, James. (2002) "Parties and Party Systems", in Zoya Hasan (ed.) *Parties and Party Politics in India*. New Delhi: Oxford University Press, pp.431-474.

13 Payne, J. Mark, Daniel Zovotto G, Fernando Carillo Florez, and Andres Allamand Zavala. (2002) *Democracies in Development: Politics and Reform in Latin America*. Washington DC: IDB.

14 Pedersen, Mogens N. (1979) "The Dynamics of European Party Systems: Changing Patterns of Electoral Volatility", *European Journal of Political Research*, 7(1), pp.1-26.

15 Przeworski, Adam. (1975) "Institutionalization of Voting Patterns, or is Mobilization the Source of Decay", *American Political Science Review*, Vol.69, No.1, pp.49-67.

16 Roy, Sanjoy K. (2005) "Conflicting Nations in North-East India", *Economic and Political Weekly*, Vol.40, No.21, pp.2176-2182.

17 Sarangi, Prakash. (2005) "Economic Reforms and Changes in the Party System", in Jos Mooij (ed.) *The Politics of Economic Reforms in India*. New Delhi: Sage Publications, pp.71-95.

18 Sartori, Giovanni. (1976) *Parties and Party Systems: A Framework of Analysis*. Cambridge: Cambridge University Press.

19 Suri, K.C.(2007) *Political Parties in South Asia: The Challenges of Change*. Stockholm: International Institute for Democracy and Electoral Assistance.

20 Taagepaera, Rein, and Bernard Grofman. (2003) "Mapping the Indices of Seats-Votes Disproportionality and Inter-Election Volatility", *Party Politics*, Vol.9, No.6, pp.659-677.

21 Wallace, Paul. (2003) "Introduction: The New National Party System and State Politics", in Paul Wallace, and Ramashray Roy (eds.) *India's 1999 Elections and 20th Century Politics*. New Delhi: Sage Publications, pp.1-21.

22 Weiner, Myron. (1957) *Party Politics in India: The Development of a Multi-Party System*. Delhi: Low Price Publications.

23 Wolinetz, Steven. (2006) "Party Systems and Party System Types", in Richard S. Katz, and William Crotty (eds.) *Handbook of Party Politics*. London: Sage Publications, pp.51-62.

24 Yadav, Yogendra, and Suhas Palshikar. (2003) "From Hegemony to Convergence: Party System and Electoral Politics in the Indian States, 1952-2002", *Journal of Indian School of Political Economy*, Vol.XV, Nos.1&2, pp.5-44.

APPENDICES

Appendix: 1

Effective Number of Parties for 2014 Election by Votes and Seats in Tripura

Party	**Percentage of votes secured**	**Pi**	**pi²**	**Seats won**	**pi**	**pi²**
INC	15.2	0.152	0.023104	0	0	0
BJP	5.7	0.057	0.003249	0	0	0
CPM	64.0	0.64	0.4096	2	1	1
AITC	9.62	0.0962	0.009254	0	0	0
OTHERS	5.48	0.0548	0.003003	0	0	0
Total	100		0.44821	2		1
ENP			**2.231095**			**1**

Note: The Effective Number of Parties (ENP) (denoted as 'N') is calculated using Laakso and Taagepera formula which is as follows:

$N= 1/\sum p_i^2$

Where '$\sum$' stands for the summation and 'p_i' stands for the proportion of the 'ith' party. Therefore in the above case the ENP by Votes (N) = 1/0.44821=2.2 and by Seats (N)=1/1=1.

Appendix: 2

Electoral Volatility for the Election Period 2009-14 by Votes in Assam

Party	2009 % of votes secured	2014 % of votes secured	Change
INC	34.89	29.6	5.29
BJP	16.21	36.5	-20.29
CPM	0.7	0	0.7
SP	0.21	0	0.21
AGP	15	3.83	11.17
ASDC	1.02	0	1.02
NCP	0.23	0	0.23
AUDP	16.1	14.83	1.27
BPF	5.41	2.19	3.22
OTHERS	1.08	2.53	-1.45
Total			44.85 (by ignoring negative signs)
Electoral Volatility			**22.425**

Note: Electoral Volatility is calculated by using formula given by Pedersen, which is calculated by dividing the Total Net Change (by ignoring the signs of the deviations) by 2. In the 2009-2014 election period, the electoral volatility rate is 44.85/ 2 = 22.4 (by percentage of votes).

(9)

Developments and Changes of Tribal Languages in Tripura before and After Joining with India: A Journey of Success

Monoranjan Das

Introduction

Tripura, an ancient province, located in the North–East region of India was princely state and had merged with Indian union on 15th October, 1949. Its three sides are encircled by Bangladesh on the North, West, South and South-East; on other side, in the East, it has common boundary with the states of Assam and Mizoram. Tribal of Tripura are known to be migrated to Tripura during an unknown phase, recorded in the ancient era of Indian history in the chapter of North-Eastern territory from a place in between *Chaina-Tibbet*, *Mongolia* and *Shan* state of *Brama* and *Chittagong* Hill Tracts. The renowned polilotist Professor Suniti Kumar Chatterjee has enlightened some fact on this issue. He says, "The *Boro* section of the *Tibeto-Burman* branch of the *Tibeto Chinese* people (*Boro, Mech, Kachari, Radha, Garo, Tripura*) came to Assam and East Bengal, and were spread all cover East and North Bengal. The time of the *Tibeto- Burman* incursion and settlement in Assam and East-Bengal is not known, but it could not have been long before the beginning of the *Christian* era, at the earliest."[1] (O.D.B.L. introduction,p.3) Their languages are divided into Boro language groups, Kuki-Chinese language group and Arakan language group. He also noted that "Kokborok as *Tipra* of *Mrung* in his '*Magamoupopus' Kirata-Jana Kriti* written in the year 1950. According to him, "Tripura of *Murng* is akin to told *Bora language*." [2] He also stated that this language by saying "Nearly 303,030 people in the state have still kept up their old *Boro* language, the

Tipra or Mrung." [3] The major tribes [4] of Tripura namely Tripuri (5,92,255), Reang (1,88,220), Jamatia (83,347), Kalai (12,011), Rupani (57,210), Uchai (2,447), Noatia (6,290) and Murasing (8,008) among tribal population (11,66,813) of Tripura. These major tribal are Bora groups of tribes of mongoloid origin and their language is categorized as Tibeto-Burman group of languages under Sino-Tibetan group of tribes. The other tribes of Tripura namely Darlong, Halam, Kuki, Lusai, Molson, Kipeng, Bong, Kor-Bong, Bongcher etc. are Tibeto-Burman language of Kuki-Chin groups which is mainly akin to Chinese origin. The rest tribes of Tripura namely Mog and Chakma are Arakanese language group. The *Boro* group of tribes contributes 81% population of the tribes of Tripura and the rest 19% are from other two language groups in Tripura. Beyond the memory record, *Boro* group of tribes who are speaking in Kokborok as the fourth generation language of *Sino-Tibetan* family; where *Sino-Tibetan* group was at the initial stage, then it transformed into Tibta-*Tibeto-Burman* group, then *Boro* group and thereafter finally the Kokborok group. In Tripura, 9, 49,788 tribal people speaks Kokborok language out of 11, 66,813 tribal population. Moreover, in total 11, 88, 041 people speaks Kokborok language over different countries Myanmar, Bangladesh including Tripura, Assam, Mizoram and Utter Pradesh. Interesting, here it is to be referred that as per the linguistic Atlas of India [5] 1991 census had witnessed 6931 people speakers in Kokborok in *Pithorgarh* district of Utter Pradesh paving the way for controversy over the original domicile of these Kokborok speaking people and also their path of migration to Tripura from China via Tibet. As per census 2011, *Tripuri* or *Tripura* or *Tippra* or *Debbarma* (5,92,255) are the major sub-group speaks Kokborok as linguistic identity in Tripura. The dialects of other tribal communities are similar with Kokborok and they understand each other's dialect having diminutive variation. So,eminent polilotist Suniti Kumar Chattopadhay, Dr. Sukumar Sen, Mr. Grierson. and W.W. Hunter mentioned all the tribal language as Tippra or Mrung [6] commonly called as Kokborok. On the other hand, for Kumud Kundu Choudhury, Kokborok means the language of Kokborok speaking tribal community.[7] The tribes Bhil (3,195), Bhutia (19), Garoo(12,952), Lushai (5,384), Mog (37,893) and Munda (14,544) migrated from South and North India does not speaking Kokborok as because they have their own dialect. However, few dialects of these tribes reveal same meaning with Kokborok.

Kokborok, therefore, is not only a language of major group rather it is a language of Tripura and irrespective of caste and creed shall have the right to go insight into the language.

This princely State Tripura had one hundred and eighty four kings [8] belonging Borok racial group. But, Kokborok remained neglected by royal groups. Over the periods, these kings, their family members and their executives had merged with different inhabitants outside their own languages. They had not popularized their mother tongue Kokborok among other communities rather they adopted language of other communities and patronized those with great satisfaction and practice. Unfortunately, no fundamental works for development of Kokborok was done either by the royal kings or by the democratic Government in Tripura before 1979. As a result, this language remained weary and exists only in oral form over the periods. So, the language could not perceive free developments and progressive changes under British colonial phase. In spite of this it moves forward in collaboration with non-tribal languages though often not spoken by the mainlanders. The accountability of the time-consuming developments of this tribal language lies its historicity, where the conflict between NEP (National Education Policy) and WME (Western Model of Education) can be witnessed, notwithstanding the benevolent approaches of the kings of Tripura in the developments of its socio-cultural relations among the masses of Tripura. No remarkable attempt had been made so far for development of tribal language still then. The successful journey of developments and progressive changes of Kokborok has taken by the present ruling Government of Tripura since after the year 1979.

The developments and changes of the status of language are very important, because, the identity of all people is depended in their socio-economic, political, educational and cultural status. And their socio-economic, political, educational and cultural identity is depend and survives in their language, traditional practice of livelihood, folk culture. Tribal language of Tripura is not different from this scenario. Consequently, traditional socio-cultural peculiarities, ethnicity, religious belief, psycho-social adoptability, language variation, economic factor etc. cannot be developed without developing of the language.

Objectives of the Study

- To study the status of developments and changes of tribal languages before and after of joining with India.

- To find out the problems and obstacles for developments and progressive changes of language.
- To find out suggestive measures to come out from problems and obstacles.

Method

Analytical and conceptual method was used in the study. Both quantitative and qualitative approaches were used.

Instrumentation

- Primary data has collected from different experts on the matter.
- Secondary data have collected from different write up.

Implications

As in this study it has been observed that tribal languages in Tripura have been developed and progressively changes after joining in India. In spite of that there have been some problems. Therefore, suitable plans and programs should be implemented for solving the problems and for bringing further quality system of development of tribal language in the state of Tripura.

Findings

The position of development and progress changes of tribal language (Kokborok language) in all sectors socio-political, economic and education, cultural and literatures in Tripura before and after joining with India. This paper would be very useful to go insight into the problem and finding new path to resolve major issues related to language development.

Developments and Changes of Tribal Language in Tripura before of Joining with India

Language has always a place in human dealings and in fact; it is a great tool of thinking which has made human civilization possible. Thus, one of the greatest achievements of the man is his ability to use language. We usually know mother tongue as our language which is as healthy as mother's milk, it is also true about Kokborok for Tripura tribal. In Tripura, beforehand it is noted that primarily Kokborok language was in oral and this stage passed from century to century. Finally, it evolved in the written form from 1703. It is whispered that at first Durlavaendra Narayan

Chantai (priest) had wrote a book (***Rajmala***) in Kokborok to glorify Mahendra Manikya Debbarma, but it was not published publicly and there is not existence in manuscript. There was the proof that Prince Radhakishor Manikhya finished Kokborok dictionary in the year 1876-1877. In this context Mr. C.W. Bolton said, "The Yubaraj (Radha Krishor) is still engaged in complication of a *Tipperah-Bengali* dictionary, and he has of late become a member of the Asiatic society of Bengal" [9] Political agent T.E. Coxhead also reported, " The Yubaraj has, moreover, at my suggestion, set about the compilation of a *Tipperah* vocabulary. He is perfectly acquainted with the vernacular of the hill people." [10] It is unfortunate that, we are not able to trace out the manuscript of Yobaraj's work in Kokborok and the text was not found either in the form of print or in manuscript, as because, Yubaraj's compilation activities was not noticed by anybody except the British agent. Since, the first decade of the twenty century, Kokborok language and her literature and research work slept a Ripvan winkle's sleep up to 1954 due to above mentioned some mysterious reasons. That is why, it may be said certainly up to 1896 Kokborok language was in oral form since it had not any written script, although it adopted the Bengali alphabet written scripts and published its literature '*Kok Boroma*' (Kokborok grammar) by Mohammed Doulat Ahamed in 1897, which was a century and seventeen years ago. Therefore, basic learning on the Kokborok actually had been begun from time. From this phase, Kokborok, the mother tongue of Tripuri, Jamatia, Noatia, Reang, Kolai, Rupani, Uchai, and Murasing communities embarked to enrich and popularize among the Kokborok speaking communities with identity and self reliance. The then contemporary, Thakur Radhamohan Debbarma(1900) had given its full form by writing three books: *Kok Borokma* (grammar of Kokborok), *Traipur bhashabhidhan* (small dictionary on Kokborok) and *Traipur Kathamala* (compiled of stories and translation of Traipur). Therefore, in the beginning of the twentieth century, the authentic renaissance in modern Kokborok literature began with the researcher oriented books on Kokborok by Thakur Radha Mohan Debbarma and Daulat Ahmed. Approximately, in the alike period, Dr. G.Grierson [11] built up India's linguistic survey giving due regard of Kokborok language. Parenthetically, it may be articulated that W.W. Hunter, piled up a comparative Kokborok and language about in 1876, which enables us to have a look into the character of Kokborok's development. Recently, nonetheless, we have getting information which is related with description the rulers' histories in Kokborok which were subsequently written in the form of '***Rajmala'*** by various writers. There are available occurrences in history Kokborok of literature of Tripura that folk tales, war song, *jhum* songs, festival songs, wedding song, love song etc. also developed in written form in Kokborok for the common people by some well known personalities. For instance, Bir Chandra Manikhya wrote Tripura Smriti (1927) (The memory of Tripura). Hereby a beautiful song may be noted from this book,

"Hadukduk kolok maisui pingjaoi //
Pagri nuruglia, jadu parsari nuruglia. //
Hadukduk kalak gunthu pingjagoi //
Yakurai nuruglia jadu Yakurai nuruglia" [12]

(For the growing paddy (*kawin*) plants spread across the high extensive hilly path. // I could not see turban, soul mate could not see your turban. // For the dapati plants grown across the high extensive hilly path. // I could not see your passing heel, soul mate could not see your passing heel //)

From the above mentions song, it makes known that the tribal soldiers of Tripura were extremely brave and duty bound. In the time of battle, they did not only lament over their sacrifice. In summary of this song, their charming reminiscences of near and dear ones had voiced by them. And another Kokborok song may be narrated and observed,

"pachim paro' sipai chamtory //
pub paro' bothai chai kurung" [13]

The inhabitants of the east side are proficient in weaving where as in west side warriors are always engaged in battle). In this song, we observer the words of the village youth ladies who pronounce that the inhabitants of the east are proficient in weaving while there is always war in the west. Yet, again in 1942, Khushi Krishna Tripura was wrote '*Kha Kachang Khumber'* and published. We may be pronounced that triumphant journey of the changes of status and development of Kokborok language and her literature progressive work is started by the Janasikha Samity movement, which was constituted at Durga Choudhury Para, Jirania Sub-Division under west Tripura on the 27th December,1945 (11

Pous,1355 Tring)[14] under the leaders of Sudhanna Debbarma, Dasaratha Debbarma, Agore Debbarma, Biren Datta and Lahxi Biswari Debbarma to develop those cultural traits. Since the motto of this Samity was yeomen service to illiterate Kokborok speaking tribal men-women who are in miserable conditions owing to curse of illiteracy and thus it paved away for spreading light of education among Kokborok speaking distressful tribal people living in remote hilly impassable terrain. Janasikha Samiti (1945) and Ganamukti Parisad were played very important role in the state of Tripura where Kokborok language found an ample opportunity to become the voice of the movement which started for the spread of educational consciousness and against poverty. Tribal language became the tool of this movement. These samities took movement for socio-economic, educational under the language and literal reformation to build up self reliance among tribal of Tripura. The use of the word '*Michhil'*(marching) in Kokborok song does testify this fact. We do not find out such '*Michhil'* word in any written records of Kokborok language before completed second war (1945). Hence, Janasikha Samity took a massive effort to popularize education among the common people in Tripura. Being active means for expansion of Kokborok language in written form as well as literate the common people, the Samity established 488 primary schools in non-government level which was situated in very remote places in the state Tripura where Kokborok was used as a language communication for teaching as medium of instruction. After that for the developments of Kokborok, Sudhanna Debbarma one of the founder leaders of Janasikha Samity, wrote and stage a small *drama* in Kokborok in popularize the tribal language. Between 1945 to 1957 he wrote many books in Kokborok and published literary magazine '*Kwtal Kothama*' (New story), '*Hachuk Khurio*'(foot of hill). In1954, keeping pace with the great Janasikha Samity's movement for education for the first time a literature was published and edited by sudhanna Debbarma. The literary magazine '*Kwtal Kothama'* (1954) gave rise to lots of writings of different literary verities. But, this historical Kokborok magazine was short-lived. According to chorological developments of Kokborok literal works scientifically was started, since and after 1960 through publication of '*chethwang*' (tree) a periodical in Kokborok where in poem, short stories, plays in Kokborok were published. Then came during of 1970, Kokborok opened her literary flood-gate giving birth to every branch of Kokborok literature and that literacy flow is still continuing. In 1972, Govt. of

Tripura was setup Tribal Language Cell for writing text books in Kokborok language to be introduced at primary level. The motto of State Government was some arithmetical and juvenile knowledge in primary education to the Kokborok speaking people in the mother tongue. Ajit Bandho Debbarma's written very much popular book '*swrwngma*' had supplied for on experimental basis. But there was no socio-scientific systematic examination arrangement for the Kokborok students reading at primary level. This test acts as a prelude to the mother tongue teaching process as medium of education in a later period. Again, in 1977, Dasaratha Dev wrote '*Kokborok Chwrwng*' (learns the language of people or learns Kokborok) for the common people which really worthy book for Kokborok speaking people. Just then we come across a Kokborok song an under

"nini numale balonga thangkha
nini nuphale mishhil o thangkha
takabdi takabdi o mwnai o"

Your mother is now in forests, your father is marching with the mass, so beloved child! Do not cry please). [15] It will be evidenced that the language also inspired the political consciousness of the common people. As a result, Mahindra Debbarma published "*Yapri*" (Marching/Footstep), newspaper composed some innumerable songs in multi language (Kokborok, Bengali and Hindi). So, Janasikha Samity movement through which tribal people in whole state of Tripura in general got inspired and understood the important of language, culture, education and democratic rights. But at that juncture development and progressive changes tribal language was facing ups and downs due to some unavoidable circumstances like after merged with India, place of Kokborok deteriorated and openly activities of Janasikha Samity could not performed in public place due to administration i.e. terror of police. Even few times tribal people were afraid of speaking their mother tongue in public place especially in town in form of other men. Even tribal people especially students had to face humiliation in academic institutions and government offices. However, things changed gradually after continuous movements launched by tribal students, youths along with other progressive youths. In spite of that it may be draw that Janasikha Samity movement contributed their knowledge to this to fulfill the preconditions of Kokborok making it fit for becoming medium of instruction.

Developments and changes of Tribal in Tripura language after of joining with India

When Tripura was emerged as state to Indian union in 1949 on 15th October then number of schools was found to be around three hundred under semi-urban areas where medium of instruction was English and Bengali but tribal language-Kokborok was totally neglected as medium of instruction. Meanwhile Janasikha Samity movement established (1945) as many as four hundred eighty eight primary schools in tribal dominated remote hilly areas with a view to spreading education among the illiterate Kokborok speaking tribal people. Besides Mr. Brown Sahib, Education Minister, was willing to give approval of those primary schools run by the Samity and, as a result, three hundred of said those primary schools became Government schools at the behest of the then Education Minister. In 1979, Government of Tripura, without waiting the constitutional amendment, decided to set up Autonomous District Council and recognized Kokborok language as official language in addition to Bengali and English and unanimously constituted the TTAADC, Act, for the Compact tribal areas in the state for betterment i.e. to protect the socio-political, economic, cultural and educational interested of tribal population who for historical reasons presently belongs to the weaker sections of society and thereby, to free them from all sorts of social injustice by passing a bill in assembly floor with the full support because a nation or tribal could not progress in world without recognize, development and scientific changes of their mother tongue as people can easily expose themselves in any field. Language, being one of the important instruments of social upliftment of scheduled tribe. So, the council of ministers has taken a policy decision (1980) to implement Kokborok as a medium of instruction in the primary level and also as official language for the benefits of Kokborok speaking common people so as to they can used their mother tongue in the of educational and official works. The State Government has taken action to getting education in mother tongue as per constitutional right and in Tripura situation is equally important. As a result, not only had this among tribal along listed Kokborok writers begun to enrich this language by contributing in all sections of language and literature but also the stage of developments and progressive changes of Kokborok and it traditional culture to be got its status and national level and international recognition for its store house of rich vocabulary, literal entity and folk tradition. The state government has taken a decision as well not for any particular script rather believes on scientific approach and popular sentiment of its speaking communities and continuing the old practice only in lieu of offering the issue in the uncertainty. The use of Kokborok is the primary object of language development of tribal people in Tripura because it is main stream line language among the tribal and even there are eleven tribal communities who do not know Kokborok. Govt. of Tripura (1991) has setup four units of educational directorate under a common umbrella of State Council of Educational and Research Training. These units are State Institute of Education (STE), Tribal Language Cell i.e. TLC (1993), Educational Publication Unit (EPU) and Bureau of Education and Vocational Guidance (EVGB). For four decades under a Polit Project Officer (PPO), TLC worked independently for development of different tribal languages in the state Tripura. The State Government has setup (2012) Directorate for Kokborok and other minorities languages instated of Tribal Language Cell for survive; developments and progressive changes in Kokborok as well as other minorities' languages. Directorate for Kokborok and other minorities' languages has written and published books on different titles from class I to VIII in Kokborok and from class I to V for *Chakma, Kuki-Mizo, Monipuri, Bishupriya-Manipuri, Halam* and *Mog* as per syllabus by the TBSE as per NCERT guideline.[16] It is also decided by the administration of Tripura Tribal Areas Autonomous District Council (TTAADC) that Kokborok language has introduced from class I from in the academic in 2006 as medium of instruction. All the primary schools under TTAADC have been identified for teaching Kokborok from Class I to Class VIII as an independent language. Kokborok language are being taught to more than 75,858 students by 6,216 numbers including 6,566 numbers Kokborok teachers in 1,719 numbers primary schools in all over Tripura as a subject and also as a medium of instruction and tribal culture like folk song, folk music, folk dance and other cultural art form of tribal of Tripura were rejuvenated right from then.[17] As a result, at the present, Kokborok not only in tribal dominated in schools but also in often all primary schools, so that, children outside the Kokborok speaking group could also learn this language as well as TTAADC had built Tribal Folk Cultural Academy for develop and expansion the Kokborok along with other tribe linguistic culture. Some Kokborok writers are writing Kokborok dictionary and other important books as similar to one world, one dictionary' with the help of TTAADC for development of Kokborok. On other hand, TTAADC has provided study for *Chakma, Manipur, Mog, Miza* and *Muslim* students who are willing to study their own languages and their literature in addition to as per TBSE under NCRT Syllabus. So, *Chakma* and *Manipuri* students are studying in classes I to VIII which areas are respectively *Chakma* and *Manipuri* dominate, *Mog* students are studying in classes I to X and Ramthukur College in Pali language in addition to other languages especially for Mog. Mizu students are also studying in their language under *Jampui* and *Dasda* block. Muslim students are studying *Pazil* in *Madrassas* and schools from class I to XII in Tripura. Tripura University also desires for the development of Kokborok. As a result, University has been introduced six month Kokborok certificate course in 1993 and a one year diploma course in 2003 and as an elective subject in 2012 and foundation course for all under graduate degree colleges. Also, the State Government attaches topmost priority for overall development of tribal language and also implementing various developmental initiatives in a more systematic manner. Besides, existing sachems are also being renewed and modified to suit the demand of time. To achieve overall development of the tribal people, the Government of Tripura had launched twenty-five points development package (1999-2002). [18] The thrust of the program was to create social, education, and economic infrastructure in tribal areas so that employment opportunities in tribal areas can be ensured. With views to expand its purview further, the State Government had announced thirty seven points development package (2003-2007) and the same was successfully implemented also. To accelerate the efforts of the State Govt. towards development of tribal people, a special package for welfare of tribal is being implemented in state. In the special emphasis has been on Kokborok language and culture development. [19] Evaluation, research, documentation, presentation and promotion of tribal language are being done through tribal research institution. Thus, to maintain, promote and revive the tribal language as well as traditional culture of the tribal, various program viz. seminar, recitation, exhibition etc. has been organized in the tribal research institute. It is first part of development of Kokborok.

On other hand, nationalism movement begins in the end part. News writers and electronic Medias begin public appearance. To develop and promote the tribal language and culture, Tripura State Academy of cultural was setup (2009-2010). At present Tripura state museum is function of preserving and spreading of language and culture of the tribal. As a result, All India Radio and National Dooradashan News and others local news channels have come forward to broadcast Kokborok literature and socio-culture regularly. Jahar Acharjee, Shyam Lal Debbarma etc. are regularly participating in the Kokborok section in different Medias. In the meantime, 'Aitarma', 'Hanikok', 'Hawjlai', 'Khumber', 'Lama', 'Sachlang', etc. periodical literatures also appeared. It is true that the life span of many of the above mentioned did not extend extreme far except "Lama" which published by Nirajan Beddarma, president of Tripura Upajati Gana Mukti Parishad. There were two organizations appeared; namely Kokborok Sahity Sabha and Kokborok Unnayan Parishad, during the first portion of seventies for development of their mother tongue. Dey Kokborok Publishers, Hachookni Khoranmg, Jura Publishers, Kokborok Sahitya Sambad, Kokborok Tie Hukumu Mission, Nava Chandan Prakashani etc. are doing publish Kokborok as develop of this language. Not only that the Kokborok writers, singers, dancers are respectively writing, singing and dancing in their respective field, in addition the writers of this language pay attention to translate the Indian and foreign literatures. As a result of success, meanwhile, Chanda Kanta Murasing had obtained Language honour award from Sahitya Academic, but also drama and cinema are started their successful journey. Lantharai, Kochuk Hachikham, Chamri Ompa, Nwng Bai, Khumpui, Raima Saima, Bukhuknwi, Lamani Haduk, Kwmajak are consequently famous cinema in Kokborok. So we can say that developments and progressively changes of Kokborok are forcedly going on, all blossom should be stimulated into flowers afterward fruit in future.

Problems

The problem of medium of instruction is still there at the elementary stage because after studying in Kokborok language up to class VIII, there is no further scope to study in mother tongue for Kokborok speaking tribal students in all schools in Tripura. They are bound to study in Bengali language from class IX onwards. On other hand, a non-tribal teacher who has no skill in Kokborok language, has been posted at Kokborok speaking tribal population dominated schools and a lot of students of these school who have no exposure to Bengali language and unquestionably, there may be communication gap between the students and teachers. Consequently, transaction of lesson in the class room are obstructed; hampered to a great extent. It is one foremost sort of obstruction that Kokborok is the main stream line among eleven tribal communities in Tripura whereas some of them cannot speaks or interested to develop of their mother tongue. Though Government has taken initiatives, but, official machinery should be improved further for giving equal importance to survive and grow for Kokborok and all other minorities' languages in Tripura.

Conclusion

"Language is not only mere a communication medium but it is more, it is certainly freedom, justice, culture and to grow at owns Aspiration." [20] As per census report 1991, it is found that several tribal languages were in existence in the state since the rule of Masnikhya dynasty. But, Tripura's tribes usually Kokborok speaking people had to face identity crisis as marginalized speaking communities. Moreover, though Tripura's kings were rich in wisdom and learning from generation still they had neglected the mother tongue-Kokborok rather they encouraged counterpart Bengali language. The most important point is that if language and culture were not nourished and given exposure then an identity crisis might be developed among the language speaking communities. So, Kokborok had been recognized [21] (1979) as official state language of Tripura after prolonged struggle of Kokborok speaking communities under the leadership of Dasaratha Dev and different democratic organizations. It is my judiciousness that there is no end of struggle and some initiatives are to be taken to survive their language as follows:

(1) The administrative patronization is gradually more necessary to develop the tribal languages. All possible effort shall be taken to implement and for inclusion of Kokborok in 8th schedule of Indian Constitution. Within short period, attempt should be taken for Kokborok in B.ED. course, as well as in core subjects for all under graduate and post graduate degree courses under Tripura University and would be in future new University.

(II) Kokborok speakers should have sincere effort to develop their mother tongue. Extensive use of print and electronic media would be useful for language development and participant of mass people. Un-printing folk literatures, oral tradition etc. need to be collected and focused to highlight in written form and as well as all writers, poets and literarists inside and outside the user communities shall be encouraged for creating high standard literature in Kokborok.

(III) Kokborok, now is taught in a small number of primary and high schools up to class VIII, but it has no proper use, because there is no capacity to teach in Kokborok from class IX in all general schools. This deficiency should be eliminated to reduce the dropout due to language.

(IV) Directorate of Kokborok and other Minority Languages under Department of School Education need to perform their activities properly throughout Tripura by incorporating in all schools and also social education through proper approach at nursery label.

Therefore, issues of improving quality of education and effective functioning of schools by engaging the attention of the Government at the highest priority. This is essentially required to address major concerns of the community and stakeholders regarding classroom teaching, effective learning by students, and attendance of students etc. several instructions were issued on specific issues from time to time. All Headmasters and teachers in charges have to need to give more concentration for improving functions of schools by involving all. The teachers of Kokborok medium schools may not be inadequate, but in many schools teachers are not skilled and well trained, as because, most of the teachers has not obtained the B.T. and B. Ed training as requirement. We have to remember that the people of world where living is pacing very quickly. The third millennium's inhabitants of Tripura are also enthusiastically waiting for a vivid future and glowing dawn of a new day with a dream to raise their head and place their position within international community. In spite of that it would like to say Tripura is also trying its level best in the Government and Non-Government level to develop different tribal languages for the developments and changes of all the scheduled tribes' communities to keep pace with their other counterparts; with a view to this. People cannot reside in the den. Indeed, we are surviving under the wide-reaching atmosphere where our dream is also soaring high but we have to keep in mind that emotional hurry for language's development is not the merely means. We should not think for a particular community and learn to walk off with all. Our thinking should be remained for man and mankind for society and it inhabitants. Thus, Kokborok speaking community, at present at the door-gate of national recognition at full fledged. A full blown Kokborok elite class, please be catch her hand. In this way long lives the Kokborok speking community.

" Hani maya chwng narwknai
lekhaapara chwng swrwngnal"

(We shall love our country, we shall read and learn)[22]

References

1. Acharyya, R.K.(2007),Development of Tribal Languages: A hope for the Mission, TRCI, Govt. of Tripura, P.79
2. Ibid, P.80
3. Ibid, P.80
4. Directorates of Census(2011), Agartala, States Primary Census Abstract For Individual Scheduled Tribe, p.15
5. Census Report, (1980)Atlas of India Based on 1991,Choudhry,K.K.,"The Origin and Development of The Bengali Language," Agartala,P.78
6. Acharyya R.K.(2007),(Editor), Development of Tribal Languages: A hope for the Mission, TRCI, Govt. of Tripura, P.137
7. Ibid, P p.178-98 referred from Gabeshaker Dairy by Choudhury,K.K.. Akhara, ,Agartala, 2006
8. Kali Prasanna Sen, Rajmala
9. Administration Report Of The Political Agency, Hill- Tipprah, 1976-77, Vol.1, P103
10. Administration, A Report From T.E. Coxhead, 1876, Vol., P,78
11. Grierson, Dr. G., Linguistic Survey Of India, New Delhi, Vol V, Part-1,Page.132
12. Debbarma, N., Kokborok Bhasha Sahityeer Cramabikash, Naba Chandana Pukasani, Agartala, Tripura, ,P. 56
13. R.K.,Acharyya, (2007), Development Of Tribal Languages:A Hope for the Mission, TRI, Govt. of Tripura, P.125
14. Ibid, P.125
15. Chakraborty,S.K. (1994), Goutami Sahitya Samskriti Bishaka Patrika, Dasaratha Dev's Article: No.3, Murdha Mlan Muk

Mokhee Ditee Habee Bhasha, Sudhanna Debbarma Smaree Sankhya, Govt.of Tripura, Kyuik Print , Agartala, P.5

16. Debbarma, K. N.(2013),An Article: Kokborok O Anyaanya Sanyaloghu Bhasa Unnayana O Tripura, In Sikha Samachara, Smaranika, 52th Sikhak Dibasha, Dept. of School Education, Govt. of Tripura, P.45
17. Acharyya,R.K.(2007),(Editor)'S Development of Tribal Languages :A hope for the Mission,TRI, Govt. of Tripura, P.127
18. Secretary (2015), Developments Initiatives, 1982-2014, TTAADC, Display Report of Tripura Statehood Day, P.20-23
19. At A Glance-(2014), The Achievement Of Tribal Welfare Department, Tribal Welfare Department, Government Of Tripura, Print :RB Group # Www.Twdtripura.In , P. 3 Hand Bill
20. Jitendra Choudhurty',(2006),Minister of Tribal Welfare Dept.)'S Presidential Speech In The Seminar Of "Development Of Tribal Languages : Sharing Of Experiences' On 27th -28th May, 2006, R.K. Acharyya, (Editor) Development Of Tribal Languages: A hope for the Mission, T.R.I., Govt. Of Tripura, P.17
21. Edited By The Eassayist,(1980) Education Department Of Formed Kokborok Advisory Board And Kokborok Text Book Writer Committee,p.9
22. Debbarma, M., Debbarma, N., Debbarma, A & Roy R.,(2007) Theatre Song, Referred By Debbarma S.L., His Article- An Evolution of Kokborok Language And Literature, R.K. Acharyya, (Editor) Development of Tribal Languages: A hope for the Mission, T.R.I., Govt. of Tripura, P118

(10)

The Liberation Movement of Bangladesh (1971): Through the Debates of Tripura Territorial Assembly

Md. Mojahid Rahman

With the merger of Tripura, a native State with special status, with Indian Union in October, 1949, it was categorized under Group 'C' and was being administered by one Chief Commissioner on behalf of the Govt. of India(1). After certain changes in the administrative structure, Tripura was declared a Union Territory in 1957 and by 1963 the first Territorial Assembly starts its functioning with 30 members in total. Congress was in the Treasury Bench. The 2nd Territorial Assembly came into being in 1967 and it remained in function in 1971. The party position was as under--- (2)

Congress	....	27
CPI (M)	....	02
CPI	....	01
	Total	30

The Congress party formed the ministry with allegation of poll-rigging. *The 6- member ministry was as follows:-*

1. Sri Sachindra lal Singh - The CM
2. Sri Krishnadhan Bhattacharjee - The Finance minister
3. Sri Tarit mohan Dasgupta - The Labour Minister
4. Sri Rajprasad Choudhury - Deputy Minister
5. Sri Prafulla Rn Das - Deputy Minister

6. Sri Mansur Ali - Deputy Minister(3)

The Opposition MLAs were :-

1. Sri Bidyachandra Debbarma - CPI (M)
2. Sri Abhiram Debbarma - CPI (M)
3. Sri Aghore Debbarma - CPI

Speaker/ Dy. Speaker

1. Sri Manindra lal Bhowmik - The Speaker
2. Sri Usha Ranjan Sen - The Dy. Speaker (4).

There was only one lady member and she was Smt. Renu Chakraborty.

The Second Territorial Assembly was in function up to June, 1971 and was dissolved in October, 1971, when President's Rule was imposed in Tripura. The Assembly met twice in 1971(5).

By March,1971, the all-out situation in Pakistan was very much grave as Awami League was in a position to form the National Government with absolute majority in the National Assembly as well as in the Provincial Assembly of East Pakistan. The Military Dictator Mr. Yahya Khan under the advice of Mr. Z.A Bhutto unleashed reign of terror in East Pakistan instead of handing over power to the Awami League and its unquestioned Leader Sheikh Mujibur Rahman. On 25th March, 1971, army was on the street with full arms & ammunitions and initiated brutal mass-killing of the people of East Pakistan. This sudden change in the attitude of the ruling Junta of Pakistan created panic everywhere in East Pakistan especially in Dhaka .People started to flee from Dhaka to save their lives and prestige(6).

The 9-month long Liberation Movement of Bangladesh (March-Dec, 1971) was an epoch-making incident in the History of South- East Asia and it was really the *partition* of Pakistan which was created on the basis of Two-Nation Theory in 1947. Immediately after the establishment of Pakistan consisted of two geographically separate Territories like West and East Pakistan with a land and sea- route distance of about 1200 miles, and 2400 miles respectively, the Bengali- speaking people of East Pakistan received a heavy shock while Mohammed Ali Jinnah, the Farther of the Nation, made one statement in the Constituent Assembly on Feb 15, 1948 that "Pakistan being a Muslim State, Urdu will be its State language." This declaration ultimately led to the LANGUAGE MOVEMENT in East Pakistan on Feb. 21, 1952 claiming the lives of some energetic students like Barkat, Salam, Rafiqur and others. "Thus, the language issue brought all the East Pakistanis together and created a sense of Nationhood in their minds" (7).

The Western Wing with their dominating and colonial attitude did not try to understand the sentiment of their counterpart in the East. As a result, the *Cultural Heritage* of the East was time and again discouraged; sometimes thwarted. In the 60's, the Pakistan Govt. put a ban on the literature and Music of Rabindranath Tagore; the same Govt. banned some popular books; e.g.. "The social History of Bengal" by Kamruddin Ahmed, "Sanskritik Sankat" (in Bengali) by Badraddin Umar etc (8).

In other aspects of life like economy, politics, society, civil & military administration, British colonial exploitation was just replaced by West Pakistani one. West Pakistan practically treated East Pakistan as its colony. So, in all important issues, West Pakistan was dominant while East was a mere on-looker. The west Pakistanis had strikingly superseded its counter- part in controlling armed forces. Actually, the Army selection Board closed its doors on the Bengalis on the plea that there was a 'lack of manpower with qualities of leadership among them (9).

Statistics show that even by 1968, the representation of East Pakistan in the Civil Service of Pakistan was only 36%; in class I officers' cadre in the various Ministries and Departments of the Central Secretariat, the percentage of East Pakistani officers was on an average less than one-third of the total number.

Various research works has been done on the economic system of Pakistan. Only one example is set here to understand the nature of colonial attitude of the West. Harvard economists, namely, Edward S. Mason, Robert Drofman and Stephen A. Marglin have pointed out in general:-

The per capita income in West Pakistan in 1969-70 was 61% higher than that in East Pakistan.

In 1950-60 East Pakistan received only 20% development expenditure and West 80%. East Pakistan was lagging far behind the West in respect of Industrial Development and Export-Import balance.

Maximum foreign economic assistance was utilized in the West wing. Glaring disparity is found between the East and West wing in respect of Agricultural development. West was very much ahead in this respect.

Bengalis of East Pakistan could not swallow all such glaring differences in the name Pakistan or Islam or Muslim League (10).

Disillusioned and disgruntled, Bengalis began agitation just after Jinnah's declaration on the language issue and the agitation was intensified in the 60s while the popular Awami League party started Autonomy movement under 6-point Demand. The Marshall Law Administrator General Ayub Khan failed in his attempt to curb the popular movement. The Agartala Conspiracy case was lodged against the Great leader Sheikh Mujibur and others proved to be boomerang to the Pak Goverment and General Ayub had to quit. Under tremendous pressure from the East wing, the Army Administration under Yahya khan became bound to hold General Election in Pakistan in 1970-71 where Awami League acquired absolute majority and its leader, elevated now as Bangabandhu, was supposed to be the Prime Minister of Pakistan. But the ruling Junta under pressure from Mr. Z.A. Bhutto, the leader of Pakistan Peoples Party, denied to hand over power and instead, unleashed a Reign of Terror in East Pakistan. Armed forces came out on the street and began to gun dawn general people, students, teachers, and intelligentsia. The old, the children, the women were not excused. At this, the Bengalis became perturbed and began to flee to the neighbouring India (11).

Tripura, a North-Eastern state, backward in all aspects of life, situated strategically at the heart of East Pakistan, opened its border to save the lives of the refugees. Influx of refugees started pouring in Tripura (12). The Territorial Council was not sitting idle about the developments in East Pakistan. On the Adjournment motion put forward by Sri. Bidya Chandra Debbarma, a CPI (M) MLA, the Speaker requested the Leader of the House to make a statement (13). At this, Sri S.L. Singh, the CM, made an emotional statement supporting the cause of the people of East Pakistan and condemning the massacre of unarmed civilian by brute force of a modern army. The CM (Leader of the House) explained the philosophy for their support to the movement of the people of East Pakistan. He expressed his feeling thus: - "I fully realize the feeling of the House on the present situation in East Pakistan. We are a democratic country and in the Fifth General Election our countrymen have again demonstrated their unflinching faith in democracy and --------. It is, therefore, but natural that our people will express great concern at the development in East Pakistan where the recent happenings have stood in the culmination of the democratic process that was ushered in the general election in Pakistan that was held in December last and the people have been undergoing a severe trial for their faith in democracy. It is well known that we are all for a democratic way of life and whoever fights for democracy will always has our moral support. We have always condemned the massacre of unarmed civilians by the brute force of a modern army in any part of the world. Our heart goes out in sympathy for the people of East Pakistan at this hour of their trial. And I have no doubt that I voice the feelings of all of you when I say that we hope that the future generations of the people of East Pakistan will proudly say that their forbears did not fail them at the hour of their greatest trial." He finished his statement on that day (on 29th March, 1971 i.e. on the 5th day of the Crackdown in Dhaka) in a very strong tune: *"I may reiterate that we stand for democracy and socialism and we shall condemn any forces that stand in the way of these noble ideals in any part of the world*"(14). The important Budget session had thus been adjourned and the Bangladesh issue was taken up for discussion. The Speaker first allowed 20 minutes for discussion on the issue but on strong demand from the members allowed 1 hour 15 minutes for the Opposition and 45 minutes for the ruling Party. But all most all the members crossed the time limit to express their great concern over the unwanted developments in East Pakistan; they condemned the Yahya Govt. and expressed sympathy towards the cause of the Bengalis. The members understood the limitation of the House, *so they requested the leader of the House to draw the attention of the Govt. of India so that Govt. of India took the issue to the UNO for its intervention for putting a stop to the untoward situation that was going on in Pakistan (15).* Some members cited the examples of Korea and Vietnam where UNO involved its all forces to solve the crises. Likewise, UNO should come forward in respect of Bangladesh issue. Some members requested the Govt. of India to recognize the Government of Bangladesh while it put forward such demand. From the discussion it is also revealed that the students as well as the youth of Tripura were very much anxious on the brutal killings of the Bengalis in East Pakistan (16).

What is astonishing is the fact that each and every member was very serious in assessing the situation in the neighboring country on the 5th day of the commencement of brutal killing in East Pakistan. The names of the Hon'ble Members and their statements in very short form are placed below to show their eagerness in this aspect (17):-

Promode Ranjan Dasgupta:-In his speech he expressed his great concern over the Bangladesh issue and demanded the intervention of the UNO and the Govt. of India as well as of the PM of India so that genocide may be stopped in any way.

Abhiram Debbarma:-All most in the same tune Mr. Debbarma condemned the fascist force of Pakistan who flooded the country with human blood and appealed to the Govt. of India to draw the attention of the UNO to put an end to the developments that made East Pakistan all most a hell.

The other Hon'ble Members expressed their concern almost in the same spirit. We find Hon'ble Member *Sri Naresh Roy* initiating his speech with a very popular slogan of the Bengalis of East Pakistan, *JOY BANGLA*. *Sri Kshitish Ch. Das and Sri Benoy Bhusan Banerjee* informs us about the anxiousness of the Students and Youths of Tripura on the plight of the people of East Pakistan due to the brutal atrocities committed by the Military Junta of Pakistan. *Smt. Renu Chakraborty*, the only woman member of the Assembly, expressed her emotion boldly that the people of Tripura had their blood-relation with the people of Bangladesh. She asserted that genocide might not be the internal problem of a country and she demanded intervention of the Govt. of India in Bangladesh issue. *Sri Kshitish Ch. Das* recalled that Bangladesh was once their *MOTHERLAND (18)*. The other Members who anxiously expressed their views on the issue were:

Sri Sunil Chandra Datta,

,, Aghore Debbarma,

,, Upendra Kr. Roy,

,, Debendra Kishore Choudhury,

,, Jatindra Kr. Majumder,

„ Tarit Mohan Dasgupta,

„ Suresh Chandra Choudhury,

„ Bidyachandra Debbarma,

„ Radhika Ranjan Gupta,

Sri Bidyachandra Debbarm brought an ADJOUNMENT MOTION demanding immediate intervention of the Govt. of India in the Bangladesh issue but that was defeated in the Assembly (19).

Summing up of the reaction of the members of the Assembly on 29th March, 1971:

(1) The Military Crackdown started in East Pakistan under Yahya Regime on 25th March,1971, was highly condemned in the TLA,

(2) The Liberation Movement started spontaneously under the leadership of Awami League especially Sheikh Mujibur Rahman was wholeheartedly supported by all the Members of the Treasury Bench and the Members of Opposition.

(3) The Members were conscious about the limitations of the Territorial Legislative Assembly to support the Movement directly

(4) So, they appealed to the Govt. of India, its PM Shrimati Indira Gandhi to support the Movement strongly and to offer recognition to the Govt. of Bangladesh.

(5) They also appealed to the said Authority to draw the attention of the UNO so that the UNO could put pressure on the Govt. of Pakistan to stop genocide in East Pakistan and to solve the crises in the eastern part of Pakistan.

On 31st March 1971 i.e. on the 7th day of the commencement of the brutal killing, Shri S. L. Sing, the CM, moved a resolution in the house. "*In view of the grave situation rising out of denial of human rights of the people of the East Bengal and atrocity committee (sic) by Yahia (sic) and his followers on the people of Bangla Desh, this House extends its full support to the freedom loving people of Bangla Desh in the struggle for establishing democratic right and requests the Govt. Of India to recognize the newly formed Govt. of Bangla Desh headed by Sheik Mujibar Rahaman (sic) and extends all kinds of help to the people of Bangla Desh in their struggle for freedom.*

This house also keeps on record its sorrow and for those who laid their lives for the cause of freedom and democracy of Bangla Desh (20)."

What a spontaneous zeal! The peoples' representatives of the state of Tripura was so anxious that they might be the first not only in India but in the World to request the Govt. of India to recognize the newly formed Government of Bangladesh headed by Sheik Mujibur Rahman. Almost each and every member of the Assembly participated in the discussion and supported wholeheartedly the resolution moved by the CM. The Members could not restrain their emotion on the resolution and spoke & expressed their solidarity towards the freedom fighters of Bangladesh. The Members who stood to support the resolution were (21):

Shri Tarit Mohan Dasgupta,
,, Aghor Debbarma,
,, Prafulla Kr. Das,
,, Krishnadas Bhattacharya,
,, Abhiram Debbarma,
,, Rajkumar Kamaljit Singha
,, Bidyachandra Debbarma,
,, Upendra Kumar Roy,
,, Benoy Bhushan Banarjee,
,, Debendra Kishore Choudhury,
,, Kshitish Ch. Das,
,, Promode Rn. Dasgupta,
,, Ghanashyam Dewan,
,, Sunil Ch. Datta,
,, Naresh Roy,
,, Radhika Ranjan Gupta,
,, Suresh Ch. Choudhury,
Shrimati Renu Chakraborty,
Shri Rabindrachandra Deb Rangkhal,
,, Nishikanta Sarkar,
,, Monomohan Debbarma

The Chief Minister first thanked the Hon'ble Speaker and all the Members of the House for their strong support of the aforesaid resolution put forward by the CM himself. *The CM then thanked lakhs of Freedom Fighters who were ready to sacrifice their lives to the cause of their motherland, for the cause of democracy and for the humanity of the World.* The Speaker then put the Govt. Resolution to vote and the resolution was passed unanimously. Not only that, the members under Bidyachandra Debbarma demanded adjournment of the House on that day in view of the emotional atmosphere evolved during the discussion of the Resolution. As that was Budget session and important business were awaiting, the House could not be adjourned (22).

During Monsoon Session, Govt. was bound to make a statement in the Assembly on 21st June,'71 regarding the influx of refugees in Tripura. A 6-page (point-wise) statement was read out in the House which showed Government's utmost endeavour to rehabilitate almost 10 lacks of refugees in a state of 15 lacks of inhabitants (23).

Point-wise Summery of the Statement of the CM in the Assembly on 21 June, 1971.

1) Addressing the Speaker the CM stated that in the last session he had already explained the unbearable circumstances created by the Military Junta of Pakistan which compelled the people of Bangladesh especially the women and children to leave their homeland. He had experienced the plight of that people.
2) The CM stated that the influx of refuges was still going on. In some hours in the last week in the Sidhai-Mohanpur Area, came 20,000 refugees. Most of them were Muslims. He gave the approximate number of the refugees at that time which stood to ten lakhs. And the pouring of refugees in Tripura was still going on @ 15,000 to 20,000 per day.
3) He informed the House that on the part of a small state like Tripura, which was backward in respect of economy and communication, it was really difficult to shoulder the responsibility of a huge number of refugees. Normally, Tripura was overburdened with 15 lakhs of people. The situation was aggravated with the flow of refugees' everyday.
4) With limited resources, Tripura was doing its best with unquestioned and wholehearted support from the people of Tripura which pleased the observers coming from other parts of India and abroad. He admitted that in the distant Sub-Divisions like Sabroom

and Belonia, satisfactory arrangement for the rehabilitation of the refugees could not be made. Moreover, the refugees were to face other difficulties but it was natural due to abnormal, sudden and unthinkable influx of refugees; but utmost attention was being given for the welfare of the refugees.

5) The CM acquainted the Members of the House about Govt. arrangement for the welfare of the refugees:-a) arrangement of shelter for 2.25 lakhs of refugees, b) 250 Tube-wells and 500 normal wells were dug, c) more temporary sheds were constructed; problems are there but these were to be overcome. Some camp materials were received from the Govt. of Australia.

6) The Govt. of Tripura had opened a new Refugee Rehabilitation Department with one Director, 3 ADMs, 26 Camp Supervisors and other employees. One Engineering Division was approved with one Executive Engineer, 4 Assistant Engineers, 26 Overseers and some other Clerks. Health care was also viewed seriously; due to lack of Medical personnel, refugee-doctors were being given appointment. The number of beds was being increased in the GB & VM Hospitals; arrangement was made to open one Dispensary for a Camp of 20,000 refugees. Immunization was operated to all most all the refugees.

7) The Govt. of India sanctioned till that time 3.2 crores of Rupees for the rehabilitation of the refugees and that Govt. assured to sanction more fund for the purpose.

8) Saving the 24 Camps already constructed, plan was prepared to establish 4 other camps which might accommodate 60,000 refugees each and that would be controlled by the Govt. of India. Plan was also prepared to send refugees to other states by rail from Dharmanagar if it was approved by the Govt. of India. Government of Tripura also took initiative to vacate the educational Institutions for normalcy in the said Institutions. The Govt. of Tripura thanked those near relatives who took the pains to provide shelters to their relatives who came over here as refugees. The Govt. was trying to provide some relief to those relatives.

9) Limited number of refugees was being shifted to Guahati by one American Cargo which is specially engaged for transporting foodstuff from Guahati to Agartala.

10) Demand for foodstuff was increasing day by day due to heavy rush of evacuees. The Government was very conscious about transporting of foodstuff from Dharmanagar Rail Godown to other parts of Tripura to keep the supply in order. Tripura State Transport Authority and the Military Authority arranged number of trucks for transportation of foodstuff. The Railway Authority tried to create problems but that could be averted due to the interference of the State government and support of the people.

11) The CM on behalf of the Govt. of Tripura and the people of Tripura took the opportunity to thank those friendly countries and International Organizations who extended their benevolent hands for the welfare of the refugees. The CM acquainted the House delightfully that the World-mind had awaked in favour of Bangladesh. So, Tripura received medicines, milk-powder, triples etc. by Air daily from various countries.

12) The CM assured the House that though overwhelming pressure was on the Government due to heavy influx of the refugees, the Govt. would not hesitate to take due measure for the welfare of the refugees in the face limited manpower and other facilities (24).

On this Report the Hon'ble Members demanded discussion very strongly and that was accepted by the Speaker and the CM; the discussion continued to the next day session (25).

Debate on the Statement made by the Chief Minister on the floor of the House on 21. 6. 71 regarding influx of refugees in Tripura

The Speaker intended to close this chapter immediately after the Chief Minister's Statement on the influx of refugees in Tripura. But the Members of Treasury Bench vehemently demanded discussion on this and *Shri Tarit Mohan Dasgupta* drew the attention of the Speaker saying that "Sir, *it is very important*." The Leader of the House i.e. the CM also eagerly agreed to have a discussion over the issue. So, the Speaker invited the Members to participate in the discussion (26)

It is clearly evident from the proceedings of the TLA dated 22 June, 1971, which was a continuation of the discussion of the previous day that the Members were not at all happy with the Statement of the CM on the refugee problem and the Government's handling of the refugee problem. *Shri Tarit Mohan Dasgupta* crossed his 15 minutes' time-limit to express his anger over the insufficient activities of the Government in rehabilitating the refugees in Tripura. He suggested introducing Dole System in lieu of supplying dry ration to the refugees due to heavy corruption in the present system. He gives his opinion on the registration system of the refugees by the Police which was a very delaying process. He also suggested engaging the teachers and educated persons from the refugees in controlling the refugee camps just as the Govt. had engaged the Doctors and the Compounders in maintaining the Hospitals and Health Camps (27).

Shri Aghore Debbarma was very much categorical in criticizing the Government's policy with regard to the handling of the refugee problems. He mentioned three particular problems of Tripura—A) there were 27 thousand of unemployed youths in Tripura; the Govt. could not handle the problem. B) Heavy influx of refugees created enormous problems in rehabilitating them in Tripura. C) There were communication problem in Tripura; no Railway extension up to Agartala. In the circumstances, the Govt. was a total failure in handling the situation. *So, Govt. should take initiative in deporting the excess evacuees to other States* (italics used by the researcher to show the importance of the statement). Corruption should be averted immediately and Indian Foreign Policy should be very bold in restraining the Pak Forces in their limit (28).

Shri Abhiram Debbarma was also very much categorical in criticizing the Govt. Policy over the issue. He was very much critical of the State as well as Central Govt. as both these governments followed very unconvincing policy with regard to Bangladesh. He said that the arrangements made by the Governments for 10 lakhs of refugees were very much unsatisfactory and under this condition the refugees could not leave anyhow. The refugees were not receiving the sanctioned amount of Rs.1.10 due to corruption. He categorically mentioned about 126 refugee families who were staying at Raima -Sharma area in South Tripura and who were not being provided with minimum requirement of the day. Deportation of refugees to Assam was very essential in view of the grave situation arising out of heavy influx; otherwise, this would lead to the collapse of the economy of Tripura. Unemployment problem, peasant problem, communication problems were being neglected in Tripura. Agriculture was disrupted; people suffered due to heavy rush of refugees. Repeated requests of the Speaker failed to normalize Shri Abhiram Debbarma who was vehemently criticizing the Govt. for its failure in all aspects of administration.

He argued that on one hand the profit mongers were busy in looting; on the other hand, people are going to die due to heavy price hike (29).

Shri Prafulla Kr. Das stood in favour of the CM and his Statement and he debated the arguments made by the Members mentioned above. He argued that in the face of severe abnormal situation in Tripura like weak communication system, Tripura already rehabilitated all most ten lacks of refugees; but flow was not abating. So, the problem was a National one and that should be understood by the Members. Then, there was a chaos in the House and the Speaker, the CM, Abhiram Debbarma and others debated on the issue (30).

Sri Promode Rn Dasgupta severely criticized the Govt. for its mismanagement of the refugee problem. He gave a picture of brutal atrocities committed by the Pak. Govt. in Bangladesh and he recalled the unanimous proposal of the House for recognition of Bangladesh by the Govt. of India. He argued that the Govt. of India should recognize the Government of Bangladesh and provide with arms and ammunitions to the freedom fighters of Bangladesh. He then mentioned the deplorable conditions of the refugees staying at various places in Tripura especially in Sadar North i.e. at Mohanpur area. He indicated about the corruption which led to the poor infrastructure made for the shelter of the refugees. He questioned the Government's decision which declares the opening of the Schools of Agartala Town and not the Schools of villages. This meant that evacuees would leave in the Schools of villages and the education system would be thwarted. This was one type of discrimination and that should not be continued. He also questioned the system of registration in the police station which compelled the refugees to come to the PS from a very distant camp and to wait for long hours with their children and older ones. He suggested registration in the Tehsils. The Speaker intimated that his time was over but Shri Dasgupta continued to point out the corruption in sanctioning diet to the refugees, in constructing shelters; the refugees were being squeezed in many way, even the ladies sexually (31).

Shri Jatindra Kr. Datta drew the attention of the Speaker on the sudden influx of the refugees which created real problems in Tripura in several ways. He indicated that the arrangement for drinking water by setting up of Tube-wells and other general wells was not sufficient at all. Shri Datta requested the authority to sanction dry milk for the children who were really infants. On the other issues he supported the CM (32).

Shri Debendra Kishore Choudhury also severely criticized Govt.'s failure in respect of rehabilitation of the refugees. He also requested the Govt. expand the registration to the Tehsils and arrange for drinking water; the problem of drinking water already gave birth to serious hazards leading to serious type of cholera which already ha taken 10 lives of the refugees (33).

Shri Binoy Bhushan Choudhury stood in favour of the CM. He criticized attitude of the Opposition Members because they followed the double-standard policy in respect of Sheikh Mujibur Rahman and the refugees. He said that the refugees are the part and parcel of the people of Tripura. He, however, remained very sympathetic towards the refugee children whose death rate was very high. He demanded special arrangements for the children and the refugees outside the camps (34).

Shri Nishikanta Sarker spoke in favour of the Government. He argued that it was not the corruption but the mistake in handling the huge number of the refugees in Tripura. He suggested some measures for the welfare of the refugees opposing the allegations of the Oppositions (35).

Shri Bidya Debbarma from the Opposition Bench drew the attention of the Speaker about the real condition of Tripura where starvation, corruption, ill-management in health-care and drinking were going on (36).

The CM answered to the allegations but criticized the Members of the Communist Party on the ground of their ambivalency in respect of Liberation Movement of Bangladesh. *He admitted that there may be corruption in a big issue but the Govt. was trying its best to do the best for the refugees. At the same time, the Govt. was not indifferent in respect of problems of the State itself. He expected that ultimate victory waited for Bangladesh and the people of Tripura would fight for the people of Bangladesh in their hardship condition (37).*

Proceedings on 23 June, 1971.
Grave Food Situation in Tripura.

The speaker requested the Hon'ble CM to make a statement on the food situation in Tripura (38).

The CM gave a detailed statement on the food situation in Tripura. The main points of the statement:-

1) The food situation in Tripura was satisfactory in 1970 and in the first 3 months of 1971,
2) But the sudden influx of the refugees in Tripura made the food situation very grave; Tripura with 16 lakhs of people had to shoulder the burden of additional 13 lakhs of people coming from East Bengal,
3) Moreover, railway system was not functioning well for their weak infrastructure and strike of railway,
4) *The average monthly supply of food-grain from Central Govt. to Tripura in first 3 months of 1971 was 1300 metric ton, but in June the average stood to 8000 / 9000 metric ton. The CM stated that on the constant increasing demand of food-stuff the Govt. of India increased the supply of rice and wheat per month 40,500 and 11,000 ton respectively.*
5) The flight used for deportation of the refugees was used to lift the food grains to Agartala from to cope with the food crises.
6) High price-rise was noticed due to various reasons—such as, heavy demand, communication problem, price-rice at the production place
7) The supply of ration to the refugees was curtailed from 400g to 300g due to the shortage (39).

The Member of the Opposition Bench Shri Bidyachandra Debbarma demanded debate on this grave issue but the Speaker did not allow (40).

Private Members' Business in the TLA on 23 June, 1971, on the Supply of dry ration to the refugees

At the call of the Speaker a Resolution was moved by Sarbashri Promode Rn. Dasgupta, Kshitish Ch. Das & Suresh Ch. Choudhury. That was:-'*This House urges upon the Government to supply the scheduled dry rations to the evacuees from East Bengal residing outside the camps and besides dry rations, for other items the evacuees living in camps should be paid in cash; cooking utensils, clothing should be supplied to evacuees: separate accommodation for unattached boys, girls, and women should be made and special diet should be given to the sick, sucking babies, expected mothers and infirm' (41).*

After moving this resolution, Shri Promode Rn Dasgupta offered a long statement supporting the resolution. He was followed by Shri Suresh Ch. Choudhury, Shri Sunil Ch. Datta, Shri Aghore Debbarma, Shri Jatindra Kumar Majumder, Shri Tarit Mohan Dasgupta, Shri Abhiram Debbarma, Shri Naresh Roy, Smt. Renu Chakraborty, and Shri Bidyachandra Debbarma. They supported the resolution on the following grounds:-

1) Due to corruption the allotted ration could not be reached to the refugees.
2) It was not possible on the part of the relatives to shoulder the burden of the additional members numbering more than 20/ 22 in some cases.
3) There were number of unattached children and pregnant women (42).

The Hon'ble Members offered some interesting suggestions for the welfare of the evacuees which were as follows:-

1) Partial ration in kind and partial in cash.
2) Ration should be allowed to those who took shelters in the houses of their Relatives
3) Separate seat arrangement in all PHCs, VM & GB Hospitals for the refugee- Patients.
4) For mental and physical health, sports goods, Radio and Drill system should be provided to the camps.
5) Special care should be taken for the unattached children and expectant women.
6) Camps situated at Gandachhera, Raima- Sharama, Asharasmbari should be given importance because these remained uncared for many days.
7) And, above all, corruption should be checked at any cost (43).

After that prolonged discussion, the resolution was put to voice vote and it was passed unanimously (44).

Proceedings on 25 June, 1971, in the TLA: Private Members' Resolution for shifting the Refugees to other states (45)

At the call of Mr. Speaker, a Private Members' Business (Resolution) was moved by the Hon'ble Member Shri Aghore Debbarma on behalf of other Members like Shri Jatindra Kr. Majumder, Sunil Ch. Dutta Naresh Roy which ran thus:-"*This House requests the Government of India to arrange the shifting of evacuees from Bangladesh, who have taken shelter in Tripura, to other provinces of India and to take the entire responsibility of the evacuees from Bangladesh.*" They supported their resolution showing the following grounds:-

1) Tripura became over-burdened with huge number of refugees; it could not bear any more evacuees but thousands of refugees were pouring to Tripura everyday,
2) With communication gape, unsound economy, backward location, Tripura could not provide any more shelter to the evacuees.
3) Tripura could not provide daily necessities to the refugees due to weak railway connection and other difficulties,
4) Necessary shelters could not be provided due to paucity of materials like thrash etc., refugees were to gather thickly in a single shelter which might cause -------diseases. Medical aids could not be provided properly to the evacuees.
5) Emergent necessities were clothes at that time which could not be provided to the refugees specially the women and children,

Then there followed prolonged debate on the issue; sometimes, the debate turned to be very sentimental on the point that the movers and the supporters were not real supporters of Bangladesh Movement which ushered furore in the House (46).

So, Hon'ble Member Shri Suresh Chandra Choudhury moved *an amended resolution* with the permission of the Mr. Dy. Speaker who was presiding over the session which ran as: -

"This House requests the Government of India to urge upon other states of India to share responsibilities of evacuees from Bangladesh equally with the bordering states overburdened with the problem, and to take the financial responsibility of the evacuees from Bangladesh (47)."

The debate continued unabated on this sentimental issue and ultimately the amendment was put and carried by voice vote. The following facts came out of the debate:-

1) The economy of the state of had been disrupted due to exodus of refugees,
2) Bengali sentiment had made the air heavy in the House while Shri Devendra Kishor Choudhury uttered that refugees were the part their blood and Bengali nationhood could not be wiped out from the history and from the map,
3) It was revealed from the debate that Assam, Meghalaya and Orissa were not at all interested to receive the refugees; even the refugees were being tortured in Meghalaya,
4) Tripura in the face of its own problem should provide all kinds of helps to the evacuees as well as to Bangladesh because, as Shri Tarit Mohan Dasgupta boldly said, " Our goal is to make the Liberation Movement of Bangladesh a victorious one," so, camps should be constructed on war-footing and military personnel might be appointed in organizing these camps.
5) The issue was not a regional but a National one; so, disagreement over the shifting of the evacuees came to the floor of the House,
6) Communalism was defeated and the communal elements kept themselves aloof in the digs and brotherhood won the battle (48).

From the above discussion, it is clear that the Peoples' Representative of Tripura were not only sympathetic towards the cause of the Bangladesh Movement but all most all of them thought the movement of their own. Notwithstanding thousands difficulties faced by the people of Tripura, about ten lacks of refugees were sheltered in Tripura by that time; other facilities were provided as far as possible. Almost every people of Tripura like the peasants, the students, the teachers, the administrators, doctors, engineers, cultural activists, the Tribal people, the Manipuri community, the news agencies, the workers etc. thought the movement of Bangladesh as their own Liberation Movement. That was the force behind the members of the Legislative Assembly to stand for the ultimate success of the Bangladesh movement.

The issue of the Liberation Movement of Bangladesh and other related matters like providing shelter, food, clothes & health care to a sudden influx of refugees was a serious challenge to the Law-Makers of the State. What is mentioned earlier is that Tripura was not at all fit due to its special geographic position and economic weakness to arrange all such facilities to a huge number of rootless evacuees coming from East Pakistan. So, the issue again surfaced in the Legislative Assembly on 31 March, 1972, in the Hon'ble Governor's Speech. His Excellency referred to the economic distortion of the State due to huge exodus of the refugees (49). Participating in the discussion on the Speech of His Excellency, the Hon'ble Members expressed their anguish over huge corruption and other mismanagement in handling the problems of the refugees and other related matters. The Opposition Bench was very much vehement in criticizing the Government's activities with regard to the issue mentioned above (50).

Notes & References

1. Acharya, Agni Kumar – *Tripura Prashasanik Bibartaner Itikatha,* Parul Prakashani, Agartala, 1998.
2. Ray, Samiran (ed) – *Tathya Panji and Nirdeshika,* Tripura Darpan, 2003.
3. Majumder, Benimadhab – *The Legislative Opposition in Tripura,* Tripura State
4. Tribal Cultural Research Institute & Museum, Govt. of Tripura, Agartala
5. Ibid.,
6. Ibid.,
7. Ibid.,
8. Karim, Nehal – *The Emergence of Nationalism in Bangladesh,* University of Dhaka, Dhaka, 1992
9. Ibid.,
10. Ibid.,
11. Ibid.,
12. Ibid.,
13. Ahmed, Salahuddin & others (ed)- Bangladesher Mukti-Sangramer Itihas, 1947-71,(History of Bangladesh Liberation War), Agamee Prakashani, Dhaka, Third Reprint: 2002.
14. Habib, Harun--Mukti-Yuddha: Dateline Agartala, Jatiya Sahitya Prakashani, Dhaka, 1992. Tripura Legislative Assembly: Proceedings

15. Series XX Vol. II dt. 29 March,'71 pp 10-34
16. Ibid.,
17. Ibid.,
18. Ibid.,
19. Ibid.,
20. Ibid.,
21. Ibid.,
22. Series XX Vol. II dt. 31 March,'71 pp 20-47.
23. Ibid.,
24. Ibid.,
25. Ibid.,
26. Series XXI Vol. I dt 21 June,'71 pp 26-31
27. Ibid.,
28. Ibid.,
29. Series XXI Vol. I dt. 22 June,'71 pp 22-57.
30. Ibid.,
31. Ibid.,
32. Ibid.,
33. Ibid.,
34. Ibid.,
35. Ibid.,
36. Ibid.,
37. Ibid.,
38. Ibid.,
39. Ibid.,
40. Series XX I, Vol. I dt. 23 June,'71 pp 22-46.
41. Ibid.,
42. Ibid.,
43. Ibid.,
44. Ibid.,
45. Ibid.,
46. Ibid.,
47. Series XXI, Vol. I, Dt. 25 June,'71 pp. 14-42.
48. Ibid.,
49. Ibid.,
50. Ibid.,

(11)
'Insurgency' in North-east literature- A study of These Hills Called Home - Stories from a War Zone by Temsula Ao.

Prasanta Chakraborty
Somali Saha

In a nation of mixed ethnic communities, the centre should address her marginalised people properly to root out their discontent, if any. The North-East India being inhabited mostly by the marginalised has become a region of socio-political contradictions because of economic deprivation by the Heartland. Political turmoil leading to horrendous distresses has become part of the life in North-East especially in Nagaland. Besides, AFSPA has been promulgated for a long time here in Nagaland to counter insurgency. The result is violent response and more hostility, of brutalisation and of state-sanctioned terror, minimising the chances of peaceful alternatives. A loss of confidence in the state machinery has increased the incidents of violence. Post independent India witnessed writings in English from North East coming out with poems, short stories, novels etc. describing the tale of their woes.

In her short stories Temsula Ao, an eminent litterateur from N.E. Region, attempts to study this crisis from woman's point of view. The stories depict how the patriarch- both the Indian army and the Naga patriarchal society - impose upon the women inhuman treatment. This paper focuses on how the patriarch treats inhumanly the Naga women and how these poor victims develop a resistance mechanism to counter this patriarch that uses the masque of different characters to unsettle the lives of the women.

Nationalist movements encouraged their members, who were mostly male, to assert themselves as agents of their own history as self fashioning and in control. Women were not so encouraged. They were marginalised therefore both by nationalist political activity and by the rhetoric of nationalist address.- - - women are cast as icons of national values, or idealised custodians of tradition. - - - In novels, short stories, poems, plays, postcolonial women have for decades sought to overturn preconceptions of Third World women's experience as uniformly degraded, passively oppressed, or lacking in powers of self-determination. Claiming a historical validity for the ordinary, they have situated their work alongside, and overlapping with, conventional narratives of a national, public history. (Boehmer 216-218)

Temsula Ao, a Naga by origin, has joined hands with others to overturn the image of degraded women in her short stories and other writings. Women have traditionally been considered as more efficient peacemakers as they are more adjustable than men and thus more prepared to make compromise and cooperation. At the time of turmoil, they show much more resilience to adjust and at the same time the much needed courage, willpower and intelligence in facing the opposition. In this article, a study of some of the women characters in the stories of Temsula Ao has been undertaken in the backdrop of upheavals in Nagaland in the post- independence India to assess their role in this turmoil-torn state. While doing so, Temsula Ao believes that 'the power structure within the family and society among the Nagas has always rested with the male.(Bhattacharjee 15) She adds further that 'the definition of woman, as the weaker sex , is a male construct; advocated and enforced by man to perpetuate his superiority and prestige in the society. But as the examples from Ao -Naga folklore demonstrates, such a generalisation is often discredited, not only in discourse but in reality too.' (Bhattacharjee 25)

A background study is essential to assess the role of the women-characters in Temsula's stories. As a consequence of the Naga people's reluctance to be included within the Indian Union, the then British Government declared the Naga areas as a Special Backward Area which later changed into an Excluded Area status by the British India Act of 1935 effective in 1937, as the Nagas did not agree to be treated as backward.

Subsequently, a nine-point Agreement was signed between the Government of India and the Naga National Council on 9th June 1947 which shows that the Naga people were willing to enter into a peaceful coexistence with India for a period of ten years, which will be reconsidered at the end of ten years. So, this was simply a temporary arrangement which was taken to be a permanent settlement as well as a political commitment of the Nagas to be a part and parcel of the Indian union. The Naga leaders read it in a different way and felt cheated. The Government of India felt it right to contain any other explanation of the situation. As a result, dissidence among the Naga people led to armed clashes with Indian military. On July 19, 1947, a Naga delegation led by Dr. A.Z. Phizo met Mahatma Gandhi in Delhi, where, in the meeting, Phizo categorically stated that the Nagas would declare their Independence Day on 14th August 1947. As claimed by Mr. Phizo, Gandhi agreed after a lengthy discussion. The Nagas declared their Independence Day on 14th August 1947. On 27th August 1948, no tax campaign public demonstration led by A.Dihrii was held at Mao-Gate. The 4th battalion of Assam Rifles killed three people on the spot and injured several others. They were the first Naga Martyrs. By the end of November 1949, a Naga delegation met C. Rajagopalachari, the first Governor - General of Independent India, at Shillong. Rajagopalachari advised them that India wants friendly relations with the Nagas and they are free to decide if they want to become part of India or be a separate Nation. On May 8, 1950, the Government of India offered District Autonomy to the Nagas, which made the Nagas insulted .The outraged Nagas were determined to fight against the Indian authority for their independence. With the election of Dr. A.Z. Phizo as the president of the NNC by the year-end of 1950, the Naga Freedom Movement became stronger and stronger. Phizo invited all the Naga people to join 'Non-cooperation' and 'Civil Disobedience' movements. In May, 1951, Nagaland people voted overwhelming in favour of independence. Next year on May, 1952, the Naga delegation met the Prime Minister Pt. Jawaharlal Nehru and informed him about the result of the plebiscite. In the same year, the Nagas boycotted the first Indian general election. In September 1954, Sovereign Republic of Nagaland was formed. On March 22, 1956, Phizo headed the Naga Central Government. The formation of Naga Home guards was also done. This marked the beginning of open serious conflict between the Government of India and the Naga people in March 1956. Rapid mobilization began on both sides. Extreme military repression was sanctioned when other efforts at subjugating their resistance failed. Naga population was relocated, villages 'grouped', civilians fined, arrested and killed.

But wherever there has been dominance, there has also existed some form of resistance. To resist this government sponsored violence, insurgency began to gain ground demanding more autonomy, or more powers of self-rule to counter the hegemony of communities in the ethnic hierarchy. This term 'insurgency' has its common traits which involve deeds of brutal, violent, inhumane actions, loss of home, and keeping an individual life at stake. Chandrika Singh in *North-East India Politics and Insurgency* has defined the term "as a discontent of a group of which uses violence to achieve its goal" (218). In his words, it is "not an association of armed robbers or dacoits. Rather it is born out of some committed ideologies of a particular group, a sect, a tribal or a community, religious or secular" (218). It turns out to be the motive of the marginalized group of people who have been neglected of their rights and "cherished political goals", and hence act out through the means of violence with an attempt to overthrow the existing structure, to replace it with one of their choice. Insurgency has become like a "disease" of the contemporary world which breaks down the security of a nation. It has become a "tool in the hand of the powerless" (Lalthakima 2008) section of the society to use it as a means to work against the powerful by rebelling against the constituted government. As the consequences of insurgency, centre-periphery conflicts, inter-ethnic conflicts or conflicts between the various communities in the Northeast took place where the most affected were the women.

In Nagaland, the early 1950s has been marked by unleashing of violence both by the Naga rebels and by the Indian government. Misunderstanding and mistrust also cropped up within the Naga leadership. In the late fifties, some moderates felt that it would be better for the Nagas to be with the Government of India. The NPC spearheaded the movement to create Nagaland State within the Indian Union with a high degree of autonomy. As a result, on December 1, 1963, Nagaland became a full-fledged state of India. And India effectively and decisively made its presence felt in Naga politics and history. Despite these developments, Armed Forces Special Power Act (AFSPA) was promulgated in several parts of North-East region for a long time apparently to counter insurgency. But 'these forces create more trouble for the common man than the underground revolutionaries. Power at its worst manifestation is ghastly.' (Das 292) Set in this tumultuous historical backdrop of Nagaland, the litterateurs of North East and especially that of Nagaland voice their anger and pain against the neo-colonial force mixed with a sense of disillusionment in their works. The dominance of patriarchy in different facets - the Indian army being the one- and modes of countering this patriarchy is prevalent in all these writings. The same note is recorded in Temsula Ao's collection of short stories entitled *These Hills Called Home - Stories from a War Zone.* It tells the story of everyday life of men; women and children of the society who struggle to make their survival and see the changes taking place around them. The stories depict patriarchy in one of its worst forms. The paper attempts a feminist study in terms of the representation of women's lives and experience as depicted in the short stories measured against the trouble-torn life in Nagaland in post-independent India where Indian army was looked down upon as a neo-colonial force; of their mode of resistance and the process of reconstruction of their identity.

So, one of the major themes of these fictions is violence perpetuated both by militant outfits and by the armed forces and how the same has been confronted by womenfolk there. Giving an account of the Naga people's dream and frustration, Temsula Ao makes a pertinent observation of their struggle for self-determination in her book *These Hills called Home*: *Stories From a War Zone.* In context of literature and insurgency, the first story of this book *The Jungle Major* becomes the most relevant which tells the tale of a couple Khatila and Punaba who lived in a land caught in the "new wave of patriotic fervour that swept the imagination of the people and plunged them into struggle" (Ao 2). It gives an account of the Naga struggle for independence as well as shows how an intelligent rustic woman protects her husband and the entire village from the Indian army. Khalita, the bride 'was tall, fair, slim and possessed of the most charming smile. Not only that, she came from a good family and belonged to a major clan.' (Ao 1) But the circumstances in this patriarchal society compelled her to sacrifice her own social status and identity and marry a man who was 'short, dark and had buck teeth. He was a mere driver who knew some mechanics and was employed by a rich man in town to drive a one- ton vehicle - - - . He had read only up to class five. ' But she gradually adjusted herself with the new married life.

After a year of their marriage, the Naga youth plunged into a struggle to liberate their homeland from 'foreign rule' (Ao 3). But suddenly out of a sense of insecurity, the Indian army began to ransack and burn villages one after another, regrouped villages and the villagers were herded away into the military camps to flush out extremists. Punaba, Khatila's husband too joined the militant activities and proved his worth.

Intelligent Khatila began reconstructing her identity playing a crucial role in resisting the patriarchal aggression and assisting the underground movement. Her courageous attitude, her cool nature together with her presence of mind gave her character a heroic dimension.

One early morning, as Punaba was in his house with his wife, the military marched to his house taking cue from an informer and cordoned it. But Punaba was informed beforehand of the impending danger. With her presence of mind, Khatila capitalised his ugly appearance to save his life and the entire village. Breaking out of the set patriarchal norms, she began to behave with her husband like a master. She utilised the ugly appearance of her husband, dressed him and began to treat him like her servant scolding him for his negligence of duties: 'You no good loafer, what were you doing all day yesterday? There is no water in the house even to wash my face. Run to the well immediately or you will rue the day you were born.'(Ao 6) Significantly, the words bear double meaning - directing her husband the road to escape and at the same time, adding a warning to quicken his activities lest he might be caught and killed. Simultaneously, she utilised her own beautiful appearance to convince the young military officer that she was not deceiving him at all.

The story ended with the dream of an independent Nagaland withering away when government announced ceasefire. Rightly assessing the reality, Khatila felt it suitable to get Punaba back home safe. Punaba responded to her request and along with others, surrendered to the Indian government. He was rehabilitated as an employee in the State Transport Department. A chronicle of confrontation winded up. Otherwise an ordinary girl, Khatila had no business with the political activities. Her only purpose was to keep her house safe and sound from both the Indian military and the militants. Khatila had to pass through these turmoil-torn days keeping her cool and by dint of her intelligence constructed her identity which she, perhaps, had lost marrying Punaba.

Temsula's next story, *Soaba,* powerfully depicts a different facet of woman during the days of rebellion. The story narrates how the state inflicts violence or disciplinary measures on the Naga people through the predicament of the protagonist, Supiba. This dreaded patriarch enjoyed unchallenged authority over suspected people involved in subversive activities or acting as agents of the underground outfit. Imtila, the wife of the boss, preferred a peaceful and simple life of a housewife but was forced to adopt one keeping with her husband's new status.(Ao 14) Her visits outside were restricted. Here too, the woman has to surrender her identity to a patriarch but the power drunk patriarch goes on increasingly imposing his personality on her in order to destroy her womanhood completely. 'She became a prisoner virtually. Her friends and relatives too began to avoid her sensing her discomfiture.'(14) When there was a total subversion of her identity, Imtila's maternal affection got an outlet in Soaba, meaning an idiot, who began to stay there. This affection-transferred on the idiot began to have a strange effect on Boss's wife; 'for the first time she began to think for herself and assess the true nature of her husband's work.' (Ao 15) In order to establish her identity, she resists the fearsome patriarch by withdrawing herself to an inner world of her own creating a barricade around her where there is no entry for the patriarch. But this aloofness hardly affected the lifestyle of the boss. The power-drunk boss did not take any notice of the situation. As days passed, the patronage of the Indian army made the boss more boisterous until one night he received a brutal mental blow for killing Supiba with his own gun in a drunken mood. Although Imtila tried to stop her husband from this final action, she failed here too. 'With a piercing cry of anguish, Imtila rushed to the body of the fallen idiot crying over and over again, 'Oh my poor boy, were you born for this? Why did I let you come to this evil place?' she was disconsolate, weeping and muttering these words again and again in a monotonous dirge-like tone.' (Ao 19)

The phrase 'piercing cry' is deliberately chosen. It is the last resort of a housewife, who is so long bearing the inimical atmosphere at home. Imtila was confined to her own world with Soaba alienating herself from her power-drunk husband. But her tolerance-level reached zenith when the boss shot Soaba dead. Her shocking expressions were so much touching that it made even the head strong boss scared. Perceptibly, there was a rapid change in his behaviour. Committed to keep her husband in good humour away from the repulsive atmosphere, Imtila rebuilt her relationship with her husband to keep him in the right track. But whereas in the previous story it was a happy ending, it is not so the case with Imtila. The magic of Boss's fast cars had drawn him into a world where violence was the order of the day and which eventually claimed his life. (Ao 21-22) True, Imtila failed to persuade her husband but through a resistance mechanism that she silently developed around her, she could at least restrain her husband, though too late for complete recovery. In the process, her identity that was under threat from her unruly husband was regained to some extent.

The last Song, the third story narrates the extent of brutality by the Indian force directly upon women in the name of curbing insurgency and the extent of resistance endured. The Indian army, presupposedly the defender of the lives and property of the marginalised people, are in fact playing a role of the freebooter torturing the common people more and more. On the one hand, compelled by the underground government to pay taxes every year and on the other hand, threats of dire consequences from the armed forces forced the poor villagers to lead a life of constant anxiety. Set in this backdrop, the villagers of a certain village erected a new church in their village, which they are going to open during the Christmas. The Indian army comes to know about the villagers paying taxes regularly to the underground government. They want to punish the villagers on that very special day. When the song of the choir is going on with Apenyo leading, the army comes in and orders to stop singing. Unfazed Apenyo continues her song to be conjoined by other members of the choir quickening thereby the brutal assault of the armed forces on the innocent villagers. The punishment meted on her is the raping of her body by the Captain and few other soldiers. Even her mother who has come to rescue her daughter faced the similar lot after which both are killed. A sample of the brutality is recorded in the following lines: 'But this only further aroused him; he bashed her head on the hard ground several times knocking her unconscious and raped her limp body, using the woman's new *lungi* afterwards, which he had flung aside, to wipe himself' (Ao 28). Two important issues emerge out with the singing of Apenyo - one is the power of women to challenge the power drunk state authority and the other is the extent of heinousness meted out by a patriarchal authority to destruct the unyielding woman. Temsula does not stop here. She even refers to the Naga tradition and shows how inhuman the tradition is as both the mother and the daughter who sacrificed their lives for a great cause were refused their dues from the diehards even after their death. The patriarchal Naga society was quite reluctant to bestow due honour upon the martyrs as they are women. Here, Apenyo uses nonviolence as her resistance against the atrocities of the Indian Army and gradually she and her last song becomes a legend. Her story is the stuff that grandparents narrate to their grandchildren.

In another story, *The Curfew Man,* Temsula depicts the story of another Naga woman Jemtila, the wife of Satemba who helps her husband find a suitable job for himself though it eventually could not favour him till the end. The story talks of the period when the situation was getting worse and the civilians shot dead were reported as unfortunate ones killed in the act of 'encounter' by the underground rebels or the army. Among the many that served to work as the mediator between the two parties, Satemba, a former constable in the Assam Police, in spite of his bad knee served to work as the curfew man who travelled at night to pass on important information. Knowing quite well the job he was handling and the risk in it, he did not wish to think of the future consequences, or the "reasonable payment" he was given elsewhere (Ao 40). In spite of all the trouble he went through to please his superiors, at the end when he decided to resign, he became 'history', unknown to all, and no longer the man who served his service loyally with his two smashed knee-caps.

But Jemtila realised the hard reality that innocent people like them were becoming victims of this ongoing turmoil. So, 'every time Satemba went out at night, she kept a lone vigil in the darkness of their small hut and worried until he appeared at the door.'(Ao 39) Temsula makes her readers share the amount of tension of Jemtila for her husband in this trouble-torn life particularly when he was working as a government informer. At the decision of Satemba's resigning the job 'Jemtila felt unusually light-hearted and free because now that both Satemba's knees were damaged, he would no longer be able to work for the SDO. If the first bad knee had secured him his pension from the Assam police, the second injury truly secured his freedom from a sinister bondage.' (Ao 42) Thus Temsula presented another type of woman who kept her cool and calm, waited for an appropriate moment in this patriarchal society to manage the situation favourably before it was too late. To her, the broken legs of her husband and his inability to earn his livelihood were much better than living a tension- packed life where at every moment there was a chance for her husband to be killed either by the insurgents or by the Indian army.

Jemtila and Khatila followed the same technique of resistance against the ongoing turmoil; both were concerned about the safety of their husbands, which they succeeded to manage by dint of their cool and intelligence. Imtila had her opposition at home - her power-drunk husband. It was different situation for Imtila and she played a different resistance -mechanism - by dissociating herself from her husband's life and following the path of non-cooperation. But her uxorial responsibilities activated when her husband was in utter distress.

In her next story, *The Night,* Temsula gives a poignant account of a young girl, Imnala, who has strong decision for a good upbringing of her children though she is neglected by the society. She was exploited twice by two suitors and in both the cases; they seduced her which led her to give birth to two illegitimate children. But what is transpired from the story is not Imnala's giving birth to illegitimate children twice but the differential treatment of the Naga patriarchal society towards women. Rupam Gogoi comments, 'We get a clear picture of the customs of a society which often tilt towards men in its judgement.' (Das 295) But Imnala seemed to have gathered sufficient courage by that time to face the Naga patriarchs who in the name of judgement would accuse her although the married man was equally guilty. She was determined to hold her head high. So she vowed, 'Come what may,' she thought, 'I shall devote my life to bringing up these two children in the best way I can. I shall finish my high school, get a job and educate them. I shall spend every ounce of my energy so that they have a better life than mine.' These thoughts seemed to revitalise the woman who had only a few hours ago, grappled with fear and utter despair in the darkest night of her life.'(Ao 54) Both Imnala of *The Night* and Apenyo of *The Last Song* were resolute enough in their belief and action- so much so that the patriarch considered these beauties as a menace for them. So they should be reduced to ashes but like a phoenix these disciples of nonviolence are reborn to confront the patriarchs throughout the ages.

The colonised writer should try to re-establish the right over the culture and the land that is theirs. Through the literary activities, the struggles and passions of the colonised should be represented and at the same time record the resistance of the indigenous. Set in the initial turbulent decades of the Naga insurgency, Temsula's short stories depict how the women struggle to come to terms with their identity, how her women characters evolve a resistance- mechanism in an assorted way with the hostile patriarch always forbidding to break the existing status. The Indian army, the boss and the two suitors symbolise different facets of this patriarchy. Along with the Indian army, the engineer and the contractor work as agents of the neo-colonial force who are appropriately endorsed by the Naga patriarchal society to exploit the women through their ridiculous verdict. This society put their women in the sacrificial alter in the name of justice though men are found equally responsible for the same guilt. And in all these adverse situations, Temsula's women characters show a presence of mind, a resoluteness and non-violence as their guiding principle to resist the opposition and construct their identity. So 'these stories, together with many others written on similar experiences, may not be considered as 'great literature' from the point of view of literary quality , but in a society that has been silenced and numbed by a neurotic fear of political violence and retributive justice , the voices of the women register some form of protest.'(Gill 253)

References:

1. Ao, Temsula. These Hills called Home. New Delhi: Penguin Books, 2006. Print.
2. Ao, Temsula. "Gender and Power Women- Centred Narratives from Ao-Naga Folklore." Ethno- Narratives. Bhattacharjee, Sukalpa & Dev, Rajesh. (ed.), Delhi: Anshah Publishing House, 2006.
3. Boehmer, Elleke. Colonial & Postcolonial Literature, New Delhi: OUP, 1995. Print.
4. Gogoi, Rupam. "Outliving turbulence: An Analysis of These Hills Called Home". Matrix of Redemption . Das, Nigamananda. Ed. New Delhi: Adhayan Publishers, 2011.
5. Misra, Tillotoma. "Women Writing in Times of Violence." The Peripheral Centre. Gill, Preeti Ed. New Delhi: Zubaan, 2010. 249-272. Print.
6. Misra, Tilottoma. Ed. Writings from North-East India .New Delhi: OUP, 2011. Print.
7. Misra, Udayan. The Periphery Strikes Back. Shimla: IIAS, 2000. Print. Singh, Chandrika. North-East India Politics and Insurgency. New Delhi: Manas Publishers, 2009. Print.

(12)
Tibetan Connection in Shaping the History and Culture of Arunachal Pradesh

Karubaki Datta

Arunachal Pradesh is one of the eight states of North east India. It is rich in ethnic diversity and rich tribal heritage. It stretches along the southern slopes of eastern Himalayas to the western slopes of the Patkoi hills around the Brahmaputra Valley. Arunachal Pradesh is physiographically included in the eastern Himalayan region. The Arunachal Himalayas are broadly divided into three longitudinal physiographic zones viz. 1.the great Himalayas that is above 3000 mts which actually forms the frontier of the whole region 2. The lesser Himalayas from 1200 – 3000 mts and 3. The outer Himalayas which is upto 1200 mts high. Except in the extreme south east the whole state is topographically very rugged and a considerable portion is under perpetual snow cover with several glaciers and glacial lakes.

The population is basically tribal and of the Mongoloid stock. The listing of the communities can be a problem and some confusion arise from the faulty enumeration of the communities and the sub groups in the census reports. The prepared by the Arunachal Pradesh Government consists of 25 scheduled tribes in addition to numerous sub tribes living in this state. The the XIV volume (Arunachal Pradesh) of the series people of India Anthropological Survey of India under the general editorship of K.S.Singh highlights all such controversies and gives an overall description of the ethnic and cultural profile of the state as a whole in the Foreword and the Introduction of the volume.[1]

All the tribes of the state have their own religion, language culture and custom. These tribes can be generally divided into distinct cultural groups on the basis of their socio- politico and religious affinities. Two broad divisions into which they can be divided are TBodic and non Bodic.

Among the Bodic group we find the use of stone and wood for their house and furniture. Their dress is tailored and wooden felt cap is used as head dress. Their religion is sophisticated with their temples, images sacred literatures and well organised priesthood. The non Bodic group on the other hand use cane and bamboo for their houses and furniture and do not use tailored cotton dress. Non Bodic religion is faith in spirits and deities with oral sacred literature but without an organised priesthood or centralised -place of worship.

Geography has influenced the cultural development of the place. The Northern region had little contact with the lower region particularly the valley of Brahmaputra and has been greatly influenced by the Indo Tibetan culture.

Religion wise there are animists, Buddhists, few Hindus and some Christians among them. Each religious group is concentrated in some geographically distinct area. The Northern belt of the higher Himalayan region is the area where the Buddhists live, the central the central belt or the central stretch of hills in the area where animism is still predominant and the southern belt or the foothills where the Hindus are in majority.[2] Since the theme of this paper is the Influence of Tibet and Tibetan culture on Arunachal Pradesh, we will focus on those tribes who practise Tibetan Buddhism of Mahayana school which is also known as Northern Buddhism as practised all along the Himalayan belt. The tribal group that is well known for its practice of Mahayana Buddhism in this region is the Monpas. These people are mainly found in the Indo Tibetan border area of the state. The Monpa and the other Buddhist group Sherdukpens live in the western highlands, Kameng frontier (Tawang and West Kameng), the Nah in Upper Subansiri, the Memba and the Khamba in Upper Siang and mayors and the Zakrings inhabit the Lohit frontier[3] The Monpas form a large tribal community and till recent past were isolated from the outside world. In both the districts of Tawang and West Kameng, they are in majority - 98% in Tawang and 78% in West Kameng.[4]

About the the Monpas

The term "Monpa'' is from Tibetan language, *'Mon'* meaning low or down land, and '*Pa'* meaning people, it means the people of the low or down lands.[5] Accordingly, the Monpas are found residing in the south of Tibet which coincides with the Northern part of Arunachal Pradesh. The land is also called Monyul or the land of the Mon or the lower land. The area is bounded by the towering Himalayan ranges of Tibet in the North, Bhutan in the west, Bomdila in the south and Zela range in the east.

This term Monpa contains in itself the connection with Tibet indicating that these people have migrated from Tibet in the past. However, there are some varying versions of this. One version prevailing among the Monpas of Tawang narrates that the higher or richer sections of the Tibetans conducted a *puja* called *Dokpa* (to ward off evil spirits from the village), to save their homeland from untoward incidents and for the purpose, selected some lower class Tibetans, dressed them in colourful attires and sent them towards the south. These persons are said to have carried the evil spirits along with them. Those who came to the south, later on, came to be known as Monpas and the colourful attire became their traditional dress. Today, the Monpas also conduct this *puja* called *Dokpa* but now instead of sending poor people, they throw away the statues of ghost and devils called *luth.*

A second version has it that they have come from Bhutan about 200 years ago. Following the persecution by the Chinese soldiers, a section of the people of eastern Bhutan and Monyul first immigrated to Pemako which their ancient prophecies had declared to exist somewhere on the frontiers of India. The descendants of this first batch are indiscriminately called Monpas or Drukpas. The people of Eastern Bhutan are called Drukpas by the Tibetans hence the Bhutanese immigrants came to be known as Drukpas or Daktas. [6]

On the basis of location of their settlements the Monpas are divided into several groups. In the volume on Arunachal Pradesh of the series on People of India, separate studies have been made of the But Monpas, Chug Monpas,Dirang Monpas, Kalaktang Monpas, Lish monpas and Tawang Monpas. 1. Tawang , Dirang and Kalaktang Monpas are generally known as Northern Monpas, Central Monpas and southern Monpas respectively.[7]

Barring the But Monpas all the Monopas are Buddhists. Their religious rituals and ceremonies, the most important of which is the Dongyur, are followed on a grand scale are performed as per the Tibetan calendar. Of all the Monpas, the Tawang Monpas are the most well known because of their connection with the famous monastery of Tawang.

The Kalaktang Monpas, also known as Rongnampa, too are Buddhists by religion but simultaneously with Buddhism they retain some practises of animism in the form of beliefs in a host of spirits, deities, gods etc. there are a number of such deities who are worshipped on a number of occasions to get relief from the miseries. The Dirang Monpas of west Kameng district believe themselves to be the original inhabitants of the Dirang circle of the west Kameng district. There are many folk beliefs regarding their origin related to Buddhist monks. They are Buddhists by religion even though they retain some of the pre Buddhistic animism or shamanism. Their sacred place, however, is the monastery which houses the images of Bodhisattavas and Buddha Himself in different *mudras*. The lama occupies an important position in the community and religious life.[8]

Influence of Tibetan culture is profound on the lifestyle of the Monpas. Even V. Elwin had observed in 1956 that that the influence of Tibetan Buddhism is strongly marked in the Monpa textile, ornaments, architecture and iconography, their funerary rites and the Tantric elements in their Buddhism.

Tibetan influence can be traced in the languages of Arunachal as well. Broadly, the languages can be divided into Tibeto Burman and Indo Aryan families. The first can again be divided into four categories two of which bear some affinity to Tibetan. These include the Tibetan dialects spoken mainly in the East and West Kameng districts and in the upper portion West Siang district. The second category consists of languages with elements of both Tibetan and Burmese spoken in upper and lower Subansiri, East and West Siang parts of East and West Kameng, Dibang valley and also in Lohit. There are differences among the dialects spoken by the different groups of Monpas. Tawang Monpa's language is said to be closer to Tibetan because of the geographical proximity of Tawang to Tibet, while the dialects spoken by other groups are said to ber more resemblance to the language of Bhutan. Tibetan script is used by the Buddhist communities like the Monpas for their religious scriptures.[9]

The Sherdukpens are another tribe to practice Tibetan Buddhism. They reside basically in the southern part of the Bomdilla range in the valleys of Tengapani River. Of late, some of them have settled down in Kamengbari areas under the Bhalukpong circle. These people trace their origin to the Tibetans. Myth goes that they originated from marriage of a

Tibetan prince with a princess of Assam possibly of Kachari origin.[10] As in the case of other Mahayani Buddhist tribes of Arunachal, their religion too is blended with local beliefs and shamanism even though monasteries with images of Buddha, Chenrezig (Avalokiteswara) and Guru Rimpoche and his different incarnations are their main place of worship. [11]

As said above, the Buddhism that these people practise is of Tibetan origin. The history of how it was introduced into this region to the south of Tibet is very much related to the history of Tibet itself.

How was Tibetan Buddhism introduced in the region?

History of Arunachal Pradesh is shrouded in myths and legends. The same is applicable in case of the Buddhists. The story of the introduction of Mahayana Buddhism can be constructed only to some extent from the oral sources in forms of myths and legends.

Legend has it that Buddhism was introduced in the region by Guru Padmasambhava, commonly known as Guru Rimpoche, more or less at the same time when it was introduced in Tibet in the 8th century. Padmasambhava was a great Indian Buddhist scholar who visited Tibet in A.D.747. It is believed that after establishing Buddhism in Tibet, Guru Padmasambhava marched towards south and reached the land inhabited by the Monpas and sowed the seed of Buddhism among them. He is known as Lopon Rimpoche (the precious guru) or Lopon Pema Jungne (the lotus-born guru) by the Monpas.[12] Imitating Tibet, his image and portrait are placed in all the Buddhist temples of Monpa region as well. Legends have it that he possessed immense magical powers with which he restrained most of the demons, evil spirits and supernatural powers. There are as many places associated with the visit of Padmasambhava. There are 16 places which are said to have been visited by him and his impressions are preserved till now in seven places visited by him, most of them in modern Tawang district.[13]

It is further believed that the Guru spent some time in meditation and preaching of Dhamma in the Tawang area even before he entered Tibet. So, according to this legend, some tribes had been converted to Buddhism as early as the 8th century. The sect to which the followers of Padmasambhava belong is Nyingmapa or the ancient ones.

The sect that has the greatest wide following among the Monpas is Gelugpa. This sect was introduced in the region by Thangston Gyalpo: a Gelugpa lama from Tibet (1385 – 1462) a fellow disciple and follower of the first Dalai Lama. He came to a place called Chankharegor and meditated in a nearby cave in the village of Kraling about seven miles to the Southeast from Tawang. He constructed an iron chain suspension bridge called Chaksam of Tawangchu River. The bridge survives till today. With his blessing seven sons were born to one Berkhar Terge of Berkhar hamlet near Kreling. The second and the seventh sons had their training under one of the disciples of the First Dalai Lama. They built many Gelugpa temples viz. Brakher, Ariakdun, Lhangaten, Sanglamphe, Tadung, Taidung, Surchung, all in the Tawang area and the Talung Gompa at the Monpa village of Sanglemin the Southwast part of Kameng district. Two temples were also built in Bhutan in the villages of Sakten and Mera.[14]

The Gelugpa sect thus introduced into the region gradually extended to areas inhabited by the Monpas and Sherdukpens by a series of reincarnations. The fourth incarnation was Lodro Gyalpo who received his education at Tashilhunpo and Sera monasteries. He was popularly known as Mera Lama. This was the period of Gelugpa rivalry with the Buddhists of Bhutan. The Dukpa subsect was introduced there in 13th century by the Tibetan monk Lama Phajo. Faced with animosity of this rival sect, Mera Lama planned to establish one Gelugpa monastery in Tsosum – the name by which Tawang was known those days. Karmapa, another rival sect, also extended some influence in the region. There was a Karmapa temple called Gangardung gompa under the jurisdiction of the Karmapa centre of Drosangacholing monastery of Tibet. There was also a Nyingma Thechpa temple at Tsosum established by Mindoling monastery of Tibet.

The region maintained close contact with Tibet from a very early period. In fact, the VIth Dalai Lama was born in this place. The monastery of Tawang has become the symbol of Buddhism in Arunachal Pradesh. In fact, this monastery is the fountainhead of the spiritual life of the Monpas their religious and social life being totally associated with the monastery. In fact Tawang became the symbol of Buddhism in Arunachal Pradesh. Full name of the monastery was Tawang Galden Namgye Lhatse. The VIth Dalai Lama Himself laid down the rules to be followed by the resident monks. He also deputed a learned and pious monk as the abbot and also two monastic officials. The monastery was affiliated to the Drepung monastery of Tibet. The exact year of construction of the monastery is not known for certain.[15] History has it that the Mongol troops led by one Sokpo Jemkhar came in this area to help the Gelugpa Monpas in their struggle against the Dukpas. From the History of Tibet it is known that the struggle for supremacy between the Dukpas and the Gelugpa Monpas had started in 1643. Considering all the facts it can be inferred that the Tawang monastery was constructed sometime between 1643 and 1647.

One Karmapa lama is believed to have visited the Dirang area to introduce Buddhism but probably that happened after the construction of the Tawang monastery. Most of the Dirang villages still have their *gompas* and other Buddhist shrines but those are datable to much later period of 18th to early 20th century.[16] Some Nyingmapas also exist among the village priests. But it is the Gelugpas who enjoy supremacy among the Monpas.

After the construction of the monastery, the Monpas of Tawang decided that every family, having three or more sons, would send the middle son known as *busum-barma* of as a monk to the monastery. The family which would fail to send the middle son out of three or more as a monk to the monastery was liable to fines called *shakpa.* However, the people of Rho and Jangda have to send one of their sons as a monk to Gompa Tse Gompa in Tibet if they had five or more sons. This situation continued till the Chinese occupation of Tibet (1959).

The Tawang monastery also has the supervising right over the administration of the several *gompas,* erected in various places. Amongst them, Tsangpo *gompa* and Urgelling *gompa* within Tawang town, Kimnash *gompa* of Jang, Thongmin *gompa* of Khrimu, Arya Dung *gompa* and Brakar *gompa* of Lhou, Khromtin *gompa* which lies below Gashela peak, Zharmang *gompa* which lies below Khromtin, Kharung *gompa* of Mukto and Manzing *gompa* near Bhutan border also falls under the vigilance and supervision of the Tawang Monastery.

Of these, the Urgelling monastery about 5 km from the main town of Tawang, holds a special place of importance on account of being the birthplace of the VIth Dalai Lama Tsangyang Gyatso. It is believed that the monastery was built around 1489 by one Ugen Tsangpo and it became a revered Gompa after the birth of the VIth Dalai Lama in 1683. The glory however was short lived since the Dalai was deposed in 1706 by Lhazang Khan of Khosat Mongols and replaced by Ngawang Yeshe Gyatso. The

Tibetans continued to recognise the deposed Tsangyang Gyatso.as the true incarnation.

For every three years, three *lamas* (priest) of the Tawang Monastery are appointed to each of these *gompas* by the authorities of the Tawang Monastery. Each of these these *lamas* are wholly responsible for the maintenance and up keep of the *gompa* allotted to him for the purpose. Traditionally, these *lamas* held a very powerful position in their respective areas. They had even judicial power to announce corporal punishments to the offenders.

Earlier, for the upkeep of the monastery, the Monpas had decided to help Mera Lama by donating land, grain and firewood. Initially, every year they donated grain and firewood according to their own wish.

The Monpas were earlier under the Tibetan authority and after the foundation of Tawang monastery they were put under the authority of Tawang. For the sake of administrative convenience the whole Monpa region was divided into three divisions with three offices called *dzong,* which were run by the *dzongpon*s. The three *dzongs* were- Gyangar *dzong* (Tawang), Dirang *dzong* and Talung *dzong* (Kalaktang) which were placed under the jurisdiction of the Tsona *dzongpon* by the Lhasa Government. Tsona *dzong,* 32 ¼ miles (51.9 km) from Tawang, was a place of considerable importance for trade, hence was put directly under the supervision of Lhasa *dzong*, the capital city of Tibet. It is to be noted that two monks of Tawang monastery were assigned as *dzongpons* in Dirang *dzong* and Talung *dzong* each, who collected taxes and paid it to the Tsona *dzongpon*. The main duty of the *dzongpon* was to collect tax but they even tried to settle local disputes. [17]

The taxes were in the form of grains, medicinal plants, herbs, firewood and timber. Each household had to pay five *bres* (a special kind of bowl having a capacity of one kilogram) of finger millet and wheat every year. In addition, they also paid different plants and dry fruits, as taxes. The Monpas collected these articles from other areas, mostly from the plains of Assam. They also had to pay timber logs called *dungring* of 12 feet, *dungthung* of 6 feet, *thapang* of 6 feet and bamboo sticks of 15 feet long. These were mostly used for constructing monasteries and houses in Tibet. The Monpas could not raise their voice against these obnoxious taxes and nothing could precisely be said as to when the Monpas came under the Tibetan authority. It is also said that due to the continuous pressure from the Tibetan rule, many of the Monpas migrated and settled in Bhutan. The Monpas of West Kameng also paid taxes to the Tawang monastery.

In the context of Kalaktang Monpas, it is known that these Monpas too had to pay tribute in kinds to the Tawang monastery through Talung *dzongpons*. Once they were so oppressed by the monastic officials that many of them left their village and migrated to Bhutan. After this incident, it was no longer compulsory for them to pay monastic tribute. In Dirang too, the people resented the monastic order. There was a clash between the monks and twelve leading householders of Dirang when the monks tried to construct a *dzong*. The leaders of Dirang opposed it as they wanted to live an independent life and were not ready to be under subordination. So they opposed the construction of *dzong* that resulted into an armed clash and twelve leaders were killed. Then the monks built a *dzong* and established their administration. A long prayer wheel *mane* was constructed by the people of Dirang in the name of the deceased leaders which exist till today.

The Monpa people gradually submitted to the monastic order of the Tawang monastery and it was only because of this reason that the monastery could collect taxes from the local people. There were no such taxes nor any rules or compulsions in case of the other monasteries, which force them to embrace the religious and hermit life of a monk. The Monpas however, still have the tradition of sending their wards to monasteries and nunneries to become nuns and monks at very early age.

It is clear from what is described above that the region had some kind of economic relations with Tibet and also with Bhutan. They carried their indigenous items and exchanged those with food grains and other items which were not found in their respective places. They also worked as middlemen in trade relationship between traders of Assam and Tibet. A.K.Thakur, while discussing manufacturing of paper and trade relations of pre colonial Arunachal wrote –'while they used to go to Tibetan trading marts during summers they usually visited the Assam plains during the winters.'[18] The Tibetan traders crossed the borders and traded in their region. Many of them settled down in the valleys. In 1840s the Commissioner of Assam advocated opening up of regular trade with Tibet through Tawang. He held that the trader who inhabited those tracts and had commercial intercourse with both the plains of the Brahmaputra

Valley and Tibet would welcome such development and cooperate with the Government with the prospect of more profit. He requested to send the members of the Boundary Commission then in Tibet back to India via Tawang or alternately to give him permission to send an envoy to Lhasa by the same route from Assam. Unfortunately the government did not take any step to implement the idea though the issue was discussed time and again. The specification of the Inner Line on the Darrang Frontier again put a barrier on Indian trader and the hills leading to Lhasa.[19]

The influence of Buddhism has enriched the cultural life of Arunachal Pradesh in another way. This is to say that every *gompa*, *stupa* etc. preserves manuscripts. Tightly wrapped in yellow silken or cotton long cloth and sandwiched between two wooden pieces, these are called *Pecha* in the local Monpa language. All the Buddhist families maintain a small altar called *chosam* at the back of the house and in some families these manuscripts if, one has any, are stacked beside the altar. Every village in the Monpa area has a *gompa.* As per one estimate, the number of *gompas* is about 108 in the Tawang area and all of these are said to have such collection of *pecha* in its custody its size varying according to the size of the *gompa.*[20]

The Tawang monastery is one of the main hubs of the Buddhist manuscripts in the state. However, it is difficult to ascertain the origin or the root country of these manuscripts. It is widely perceived that some of the earliest manuscripts have landed during Padmasambhava's teaching and a host of others were later recovered by the local Buddhist teachers or *Rimpoches* who were devout disciples of Padmasambhava. Most of these manuscripts are handwritten on the paper which was also handmade from the barks of a tree called *sheng*[21]

The library of the Tawang monastery is big. It contains two printed sets of *Tanjur*, three sets of *Kanjur* and five volumes of *Changia Sungbum*. Each set of *Tanjur* contains 225 volumes. Among the sets of *Kanjur* 2 sets are handwritten and one set of 101 volumes is printed. One handwritten set has 131 volumes and another 125. In one set the letters are washed with pure gold some being written with silver. Many of such manuscripts of great value are now in brittle condition with their edges broken and some are getting eaten up by insects. The origin of these manuscripts is not always known. According to some oral tradition some of these were brought in from Tibet at the time of the construction of the monastery. Some are lying with individual families also. This is certainly a rich heritage of its Tibetan connection. Now these are being taken care of by the National Mission for Manuscripts.[22] Though it is a time consuming task and will take some time, the work of digitisation and documentation has started.

Strategic Importance of Arunachal in the Context of Sino-Indian Border Dispute:

As to the question of the geo strategic importance of Arunachal Pradesh, there is serious difference of perception between India and China over the question of boundary between the two states. This difference of perception and claims has fuelled the Chinese aggression against India in 1962 and China even crossed the boundary to reach as far as Bomdilla in Arunachal. The dispute is over the question of legality of the McMahon Line – the border between the two states of India and China (erstwhile Tibet).

The McMahon Line emerged from the Indo Tibetan Boundary Agreement of 1914.[23] It runs over a distance of 820 miles of which 640 miles are between India and Tibet from the tri-junction of Bhutan, Tibet and the Kameng district of Arunachal Pradesh through the crest of the Himalayas to the Diphuk Pass to the North West of Burma where India, Burma and Tibet meet. [24]

Tawang, because of its close contact and cultural affinity with Tibet proved to be a tricky question at the time of delineation. There were disputes and difference of interpretation with regard to two places at the time of demarcation in 1914- one being Walong and the other Tawang. Alaistar Lamb holds the view that although the British did not recognise any paramount power over the North eastern tribes, Tawang was undoubtedly a Tibetan territory.[25] He also says that the Indo Tibetan agreement involved a nominal transfer of territory from Tibet to India. As for the situation and inclusion of Walong, the Government of India was at first hesitant but subsequently it was found to be outside the Tibetan province of Zayul Chu from watershed, geographical and historical points of view. Walong is situated on the left bank of the Lohit which forms the Indo Tibetan boundary there. The area was at one time inhabited by the Mishmis but later on abandoned by them. In 1914, the area was largely uninhabited but the Mishmi occupation of the region was still testified by the Muju names of the place, hills and rivers.[26]

As for the Tawang region, even though it was perceived as the 'Monyul' and its inhabitants – the Monpas remained deeply connected to Tibet through religion and also through revenue administration, it was kept to the south of the border on the basis of some basic considerations. The principal inhabitants, the Monpas, their affinity to Tibetan culture notwithstanding, were described as culturally and linguistically different from the main stream of the Tibetan population.[27] Pandit Nain Singh of the Trigonometrical Survey of India who visited the monastery in 1874-75 on his way back from Lhasa, pointed out that even though the affairs of the Tawang district were managed by a sort of parliament composed of the lamas of the monastery, termed *Kato* it was completely independent of the Dzongpon and the Lhasa government.[28] Almost 50 years later, G.A.Nevill who visited Tawang in 1914 stated the same thing.[29] It may be noted that Lochen Shatra, the Tibetan representative in the Simla conference, raised the case of Tawang region as -

" the Potala trung-Yik Chenpo and the Loseling college of Drepung monastery each get 10 Dotse (1 Dotse = rs 84) from Tawang for the right to send agents to manage the land of the Tawang monastery which right they farm out to them considered as the right of private individuals. .The Lebrang and Nyetsang get a share of about Rs 500 together, out of the supply paid by the British Government annually for the Kuriapur Duar. .. this ... may be continued to be paid to them. The families of Shewo and Sham-drung –potrang have also private estates in Tawang, which... they may be allowed to retain. The Tawang monastery.....has private estates at Dhirang and Takla jongs ... which they may be allowed to retain with the monastery's other income.'[30]

Realising that these were private estates, Henry McMahon and Charles Bell, demarcated Tawang to the south of the Line i.e in India.

In fact, given the deep historical and cultural ties the region had with Tibet, Henry McMahon and Charles Bell tried to exclude what was undisputedly Tibetan territory. While anxious to secure a frontier which would be consistent with India's strategic requirements, they tried to keep these factors in consideration as far as possible. For example, in Subansiri region, the two holy places of Tibetan pilgrimage Tso Sharpo and Tsari Sharpo together with the village Migyitun wherefrom the pilgrimage started, were kept North of the McMahon Line. To enable the Tibetan pilgrims' smooth and unrestricted entry into those –places disregarding the watershed principle.[31]

The Tibetan government agreed to the transfer without prejudice. So the agreement drawn up in Simla was agreed to by Lochen Shatra. The Chinese were not invited to take part in the discussions about the Indo Tibetan frontier and their specific acceptance was not sought.

The McMahon Line was first published by Charles Bell in his book on Tibet in 1924. The Government of India soon got engaged in the First World War and Sir. McMahon was also transferred to Egypt. It was not before 1929 that the map was incorporated in the volume of Aitchison's *Treaties, Engagements and Sanads*. Thereafter it was published in 1962 by the Government of India after the Sino Indian border clashes of 1962.[32]

India regards the McMahon Line as the official border but China does not. The difference of perception originated from the treaty (1914) between colonial India under British rule and Tibet which India considers legal and final but China does not. Since a part of the line affects Burma as well and China has already used the McMahon line as the basis for a border with Burma, India argues that China's stand is creating the perception of a double-standard on its part. China, however, views the McMahon Line as a colonially imposed boundary since India was under British rule at the time. The Chinese wish to resolve the dispute based on the "traditional line" which falls further south of the McMahon Line.

In addition, regarding Arunachal Pradesh, the Chinese continue to claim that from a historical perspective, Tibet has held administrative control over the territory, and Tibet is part of China which is to say that it rejects the arguments that Charles Bell and Henry McMahon had advanced in favour of inclusion of Tawang. From the Indian perspective however if you lose the McMahon line as the border, then you lose the ability to defend the mountains hence no compromise.[33]

The dispute is basically because all of the border areas of Arunachal Pradesh are deeply connected to Tibetan Buddhism in one way or another. Because of its traditional connection with Tibet the free Tibet movement is quite strong in the region and it is widely believed that the next Dalai Lama may come from this area.

Sensitive to the possibility as China is, this naturally contributes to an aggressive and defensive negotiating posture on the part of China, which only complicates any resolution of the border and territorial dispute. China had received strong opposition from the media and general public when it 'liberated 'Tibet' that made it conclude that India was simply trying to undermine China's drive to unify its territory. There has been a wide-held (unfounded) belief in China that India, particularly under Nehru, has had an expansionist agenda and wishes to turn Tibet into an Indian province.

As a result of all this, Arunachal (in addition to some other points in the western Himalayas) has emerged the centre of India's security concern. There continues to be an increase in military installations on both sides of the border with India upgrading the airfields and China constructing missile sites near Tibet so that the missiles can reach Delhi. They are planning to deploy even longer range missiles in the future. Military exercises have also escalated on both sides, particularly in Northeast India, where little to no such exercises occurred in the past.[34] As a result of all this there has been a fundamental transformation in the region. Geo strategic compulsions has now transformed into a high security area for India.

Arunachal Pradesh continues its contact with Tibet and Tibetan culture also through the Tibetan refugees many of whom have settled down in this state of India in course of the 1960s. . There are at least five settlements for the refugees in addition to which the Tibetans are scattered in many parts of the state outside the settlements. They are mainly concentrated in the West Kameng, Lohit, Siang, and Changlang districts. They have adjusted themselves with the local communities and even speak the Tangsa and Khampa dialects among themselves, have picked up Hindi and Sonpa dialects of the neighbouring communities but the use of Tibetan script continues to be common among them. This refugee Tibetans are basically traders and are economically stable. Most of the shopkeepers of Bomdilla, Rupa, Shergaon, and Kalaktang are Tibetans. While they have trade relations with the plainsmen like the Bengalis, Biharis, Assamese and Marwaris they have close religious linkages with the Buddhists Monpas, Khambas, Sherdukpens and others who practice Tibetan Mahayana Buddhism. The Government has also provided them with schools for the children, and also extended the developmental schemes to them. This diasporic community of Tibetans add to the ethnic and cultural mosaic of the state and carries on the old cultural linkage between Tibet and Arunachal Pradesh.

Notes and References

1. Dutta Parul and Ahmad Syed Ishteaque Singh, People of India(general editor K.S.Singh), Volume XIV , Anthropological Survey of India, Seagull Books, Calcutta, 1995
2. Bose . M.L., History of Arunachal Pradesh ,Concept Publishing Company, New Delhi, 1997,p.16
3. ibid.p.22
4. Dutta Parul and Ahmad Syed Ishteaque, op cit.p.5
5. ibid. p.216
6. Nair., P.T. Tribes of Arunachal Pradesh, Spectrum Publications, Guwahati, 1985, pp.70-71
7. Dutta Parul and Ahmad Syed Ishteaque, op cit. p216
8. ibid.pp.228 -231
9. ibid.p.23.
10. Ibid.p.288
11. ibid.p.291
12. Padmasambhava is believed to have visited parts of Sikkim and Bhutan as well. He is generally known as Guru Rimpoche and even considered as second Buddha.
13. Tripathy. B. and Pema Deki Mize –'Mahayana Buddhism in Arunachal Pradesh – A study of the Dirang Monpas , in Religious History of Arunachal Pradesh, Gyan Publishing House, Delhi, 2008, p.287.
14. Information about the early history of Buddhism in Arunachal can be collected from the several books and articles on either the religious history of the state or the ethnographic accounts of the various communities. In addition to the book mentioned above, information is available also in Sarkar Niranjan ,Buddhism among the Monpas and Sherdukpens, Shillong, 1980 and Kazuhuru Mizuno and Tenpa Lobsang , Himalayan nature and Tibetan

Buddhist culture in arunachal Pradesh, ndia : A study of Monpa, Springer, Japan, 2015

15. For a history of the Tawang monastery , Sarkar Niranjan, Tawang Monastery, Shillong, 1981
16. B.Tripathy and Pema Delli Mize op cit. pp.295-96
17. For an overall history of the Monpas, their history, their relation with Tawang and village administration, see Kazuharu Mizuno and Lobsang Tenpa , Himalayan nature and Tibetan Buddhist culture in Arunachal Pradesh, India : A study of Monpa, mentioned above.
18. Thakur, A.K., NEIHA 25th session, Shilling (NEHU), 'Indigenous paper in pre colonial Arunachal : A study on manufacturing, trade and other usage. p.260. Also by the same author, 'NEIHA 21st session Imphal (Manipur), 'Patterns of pre colonial trade and polity formation in Arunachal Pradesh: A study of their relationship'. p.293
19. Bose. M.L.op cit. p.34-35
20. Maltesh Motebennur, 'Digital preservation of Mahayana Buddhist manuscripts of Arunachal Pradesh : Strategies, issues and challenges', www.inflibnet.ac.in/caliber2009/caliberPDF/16pdf
21. Maltesh., M. and Satyabati Devi Th., 'Buddhist manuscripts of Arunachal Pradesh and Manipur' ir.inflibnet.ac.in/bistream/1944/1192/1/71-74.pdf
22. Ibid.
23. Bose., M.L. op cit. pp133-136
24. ibid. p.137
25. Lamb., Alaister, India China border : The origins of the Disputed boundaries, London, 1964, The McMahon Line : A study of relations between India, China and Tibet 1904-1914, London 1966
26. Bose., M.L. op cit. pp137-38
27. This was pointed out by Murty., T.S. the Political Officer in the NEFA. Quoted by Bose., M.L.,op cit. p. 140
28. For Nain Sing's explorations of the Himalayan region , Madan., P.L. Tibet :Saga of Indian explorers (1864 – 1894), Manohar, New Delhi, 2004

29. Bose .M.L. op cit. p.140
30. Quoted by Bose., M.L. op cit, p. 136
31. Bose.,M.L. op cit. P.135
32. The reasons behind India's failure to make the McMahon frontier effective and the origins of the subsequent border dispute with China over the issue have been analysed by Mehra Parshotam in 'Tawang : A brief sum up' in Essays in frontier history, India, China and the disputed border, Oxford University Press, New Delhi, 2007, pp. 136 – 139.
33. Bose. M.L. op cit. pp142-149
34 The volume of literature on the issue of India's security concerns in the eastern sector vis a vis China is vast and these include the publications of IDSA, To cite one example – Goswami Namrata , China's territorial claim on Arunachal Pradesh : Alternative scenario 2032. Occasional Paper 29, IDSA, New Delhi, 2012.

(13)
The Revolutionaries of Anushilan Samiti and Their Inter-Provincial Connections with Tippera (1935 -47)

Keka Dutta Roy

The Anushilan Samiti was one of the premiere organizations of the Indian revolutionaries which drew within its fold numerous brilliant revolutionaries and patriotic heroes who had left an indelible impression on the minds of the people and in the history of the Indian Freedom Movement. Founded in 1902 by Satish Chandra Bose with Barrister Pramatha Nath Mitra, it was wedded to the faith of emancipating the motherland through a nationwide armed revolt. Originally it had twin centres at Calcutta and Dacca, but it gradually established its 116 branches and enrolled more than 9000 members. The Anushilan Samiti made the British tremble and the latter had to acknowledge that it was one of the most powerful amongst revolutionary associations spreading from Bengal, Assam, Tippera, Bihar, Punjab, U.P, C.P down to Poona. Its activities were carried with strict secrecy. [1]

Based on archival records, proscribed literature, and a host of secondary sources, including personal memoirs and biographies of revolutionaries, the paper evaluates the role and trends in the activities of the Tippera Anushilan Samiti highlighting the facts and events which captured the imagination of the students and youth of the period.[2]

Tippera had always been in the forefront of the revolutionary movements in India. The tide of the Anushilan Samiti was started by Pulin Das of Dacca having its usual sways in Tippera. Starting with the Manicktola Bomb Case in 1908 in which Ullaskar Datta of Tippera played an important part, the youth of Tippera were prominently active in the revolutionary movements of 1914, 1921-22, 1925 -27.[3]

Prior to 1914 there were incidents of robbery and dacoity for collection of money and arms. As early as 1909, in a concerted drive to collect money and arms, the Anushilan members with guns and bombs looted a few shops at Mohanpur market place at Tripura and carried cash and ornaments. The most interesting aspect was that the intelligence failed to detect the actual participants, though official records identified Anushilan as the actor of the operations. Tripura, being a native state, had certain advantages for secret revolutionary organizations. The absconding members of the Samiti had selected the hilly area for its underground activities. Two agricultural farms were built up at Udaipur and Belonia in Tripura by Trailokyanath Chakraborty, which were used as cover to train the cadre in revolutionary activities. These farms were also owned and maintained by the revolutionaries. Three revolutionaries disguised as sanyasis followed the Lieutenant Governor of Eastern Bengal and Assam during his visit to Agartala in November 1909. But the mission remained unfulfilled as they had been detected by the police who were loitering there. By 1912, the Anushilan Samiti had drawn up the District Organization Scheme and the rules for membership. New batches of young men were recruited. Men like Jogesh Chandra Chatterjee, Nalini Bagchi, Atindra Mohan Raychaudhury were recruited during this period. The murder of Sarat Chandra Basu, head master of Comilla Zilla School, and the Gossainpur dacoity in Tripura district were among the notable outrages of the period.[4]

It was a Tippera youth, Atindra Mohan Raychaudhuri who is often acclaimed as a 'hero' by the revolutionaries and their sympathizers, emptied his revolver on 30th June 1916 on Basanta Chatarji, the DSP, Intelligence Branch, the right-hand man of Sir Charles Tegart in his campaign against the revolutionaries of Bengal. However, Atindra Mohan escaped and was arrested later.[5]

Between 1928 -30, Pratul Ganguly of Dacca Anushilan and Pulin Das visited Tippera to build youth organizations. These became centres for recruitment, shelters for absconders, custodians of revolutionary books and proscribed literature. The Tippera Yuba Samiti was formed having smaller units all over the district wherever there was a High English school. The Tippera Students Association was formed to keep the students within their pernicious fold. This was a branch of All Bengal Students Association patronized by J.M Sengupta.[6]

A number of gymnasiums and libraries were set up. Students were encouraged to take physical exercises. Gymnastic teachers were appointed for this purpose who displayed their physical feat in student conferences. Youths were trained in lathis, sword and dagger and even girls joined the military drills. They followed the example of students in Russia and China. A number of student meetings and conferences were held where Anushilan leaders addressed them to unite and fight for the liberty of the motherland. The libraries housed stocks of revolutionary and proscribed literature and boys were encouraged to read them. However, these organizations often suffered due to rivalry between Anushilan and Yugantar parties.[7]

The Chittagong Armoury Raid of 1930 served as an eye opener to the government and the Bengal Criminal Law Amendment Act of 1930 was promulgated to equip the police to deal with the revolutionaries who had engulfed the youthful intelligensia of Bengal. The Anushilan Samiti had already drawn up a programme which was to instil revolutionary ideas in youths in order to build an organization to free the country from the hands of the British[8].

The House of Labourers and Allied companies was started in 1922 by Tippera Anushilan revolutionaries led by Jogesh Chatarji. About this venture, Jogesh Chatarji writes, "Owing to our faith in socialism, we ran the factory on socialistic lines. All those who believed in socialistic thinking there, were considered as members of the Brotherhood which was the main executive body." Here the revolutionaries worked on a community basis with each worker sharing the profit. Soon it grew into a flourishing business and rose to a limited company. Trouble arose about the division of profit and at the intervention of Pratul Ganguly, all workers were converted into salaried employees. The workers toured all over the district in connection with steel construction work in Tippera and Assam encouraging the ramifications of the Anushilan Samiti. Gradually other companies emerged like the Peerless Tea Co., Comilla Electric Supply Ltd, Bholachand Pallimangal Bank Ltd, Inland Transport Co, Ltd. and many youths were given employment in these concerns. With perfect ease and security of employment, the youth carried on the organization of the Anushilan Samiti.[9]

Revolutionaries found an easy shelter in Tippera. The Abhoy Ashram sheltered the Anushilan members along with their revolutionary literature followed by their arrest and seizure of proscribed literature. To carry on propaganda, the Anushilan members held Swadeshi Jatras,

Lantern shows, meetings along with the growth of student organizations, gymnasiums, akhras, reading clubs and military-drill units. Social service units like Tripura Hitaishini Sabha were also encouraged by the Anushilan of Tippera. There was a network of Sanghas at Agartala and other important places. The Sanghas were something like a martial organization with strict rules. The general work included organizational propaganda and agitation. Organizational work included recruitment of new members and arrangement for their training. Collection of arms and money and the commitment of political dacoities were the important activities of the Sanghas.[10]

The most powerful and dreaded Sangha was the Milan Sangha which sprang up as early as 1930 in Banamalipur area of East Agartala. The founder members were Anantalal De, Prabhat Chandra Ray, Jitendra Chandra Datta, Prafulla Kumar Nandi, Rajkumar Mazumdar, Biren Dutta, Sachindra Dutta, Asit Chandra Bhattacharjee, Debaprosad Sen, Sukumar Bhowmick etc. It was a branch of the Anushilan Samiti at Comilla. The object of the Sangha was to attain the freedom of the country by means of violence in the Sangha, members were trained in lathi, dagger and sword play. Sometimes the members used to go to the hills in order to practice revolver shooting. To serve their purpose, the revolutionaries took recourse to stealing pistols and arms from the state armoury and the police officers. Debaprasad Sen, a underground activist gave a list of 5 members who were entrusted with the responsible duties of the Sangha. They were Hari Kumar Ray Chowdhury, Deboprosad Sen, Niranjan Ghosal and Sachindra Dutta but they failed to take any firm decision.[11]

Among the Sanghas the Matri Sangha was set up by those who had belief in the Anushilan ideology and who kept contact with elder women folk of the adjoining districts. The female members of the Sangha included Nirupana Das, Saibalini De, Nirupama Datta, Hema Prava Singha and others.[12]

The Thakur Sangha heralded by Prabhat Ray, Harendra Debbarma and Haridas Banerjee kept links with the Anushilan Samiti of Comilla and also worked as a branch of the Milan Sangha, Agartala.[13]

The Young Men's Association called Milan Sangha affiliated to the Anushilan Samiti thrived along with the Agartala branch of the Tippera Anushilan Samiti collected arms and ammunitions through state borders and raised funds through dacoities.[14]

The Melaghar centre was set up in a dense forest at Melaghar, Sonamura on the southern side of the river Gomati through the efforts of Jogesh Chakraborty, Jogesh Chatterjee, Atindra Roy, Prafulla Chakraborty. During the middle of 1920's it was a charcoal making place set up by Jogesh Chatterjee, Naren Sen, Kamanijya Singha in 1922 in Comilla. It was an ideal House of Labourers where all worked equally on the likes of Robert Owen of England. Melaghar centre of the Anushilan was outwardly a feeding centre of charcoal but actually shooting, drill, physical exercise were its regular features. It had many members as workers. Its inward activities remained unexposed for a long time. It acquired financial solvency through the production and supply of agricultural goods and charcoal.[15]

In the Tripura State of the Tippera district, the Anushilan revolutionaries took shelter with ease because the state police was naturally less enthusiastic to curb their activities entertaining a spirit of sympathy with them.[16]

At Rajababu's house at Krishnanagar, Agartala, a camp of Anushilan Samiti of Comilla was established as early as 1931 to give shelter to absconders from the districts and to help them to practice revolver shooting in hills. Prabhat Chandra Ray a member of Milan Sangha and Thakur Sangha was associated in its establishment. Other founder members included Sushil Debbarma and Kanti Debbarma.[17]

The Tippera Anushilan gradually established a inter-district connection with Chittagong, Comilla, Noakhali, Faridpur, Rajshahi, Dacca, Bakarganj, Senior Anushilan leaders from Dacca like Troilokya Chakraborty, Pratul Ganguly, Ramesh Acharji came to Tippera as tourists to help in organizing the Tippera Anushilan Samiti.[18]

To raise funds, thefts, robberies and dacoities were committed to raise funds and to obtain fire arms. The Anushilan centres at Tippera continued work in secret groups to evade arrests. In 1932, the Students Association and Youth Association were declared unlawful and banned. Collection of arms and ammunitions by the Anushilan members was rampant and many Anushilan members possessing arms and ammunitions were arrested and convicted under the Arms Act and Explosive Substance Act as well as the Bengal Criminal Law Amendment Act of 1930. To raise funds, the Anushilan members committed a number of dacoities as recorded in the Agartala Robbery Case(1932), the Mograbazar Dacoity

(1932), Nayanpur Bazar Dacoity (1932), mail robbery, murder of police officers and European Government officers took place as seen in the Ellison Murder Case of 1932, burning of the Comilla European Club, 1930 etc. took place.[19]

In Tippera, the Anushilan till 1934 was a formidable organization having close connections with its central body in Bengal. The policy of Tippera Anushilan upto 1934 was (i) to recruit members for an armed mass uprising (ii) to collect funds by stealing ornaments and cash and by committing dacoities to secure firearms and (iii) to murder both European and Indian officials-[20].

A major setback came with the arrest of Prabhat Chakravarty in 1930's in the Inter Provincial Conspiracy Case followed by the arrest of a number of leaders in the Titagarh Conspiracy Case in 1935. But this did not retard the progress of the movement. Young or workers took up the place of the seniors and organizational work included military drills, lathi and dagger play, training of male and female volunteers and secret work of the Samiti continued[21].

Here is a list of political suspects involved in the Inter-provincial Conspiracy Case (Anushilan) and the Titagarh Conspiracy Case (Anushilan):

1. Parimal Kandti Datta living in Agartala
2. Santi Bhusan Bardhan of Anushilan Comilla who left for Rangoon for occupation.
3. Sukumar Chakraborty of Anushilan who was a compounder working in Mohesh Bhattacharya & Co.
4. Labanya Chandra Roy of the Inter Provincial Conspiracy Case workers in a Homeo Dispensary, Roy & Co.
5. Lalit Mohan Datta Gupta of Anushilan practicing as a homeopath in Comilla.
6. Baroda Kanta Bose of Tippera Anushilan, Chandpur who was a vegetable dealer acting as a post boy for the group dealing with arms.
7. Jagadish Chandra Sen Chowdhury of the Titagarh arms conspiracy case working as a clerk in Das Bhowmick & Co. belonging to Tippera Anushilan.
8. Sanjib Kumar Datta of Tippera Anushilan, a student of Carmichael Medical College.

9. Sushen Chandra Ray, employed in Dhakeswar Cotton Mills, a clerk and a member of Tippera Anushilan, employed in the Bengal Academy of Chandpur.[22]

In connection with the Interprovincial Conspiracy Case the following ciphers were seized from Prabhat Chakraborty in a house at 11 Sitalatala Lane Calcutta which showed a list of Tippera Anushilan members engaged in this case:

1)Sukumar Chakraborty
2)Benoda Kanta Basu
3)Ganesh Mazumdar
4)Satish De
5)Paresh Guha
6)Suresh Mazumdar
7)Pran Ballav Misir
8)Atish Chandra Mazumdar (student of Sree Guru Library)

To safeguard themselves, the members were divided into self-contained groups under a separate executive leader. The programme of the Tippera Anushilan was to recruit members and to collect funds to assist those evading arrest. The leaders were in communication with those in jail and arms were coming from Agartala. These arms were collected and kept under the control of the executive leaders in order to prevent unauthorized commission of outrages. The Anushilan leaders were in touch with the village organizations having varying strength and importance. Important leaders guiding them were Prabhat Chakrabarti and Hari Kumar RayChaudhury though the latter's arrest came as a rude shock to the party's activities. The important centres of the Tippera Anushilan at this time were Comilla, Chandpur, Brahmanbaria and the Tripura State. The Tippera Anushilan decided to shift its headquarters from Agartala to Faridpur due to several arrests and with many absconding, its fire arms were also sent away to Faridpur from Tripura State. In Tripura State, this Anushilan group was known as Milan Sangha and its leader Sachin Mazumdar who was arrested. Female members included Pulina Sen Chaudhuri and Champaklata Debi leading the female group[23].

The Anushilan central body which controlled the activities of the different groups was forced out of the Tippera district to Faridpur faced need for funds leading to the Hajiganj Mail Dacoity of 1934 etc. Funds were also required for the defense of the party members in jail implicated in various criminal cases. The leader of the Tripura Anushilan, Sukumar Chakraborty too was arrested and the central body became detached from Tippera, though it flourished in small groups with younger members and gradually links with Tippera and Comilla began again. However they were primarily inactive as members were instructed not to strike before they received command.[24]

In January 1935 notorious absconders Purnananda Dasgupta who had escaped from the Alipore Central Jail and Parul Mukherjee of Tippera were arrested with firearms in a den at Titagarh and other Anushilan revolutionaries namely Debaprasad Sen of Agartala at Belgharia following an explosion and Prafulla Sen of Tippera at Sukchar, all in the district of 24 Parganas. These arrests followed by many more, gave a death blow to the Central Body which could not manage to send any more district leaders to Tippera but this district continued to have small groups which were led by minor leaders who made occasional attempts to get connected with the Central Body in early 1935.[25]

In February 1935, Sukumar Chakraborty of Bordia came home to Tippera from jail and mixed with Raj Kumar Raychaudhury (brother of Hari Kumar), Hemanta Singh, Nirmal Singh, Lalit Duttagupta and Krishna Chakrabarty of Chandpur. They began a talk of reorganization and collection of funds by dacoity. [26]

Later, at Rajargaon, Hajiganj, Lalit Dattagupta, Nirmal Singh, Rajkumar Raychowdhury, Hemanta Singh and Nitya Gopal Datta planned a dacoity but were hauled up and detained under BCLA Act. This group possessed fire arms and had planned to take revenge on the District Intelligence Branch officers. However this plan did not mature.[27]

Smaller groups with young members continued to flourish at Chandpur, Comilla Brahmanberia and Agartala. Krishna Chakraborty ran an organization at Matlab. Makhan Datta at Chandpur, Dhirendra Karmakar and Manmohan Ghosh at Comilla and they tried milder methods of stealing ornaments and cash from the houses of members for party funds and attempted to secure firearms from the Tripura State. Bimal Sen and Sunil Chaudhuri tried in vain to find a link with the Central body. Abinas Chandra Bhaumik was running the organization at Chunta but could not find a link with Comilla and Agartala parties. Bhupendra Chanda tried to form a group in his village. One Bimal Dutta of the

Chittagong Anushilan was arrested at Mogra where he was carrying party work with Gopal Shah and others. He was introduced by Abinash Bhaumick to work for the party and establish a link between Comilla and Agartala Anushilan. However he was arrested and convicted.[28]

In the Tripura State, the activities of the Agartala Milan Sangha were checked to a great extent owing to the arrest and detention of Sachindra Majumdar , Ganesh Chakraborty, Nalini Ranjan Das Gupta, Ashit Bhattacharya and Asha Ranjan Chakraborty who had taken part in at least two dacoities at Nalua and Gauripur and were also booked for the Hajigunj Mail dacoity and remained absconding and were not to be found in Tripura State. [29]

However Asha Ranjan maintained a link with Sylhet Anushilan. Tinkowri Ganguly and Gopal Datta formed a link with the Mogra group. The Anushilan group at Belonia which was working in close touch with the Noakhali Anushilan received a shock with the arrest of Ananda Acharji who was in possession of fire arms. [30]

From July 1935, Mahendra Das of Tarapur who was connected with Tippera- Noakhali Anushilan for a long time wanted to abscond for party work. He was restrained along with Rajendra Chakraborty of Chandpur for revolutionary activities. Siddiqur Rahman of Chandpur talked of committing dacoity but his plan never matured. Hirendra Dutta took charge of the party at Comilla and Agartala. More fire arms were required for party members like Hirendra Dutta, Haripada Bhatatcharji and Manindra but the plans for dacoities did not mature. Krishna Chakraborty worked amongst boys at Boalia and Matlab but very little activity occurred and the little that was in existence finally stopped with the arrest of the following leaders: Dhirendra Karmakar, Manmohan Ghosh, Gopal Datta, Asha Ranjan Chakraborty, Pratul Dutta , Krishna Chakraborty under BCLA Act and Anushilan activities were stopped after these arrests. By the end of 1935 the Anushilan had no activity.[31]

After 1935, despite arrests, recruitment and reorganization of Tripura Anushilan continued. The party revived the mental and physical clubs for boys in different quarters. The clubs were named after a deceased revolutionary. This was the old Anushilan policy for recruitment. The Chandpur Anushilan party was particularly active in spreading the organization among the students and the youth in the interior.[32]

In the beginning of 1936, there was nothing going on by way of recruitment and organization. In February 1936, the Mogra Anushilan Group became responsible for theft of cash and ornaments from shops. Sachindra Datta and Pabitra Pal, who were convicted earlier in the Agartala Dacoity, were in Agartala jail and tried to pick up connection with party members encouraging them to continue their work. In March 1936, Sitanath De, a notorious absconder often started visiting Shyamnagar. However, he was arrested in a shelter in May 1936. Ramesh Ray, an Anushilan detenue had arranged for his shelter. Prabhat Roy wrote to young workers from Agartala jail and encouraged them to carry on their work. There was general talk of reorganization but no active attempt was made to reorganize the party in 1936.[33]

The first active attempt at reorganization was started in April 1937 by Naresh Deb, Benoy Bhaumick , Shayama Charan Chakravarty, Manindra Pal and Prabodh Kar who kept the party going and wanted a definite pogramme. In May 1937, Manmohan Ghosh and Dhirendra Dhar were released and moved to Comilla, Agartala and Calcutta speaking of Communism as the latest programme of the party. Circulation of Communist literature prevailed. In June 1937, Hemanta Singh of Chandpur came and spoke of the Cult of Communism and Scientific Socialism and the division of detenues in two groups on these two lines. Protima Bhadra and Prabodh Kar discussed party matters while Manindra Pal and Benoy Bhaumick were trying to procure fire arms from Comilla. In November, 1937, Probhat Ray was released from Agartala jail and took up the work of reorganizing the Milan Sangha. Monoranjan Chakraborty took charge of the Comilla Anushilan.[34]

The undercurrent of revolutionary activities continued with difference in character owing to changed circumstances of the times. The Anushilan movement was gradually taking a Socialist turn. There was a more realistic approach and a concrete program of action. The sentimentalism of the earlier period gave way to a desire for mass movements and the Anushilan of Tippera was trying to arouse the masses through propagation and action.[35]

In 1937, the influence of Communism came with the emergence of the new programme of the Anushilan party. Circulation of Communist Literature amongst revolutionaries, lectures on communism and scientific socialism influencing the recruits followed. In Tippera, the Anushilan became active in reviving and reorganizing a number of gymnasiums, public reading rooms, study circles and libraries to propagate their ideas and attract people. Well known among them were the Public Reading Room at Comilla, Abhay Asram Reading room, ABR Library at Comilla, Hitakari Sadharan Library (Chandpur), Siksha Mandir Library, Matindra Memorial Library(Chandpur), Pragati Pathagar(Chandpur), Chandpur Circulating library, Syamagram Pathagar or Vivekananda Library (Brahmanbaria), Chunta Public Library, Malai Library (Brahmanberia), Nasirabad Library(Brahmanbaria), Rasullabad Bijoya Library(Brahmanbaria), The Banipith Library, Kandirpur, Comilla etc. Book depots or book shops at Kandirpur, Chandpur were set up by ex-convicts where the ex-detenus and suspects gathered to collect revolutionary literature and earn money. Some revolutionaries worked as book canvassers in school for earning money and studying the situation. Study circles such as Pragati Lekhak Sangha , Chandpur Study Circle, Chittaranjan Jatiya Pratisthan were set up to circulate the party's ideas and read out books on Communist ideas to new members. Newspaper agencies were run by Anushilan ex-detenus where agencies for periodicals like 'New Age', 'National Front', 'Mandira', 'Comrade', 'Joysree' were undertaken. Some Anushilan detenues served as tea venders as well. Other business enterprises set up after 1935 by ex-detenues were Cotton Mills(agency of Bangasree Cotton Mills), Tea Companies(Das & Co.), Eastern Continental Bank, Ayurvedic Chemical Works, Steel works, Standard Match Factory (Chandpur) as well as hotels and mess in and around Tippera. The government at this time put forward the Detenue Training Scheme whereby selected detenues were given agricultural and industrial training at the agricultural and industrial camps so that after release from jail they could pursue a livelihood and overcome unemployment.[36]

Agricultural training included market gardening, fruit-farming as well as growing of oilseeds, sugarcanes and tobacco and large profit could be made from such undertakings. Industrial training included training in small industries like cutlery, pottery, brass works, umbrella manufacture, etc. The detenues were given financial aid to start their own business or be employed in such concerns. Industrial training camps were set up at Clive House, Sukchar, Gouripur etc (industrial) and Maslandpur(agriculture). Well known among the Tippera Anushilanites who took this training and were later employed or charted their business were:[37]

Industrial Training Scheme

	Name of Partner	Name of Firm
1	Prafulla Kumar Nandi	Pioneer Industrial Works
2	Ramesh Chandra Sil Baidya	International Brass Works
3	Punnyabrata Mazumdar	House of Industries
4	Swarna Renu Dutta	House of Industries
5	Subodh Chandra Gupta	House of Industries
6	Abani Mohan Bhattacharya	House of Industries
7	Sushil Kr. Deb Burman	House of Industries
8	Sudhir Chakraborty	Factory no.6 at Alipore
9	Pulin Behari Pal	United Potteries

Praised Agricultural Scheme

	Name of Partner	Name of Firm
1	Purnendu Sen	Factory No.13 at Belighata Main Road
2	Dhirendra Chandra Dhar	Agricultural Farm No.1 (Habra)
3	Manmohan Ghosh	Agricultural Farm No.1 (Habra)
4	Shitala Kanta Das	Agricultural Farm No.1 (Maslandapur)
5	Sudhir Bhattacharjee	Agricultural Farm No.1 (Maslandpur)[38]

After 1937, many revolutionaries having been released from jail as a result of the Gandhi-Nazimuddin pact were permeating into the Congress Socialist party or the Communist Party. Most of them resumed activity in different forms no longer believed in terrorism. Their latest doctrine was Communism or Socialism as they preferred to call it but it was apprehended that would lead to terrorism in a more extensive and vigorous scale. Most of the released detenues discussed their plans and programme of action. On 23rd December 1937, the detenues were extolled as heroes and martyrs by the Congress. Krishaks and the Congress Socialists and Nibaran Chandra Datta, a released detenue declared at a meeting, that he had the occasion to study the different political ideologies in jails and camps and came out with a complete training programme to lead the masses in the revolutionary movement on lines of Socialism.[39]

In early 1938, Nibaran Chandra Datta became the Secretary of the Congress Socialist party which called political meetings for example in memory of terrorist convicts who died in jails as a result of disease or otherwise. Most of the Anushilan detenues joined the Congress Socialist party which was working with the right-wing of the Congress. Sailendra Ray, ex-detenue organized a Students Federation conference to encourage the students to adopt the principles of Socialism. Lalit Dutta Gupta, Rai Haran Chakraborty, Gopal Datta of the Anushilan joined the left wing and worked on the Krishak front while Ranjit Raychaudhuri started the Pragati Lekhak Sangha (Progressive Writers Association) which was a Communist organization. Lalit Dutta Gupta was instrumental in the formation of a Students Federation at Chandpur. [40]

In 1939, the Anushilan members active in the Congress Socialist Party and the Students Federation of the Communist party were touring about organizing branches of the Students Federation. Soumendranath Tagore played a significant role in spreading Communism and in organizing the Students Federation at this time. The influence of the Progressive writers Associations controlled by the Communists was significant at this time.[41]

After 1939, the Anushilan leaders were averse to murder and dacoity. They did not believe in terrorism but had the occasion to study the different ideologies - the latest doctrine being Communism or Socialism as they preferred to call it. In fact from 1937 onwards most of the ex-detenues had been discussing the plans and programmes of the Anushilan. The released ex-detenues were extolled as heroes and martyrs by the Congress, Krishaks and the Congress Socialists. From Tippera, came reports that some members were preparing for 'Satyagraha' but the Anushilan members were instructed to abstain from Congress affairs only to participate when open agitation would take place. Those reserved for secret work would be kept aside so that it did not impair the secret programme of the party. Secret party meetings were held where members were talking about striking the roots of imperialism at a favourable moment. Here is a list of exdetenues/ Terrorist Convicts of Tippera who had been convicted under the

BCLA Act and subsequently arrested for possessing arms

ent and

1. Makhan lal Datta of Anushilan
2. Nibaran Datta
3. Binode Sarkar
4. Brojendra Chandra Chakraborty
5. Bimal Majumdar
6. Lalit Datta Gupta
7. Hari Kumar Roy Cowdhury
8. Mukunda Chakraborty
9. Sunil Mazumder
10. Amulya Mukherjee[43]

By 1939, many ex-detenues of Tippera had been actively working amongst labourers and peasants and committees were formed to control the labour unions organized by the Anushilan party to evade arrest under the Defense of India rules. The Assam-Bengal railway workers were particularly organized as well as the Assam-Bengal railway employees Associations. The 'New Equity' was the well known organ of the Assam Bengal Rail Employees Association run by Anushilan members like Atindra Mohan Roychowdhury, Jamini Mohan Pal, etc. In Chandpur, the Tippera District Jute Press Worker's union was started by the Anushilan party, however it received poor response from the jute workers. [44]

"New Equity" was the party organ of the Assam Bengal Railway Employees Association (Anushilan – CSP). This organ was well distributed by Dhuresh Chadra Ghosh of Comilla and then to Abineswar Ghose the Station Master of AB Railways of Chittagong. It was distributed to the Jugantar Revolutionaries as well like Sukhendu Bikash Dutta of Chittagong Steam Laundry. Ananta Lal De of Anushilan Comilla also subscribed it Jamini Mohan Pal, General Secretary of Assam Bengal Rail Employees Association distributed them to Sukhendu Datta of CSP of Chittagong Bengal publicity Syndicate. This magazine was subscribed by Amiyo Ballav Sanyal of Bipin Smriti Granthagar of Mymensingh. Jogesh Chatterjee of the Anushilan carried the New Equity to Calcutta for distribution. The Rail Guard Sailen Chatterjee received the magazine from Bhairab Bazar for distribution. Jamini Mohan Pal the General Secretary of Assam Bengal Rail Employees Association informed Amiyo Ballav

Sanyal of Mymensingh that Shib Nath Banerjee was sending him message of good wishes to New Equity urging rail workers to organise vigorous agitation against Federal Scheme which would deprive their opposition to criticize the rail administration. Utpal Ghosh, Station Master of Pahartali, Chittagong, Dwijendra Benoy Roy of Comilla Anushilan, Atindra Mohan Roy of Comila Anushilan, Tamini Mohan Pal of Anushilan CSP, Pratul Ganguly of Anushilan, Amulya Mukherjee of Comilla Anushilan – CSP, Nepal Naha of Anushilan were some of the important detenues of the Anushilan who participated in the distribution network of "New Equity". In Tippera, Assam and Calcutta many rail employees subscribed this magazine. However reports from Noakhali were not favourable. Pratul Ganguly informed of the poor response in the subscription of New Equity. Jagabandhu Mazumdar, Biren Dasgupta, Nepal Naha , Surendra Kar Bedar got poor response in getting subscription. Many Anushilan revolutionaries came forward to collect subscription for this organization. Notable among them was Rabindra Mohan Sengupta of Dacca and Calcutta Anushilan Chittaranhan Ray of Anushilan, Sailendra Mohan Ray of Bakarganj Narendra Nath Chakravarty, Ananta Bose of Netro Kona, Mymensingh, Shibnath Banerjee, President of Assam-Bengal Rail Association and Jamini Mohan Pal its Secretary to name a few. Further, subscription collectors were also engaged to run the magazine.[45]

In Chandpur, Hari Kumar Raychowdhury, Dinesh Ghatak, Jyotirindranath Mazumdar and others were active in arranging political classes thrice a weak and selected three detenues for secret party work. A number of girls too were recruited to the Mahila Sangha of Tippera by ex-convict Parul Mukherjee and her sister ex-detenue Moyna Mukherjee. The Anushilan recruited 1300 members from a union among the Bengal employees at Lalmonirhat.[46]

By 1940, 'The Thesis' and the 'War thesis' advocating mass revolution was being widely circulated in Tippera. The members were distributing leaflets among village workers which called for an uncompromising struggle for independence during international crisis.[47]

It is true that after 1937, many revolutionaries had been released from jail as a result of Gandhi-Nazimuddin Pact but there was a division among detenues into two groups having different lines of action. By 1940, the object of the Anushilan Samiti was to organize armed rebellion but opinion was divided about when this would take place. Some leaders, who were backed by Tippera Anushilan opined that the present situation was

nd that

e more

arms. Those who were not in favour opined that the time was not ripe for a open rebellion and that it should come when some foreign power should attack India, for example, when Russia would invade India.[48]

In 1940 in Tippera, the Anushilan was working hand in hand with the Forward Bloc. Many Bengal leaders of the Anushilan belonged to Tippera. They were vigorously pushing forward their plans to organize a volunteer Corp ostensibly for war-time internal defence which they would undoubtedly use against the government through the Students Federation. The Anushilan party spread itself in various parts of the district with the plea of spreading anti-illiteracy work which the unsuspecting public welcomed as a movement for their welfare. This was another weapon like the one of attending the sick and doing relief work in the time of distress both of which had been used in the past to capture the imagination of the people. The Anushilan organization at this juncture was an Indian one and its strength was increasing every day. Their latest programme of work had surpassed the worst apprehensions about them entertained in the past. There were indications that they were working hard to get arms with which they would bring about a mass revolution.[49]

Specific prosecution was undertaken and prominent members of the Anushilan were bound down while some others were dealt for delivering objectionable speeches by the British. Restriction orders under DI Rules were also tried in respect of some of the active members but those steps had not succeeded in checking their activities which were increasing.[50]

The Anushilan party members attended the Dacca Conference which was addressed by Subhas Bose in full force and the Anushilan members took steps to implement some of the resolutions passed therein. They were planning to organize a Volunteer Corp. which if allowed to develop would constitute a grave menace to the government.[51]

The Anushilan party controlled the Assam Bengal Employees Association whose headquarters were in Comila. Their aim was to foment labour unrest with a view to bring about a strike when necessary.[52]

In 1940, the arrest and externment of the revolutionaries of the Anushilan damaged the organization. There was a look out notice for many Anushilan members of Tippera who were absconding:-

1. Hari Charan De
2. Amiyo Dasgupta
3. Purnendu Dasgupta
4. Nani Gopal De (Referencing leaflets issued by RSPI were found on walls of libraries in Agartala Town)

Though revolutionaries were trying to organize the student community and reorganize the Samiti, leaders like Atin Roychoudhury were finding Tippera unhealthy and moving towards Assam. Several members went into hiding to reorganize the local groups.[53]

By 1941, Surendra Ray was acting as the adviser to the younger members who were quarrelling owing to inactivity and lack of definite programme leading to a split in the Samiti. Finally Surendra Ray drew up a detailed scheme for the reorganization of the Samiti for many parts of the district. However active members like Jatindranath Chakrabarti and Manindra Kumar Chakravarty were arrested at this time. Again in 1942, a large number of Anushilan members were arrested. During the Quit India movement group meeting were held to arouse consciousness in favour of the movement. The Samiti was responsible for organizing student agitation and outside the state as a protest to the arrest of the leaders of the Quit India movement.[54]

The Anushilan in all districts save in Dacca, Tippera and Bakharganj were disintegrating owing to central committee's lack of initiative and inability to guide. Pratibha Raychowdhury did not think it was worthwhile even to attempt any reconstruction of the tribunal appointed prisoners. Many members like Nihar Dasgupta of Tippera belonging to the central committee of Tippera Anushilan were trying to remain inactive to evade arrest.[55]

Many revolutionaries like Sushil Bhattacharya of Tippera shifted to U.P and resided in Kanpur and Allahabad and after release in 1945, had activities of wide nature. An associate of Jogesh Chatterjee, plans were made to send him to tribal areas to spread anti-British propaganda but this had to be abandoned because he would be easily recognized.[56]

The Anushilan RSP of Tippera published a number of leaflets at this time which were considered objectionable by the British Government

like "Jatiyo Saptaha" (Bengali) RSPI Tippera "National Flag" (Bengal) leaflet of RSPI Tippera "Swadhinata Diboshe Bharater Biplobi Samajtantri Dal (RSPI on Independence Day), RSPI Bengal branch. This is a tribute of respect to the RSP leaders who were behind the prison bars
 ˀomilla,

The Anushilan revolutionaries faced certain limitations too. The participants included those from upper caste i.e Brahmins, Kayasthas and Vaishaya. With them, a few Thakurs (nobles), and the Raj family members joined and the 'Bhadralok' colour could be given to only a fraction of the people though support came in large numbers during 30's. Though Anushilan revolutionaries operated primarily from Udaipur, Belonia, Sonamura and Kailasahar, Agartala remained the main centre of activities in both the early and later phases. The movement was thus localized in character. The middle class youthful boys were the active participants among the Anushilanites. Coordination between the Sanghas was lacking. To make a broad based platform an effort, for the mobilization of the tribals, jhoomias, poor peasants, workers was hardly undertaken. Above all, the participants among the Muslims were negligible though the movement was not religious in essence. The leaders of the Anushilan Samiti failed to deliver an enthusing programme of action to their younger followers.[58]

The Dhwaja-Bhaja tussle took place among the revolutionaries in Tripura. 'Dhwaja' means standard bearers of the Anushilan Samiti and 'Bhaja' means the followers of the Jugantar party. It was purely a conflict between a party and a Samiti over ideological differences, clash of personalities and a struggle for power. The quarrel between Sachindralal Singha and Sukumar Bhowmick was a pointer in that direction. Sometimes bloody feuds took place among the opposing members. Fighting and boxing became an usual matter. Both had arms and they tried to overpower each other, and the police had to intervene to settle the feud.[59], [60]

The policy of the Anushilan Samiti was to run a parallel line of armed struggle with Gandhi's non violent road to Indian freedom movement.

Note & References

1. Tarapada Lahiri, Freedom Struggle and Anushilan Samiti, Calcutta, 1991, p.1-4
2. Gopal Chakravorty, A Brief history of the Tippera Anushilan Samiti in Amiyo Samanta, Terrorism in Bengal, Volume II, Calcutta 1995 pp.1098-1136.
3. Gopal Chakravorty, op.cit.
4. Gopal Chakravarty 'A Brief History of the Tippera Anushilan Samiti in Amiyo Samanta, Terrorism in Bengal, p.1098 -1136, Volume II, Calcutta 1995, pp 1098 -1136 and Pratul Chandra Ganguly, Biplobir Jiban Darshan, pp.143(Bengali) and Trailokya Nath Chakravorty, Jele Tirish Bachor (1369 BS), pp.53-57, Bengali, and Sedition Committee Report, paragraph 43.
5. Amiyo Samanta, op.cit. and Tridib Chaudhuri edited Freedom Struggle and the Anushilan Samiti, Volume I, Calcutta, 1977, pp.129.
6. Ibid.
7. Ibid.
8. Amiyo Samanta op.cit. Tridib Chaudhuri op.cit p.129.
9. Amalendu De, Prabhat Chakravarty: Anushilan Samiti Theke Communist Party Te, Calcutta 2002, p.20, Amiyo Samanta, op.cit. and IB File no.697/36 list of Business concern owned and used by revolutionaries, West Bengal State Archives (W.B.S.A) and Jogesh Chandra Chatarji, In Search of Freedom, pg. 208-9 and Tridib Chauduri edited Freedom Struggle and Anushilan Samiti, op.cit, pp.214.
10. Amiyo Samanta, op.cit.
11. Amiyo Samanta op.cit and Ranjit Kumar Dey, Sociopolitical movement in India, New Delhi 1998, p.99-104.
12. Ranjit Dey op. cit p.103.
13. Ibid.
14. Amiyo Samanta op.cit.
15. Ranjit Dey op.cit p.103-104.
16. Amiyo Samanta op. cit.
17. Ranjit Dey op.cit p.104.
18. Amiyo Samanta op.cit.

19. Amiyo Samanta op.cit and IB File 935/36 Classified list of Terrorism cases from 1930-33, 1912-35 W.B.S.A.
20. Ibid and I.B Records W.B.S.A File No. 19/35.
21. Ibid and Amalendu De op.cit.
22. File No. 174/37 IB Records W.B.S.A.
23. Ibid.
24. Amiyo Samanta op.ct and IB File no. 935/36. Classified list of Terrorist cases from 1930-33, 1912-35, WBSA.
25. Amiyo Samanta p.113.
26. Ibid; p.1131.
27. Ibid p.1131.
28. Ibid; p.1132.
29. Ibid; p.1132.
30. Ibid; p.1133.
31. Bid; p.1133.
32. File No. IOR/L/P&J/12/401, Review of Revolutionary matters, British Library London.
33. Amiyo Samanta op.cit, p.1134.
34. Ibid p.1134.
35. Buddhadev Bhattacharya, Freedom Struggle and Anushilan Samiti, Volume I, pp.1-2 , Calcutta , 1979.
36. File No. 1056A- 33 Notes by the Bengal Government on the terrorist movement in Bengal, 1933 – 1944, W.B.S.A and 21/39 list of the activities of the ex-terrorists, 1939.
37. File No. 9C/35 IB Records, WBSA.
38. IB File No. 989 / 35(1) WBSA and File No. 989C/35, File No. 77-36, WBSA.
39. Amiyo Samanta op.cit, p.1134-35.
40. Ibid.
41. File No. IOR/L/P&J/12/401, Review of Revolutionary matters, op.cit.
42. IB Records File No. 288A/38 WBSA.
43. Ibid.
44. IB Records File no. 10R/L/P &J/12/401British Library IB Records op.cit and 96/39, WBSA.
45. IB Records File No.: 96/39 WBSA.
46. IB Records File No. 10R/L/P & J/12/4-1 British Library London.

47. Ibid and Jogesh Chandra Chatarji, In search of Freedom p.208-9 and Tridib Chaudhuri ed: Freedom Struggle and Anushilan Samiti, p.214.
48. Ibid.
49. IB Records File No. 437/40, WBSA.
50. Ibid.
51. Ibid.
52. Ibid.
53. IB Records File no. 250/40, 575/40 (2), 575/40 (2), 575/40 WBSA.
54. Review of Revolutionary matters File No. 10R/L/P&J/12/420, British Library, London.
55. Ibid.
56. Review of Revolutionary matters, File No.IOR/L/P&J/12/402, British Library, London.
57. IB Records File No. 36/45, WBSA and IB Records File No. 5/39.
58. Ranjit Dey op.cit.
59. Ranjit Dey op.cit.
60. Here is a list of Business concerns at Tippera having connections with revolutionaries:-

    (a) Banipith Bookshop Comilla (Anushilan)
    (b) Dispensary of Rajendra De
    (c) Umbrella Shop started by Dhiren De of Chandpur Anushilan.
    (d) Engineering Works at Chandpur
    (e) S.D Chakraborty & Co.
    (f) Book selling Association Tippera Agency
    (g) Arjya Oshyadhalaya – Dispensary of Kalusaj Sevabrata Ghosh of Matlab Anushilan
    (h) Datta Brothers, newspaper Agents Agartala
    (i) Eastern Continental Bank at Chandpur (Anushilan)
    (j) Eastern Continental Bank at Agartala (Anushilan)
    (k) The 'Graduate Friends' a stationary shop at Agartala
    (l) Akshoy Bhandar Chandpur
    (m) Kalika Coton Mills
    (n) Kalighat Biri Factory, Chandpur
    (o) Pallimangal Bank Tippera
    (p) Popular Engineers Ltd, Chandpur
    (q) Publicity Syndicate

(r) Sarada Pharmacy Chandpur
(s) The Standard Match Factory Tippera (Anushilan)
(t) Union Bank Chandpur
(u) Workers Union (of Arya Oushadhalaya) Chandpur[1]

ABBREVIATIONS USED

1) WBSA : West Bengal State Archives
2) IB : Intelligence Branch
3) IOR : India Office Records
4) CP : Central Provinces
5) UP : Uttar Pradesh
6) BCLA : Bengal Criminal law Amendment Act
7) DIB : District Intelligence Branch

(14)
The Depressed class Weavers of Patna–Sonepur Princely States in Assam Tea Gardens in Early 20th Century

Kishore Ch. Meher

Any visitor to rural Assam (cachar and Brahmaputra valley) may come across people especially from Sambalpur and ex-princely states of Sonepur and Patna in west Orissa. These people speak odia language even today. Moreover they are also found in Meghalaya; Tripura. They work many tea gardens of Assam even today as they did in the past. They work in Lakhimpur Dabalagarh Brahmajan Ketla Dibrugarh Tezpur etc places. Today they constitute a sizable population of Assam. Their kins and relatives in Orissa remember them and even construct memories of their kins in the form of oral songs and tales.

These people are the so called depressed class or scheduled caste people. Being branded as untouchable in Hindu society they were also narrated as people who had habit of making theft and robbery by colonial gazzateers and cenus reports. They are often known as ganda pan Dom and Tanty.[1] They are not yet assimilated in the socalled Hindu society though there is little improvement in their social position.

These people were/are traditional weavers. In almost every village of present-day west Odisha there is a Ganda Dom or Pan para or locality. Most of them still weave cloth. Their long tradition of cloth weaving, spinning carding and ginning cotton is in their folklores and oral tradition.[2] The village Birtia or castehead of these people have preserved this memory in their oral account.Apart from weaving coarse cotton cloth they were also engaged in rearing cocoon to produce tusser yarn. Infact they were major supplier of tusser to the Bhulia weavers of Sonepur princely state and Sambalpur weavers.[3]

The present paper seeks to examine the reasons and factors responsible for their emigration to Assam in the late nineteenth century and early twentieth century. How come weaver community members became coolies or indentured labourers in the tea plantations thousands of miles away from their native places? Infact, these people did not go to Assam voluntarily but they were just enticed by agents of tea planters. They were promised better life in Assam. The Sardars [sirdar] lured them and promised a very bright life. But very soon after coming to Assam, their dreams of decent and bright life were all shattered into pieces. [4]

Tea does not have a long history in India. It was not native to India. China remained the sole exporter of tealeaves until the early nineteenth century. It is understood that for the first time in 1822, the chief of the Singpo tribe had intimated about tea leaves in Assam to Major Robert. Then in 1832 Lt. Charlton himself saw tea plant in Assam. They intimated it to the Bengal government.[5] In 1834 Governor General William Bentick formed the tea committee. The first tea garden of India appeared in Assam in 1837. In 1839 the Assam Company was constituted in London to make the commercial cultivation of tealeaves. The East India Company resolved to end the monopoly of china in tea business. Hence the company took steps to cultivate tea in many other places too. By 1839, tea gardens begun to be created in many localities of Assam. But it was not until after 1850 that the company attained some success and tea gardens begun to be established.[6] The Company sold large quantity of land to the European planters in very cheap price. Even per hectare of land was sold at Rs 6 toRs12 only. By 1871 there were 205 plantations in Assam. Nearly 12,668hectare land was under tea cultivation. Total tea production was 2.83 million kilograms. [7] Later on tea plantation was encouraged also in Darjeeling district [Bengal] Travancore [Kerala] and Madras. By1910, tea was grown in almost 228,000 hectares with total production of 119.4 million kilo grams. India had now become the principal exporter of tea in the whole world.[8]

Most of the tea planters were Europeans. The Company preferred them by selling land to them at far cheaper rate. In 1911,in Bengal,158 outof176 tea companies and 46 out of 64 privately owned gardens were under exclusive European control. A sum of Rs 30.2crore was invested in this sector in 1914.Out of which only Rs4.3crore owned by companies registered in India. Many of them had floated joint ventures too. The Company came forward to help the planters to recruit their labour force. It was indeed partly due to the help and favour of the Company that the tea industry grew in massive scale in such quick time. In Assam the tea plantations were set up in highly malaria prone lightly populated areas. The local people could not be persuaded to work in tea gardens in cheap wages. So the easy solution was found in Bihar and Central Province.It may be noted here that till1905 the present day west Odisha or Sambalpur region had remained under the Central Province. In order to maintain the fast growing tea business massive labour force was required .It was possible only by bringing labourers from outside. Hence labourers were brought from the over populated areas. As we know, 19th century was an age of immense mass migration. The decaying agrarian economy of India had rendered large number of agricultural workers out of job. They formed the surplus labour. The tea planters targeted this labour force.Hence the British Govt. worked out a special type of 'indentured system; for the migrants. According to this system, cheaply available labour was transported from one region to another region under contract. Both the Govt. and tea planters were involved. Sardars or Sirdars engaged by the planters used to recruit the whole family through a contract in which the labour agreed to serve five or three years in the tea gardens. Then they used to be transported in cheapest method to Assam. Once they reached in Assam they were being treated as prisoners. There was no way to escape. Even if they tried, they used to be arrested by the plantation owners. Though in1915 this legal right of the planters was taken away,still it was in vogue. The Govt. was directly involved in this coercion. Till1926 this method of exploitation continued.[9] Labour brought from mostly Bihar and Central Provinces were assembled at the tea plantations. In 1887 some 500,000 labourers were employed. But in 1901 the number rose to 606,835, apart from temporarily employed 90,946 labourers. The Industrial Census of 1911 counts it as 703,585 labourers. Atleast four regions were chosen by Govt. to recruit labourers. Those regions were Hazaribagh, Manbhum SantalPargana and Sambalpur,all in Bihar and Central Province.[10] A report was submitted on labour recruitment from Sambalpur. In the report it was noted that a certain people of a particular castegroup had tendency for theft and robbery and stealing was their chief vocation. The village choukidar or watchmen especially asked to be careful on their movement. Generally many of them were put in the prisons for petty crimes. The Govt. thought that if these people would be sent to Assam tea gardens, their old habit of committing crime would be less. Hence, the Deputy Commissioner of Sambalpur asked his staff to visit the jails.They lured and enticed the prisoners to go to Assam tea gardens. The prisoners were assured release from jail in case they were willing to go to Assam. Though some prisoners opposed but many approved the idea and became ready to go to Assam. Local registered agents [sirdars] had been appointed by the tea planters. They persuaded the socalled criminal type to go to Assam. Later on the Tea District Labour Association was formed at Sambalpur. The Association had the responsibility to register the labourer and send them to Assam. The recruitment of labourers and their transportation was made as per clause no 90. People from the Ganda Dom, and Pan caste group were taken to Assam. People from present-day Barpali[Bargarh dist.] to Balangir in Patna princely state,and Sonepur princely state were recruited. According to data available to us, in 1901-02 11613, 1902-03 7712, 1903-041354. 1904-05 853, 1905-06 214 and 1906-07 only 64 labourers from Sambalpur had been sent to Assam tea gardens.[11] Those were only the registered or indentured labourers. But apart from the above labourers there were unregistered labourers too. The District Labour Association used to be a busy place. There were many employees. Now days the old building of Labour Association houses the office of DIG police of Odisha Police. Recruitment of labourers for Assam tea gardens is narrated by Assam Labour Inquiry Committee Report 1906, Jagdish Chandra Jha in [Aspect of Immigration toNorth-East India [1859-1918], LSS O Malley[1909] Harissan Mark and other observers.[12]

As we have noted earlier the so called criminal caste [Ganda,Pan,Dom] people had been lured to go to Assam tea gardens. A question arises what were the most important factors that compelled them to leave their ancestral villages? What was the condition of life at home? It seems there were multiple factors that had forced them to adopt the socalled criminal path. As it is mentioned the depressed class people, otherwise known as Ganda Pan or Dom all used to weave coarse cotton cloth. Weaving, spinning and cocoon rearing was their traditional occupation. In erstwhile Patna and Sonepur princely states they used to cater the need of the local weavers of tusser cloth.[13] Rearing caterpillar meant for cocoon was carried in sahaj or asan[Terminalia to Mentosa] sal [shorea robusta] sima or dhaura [largerstomemi parviflora] trees grown in the forest of the states. They were main providers of cocoons to the local weavers.[14] But towards the end of the 19th century there was the decline of tusser industry. The forest policy of the colonial government had precipitated the decline. The making of the Imperial Forest Dept in 1864 and the Indian Forest Act of 1865 and further a much more comprehensive legislation in 1878 had almost blocked access of common people in to the forest areas. Forests were now begun to be reserved for mining and timber. Now conservation of forest was given much more priority to make it a source of profit.[15] It had seriously effected the life of the Ganda, Dom, Pan and the tribal people. The rearing of caterpillars for tusser could not be possible due to severe restrictions in the reserved forests. In the Patna princely state the first rule for reserved forest was made in 1889. Similar rule was made by the administration of Sonepur princely state, Bonai state and Sambalpur. Now rearing of caterpillar became less. It had caused much damage to the tusser industry. The cocoon collectors –Dom, Pan Ganda weavers lost their livelihood to a great extend. Writing in 1901 on the silk industry of Central Provinces Dewar quoted the observations of Fuller, the Commissioner of Settlement and Agriculture-"The policy of the Forest Dept. apparently influenced the action of Government offices in Court of Wards Estates, and has also had some effects on Malguzars who are said to give fewer facilities than they used to do to the taser rearers. The only effect of these orders has been that the growth of taser within forest limits has been in many places practically prohibited altogether. It brings no income to the government. So, it has been regarded as simply injurious to the forests"[16].

Moreover the opening of railway lines too had increased the demands for sleepers. Sal trees were cut to cater the demand of the railways. The opening of Bengal-Nagpur railways in 1896 and the Raipur –Vizianagaram railway lines had caused pressure on the forest s of the region, therefore it further checked the cocoon rearing business.[17]

Another factor that had seriously affected the livelihood of the poor and marginalized was the famine of 1899-1900. Infamously known as '*Chhapan salar marudi'* the famine had almost ruined the life the people in the than West Odisha. In Patna state there was rainfall of only 7 inch, far below the average. Similarly in Sonepur and Samalpur too rainfall was far below to average. In Patna The relief measure was not enough. Though Sonepur had some relief measure but it also could not solve the problem. Dom, Ganda, Gauras, Saharas ,Dumal Kewat and Khadal castes were worst sufferers. Cattles were slaughtred by the Gandas and Doms for food. Cobden Ramsay wrote that crimes of this type were growing.18

The import of millspun cotton yarn to this locality had ruined the traditional weaving occupation of Ganda and Pan Weavers. Spinning, carding and winding jobs that involve in the weaving industry became thing of the past, though it did not cease completely.[19] While writing about the Pans of Anugul [another princely state] a contemporary commentator said that most of them were criminals and large number of them were put in the jails. Many of them were sent to Assam tea garden as coolies.

So from the above discussion it is more or less clear that the weavers belonging to the depressed class of West Odisha became indentured labourers or coolies in Assam tea gardens because of colonial policies. They were the people who were hit very severely by colonial exploitation. They lost their traditional occupations. Further, the severe famine of 1900 and the forest policy of the Govt. made them destitute. It seems prisons were only option left for them. They resorted to petty crimes. But the colonizers were not behind in making money out the human body. Hence they became the easy preys of the tea planters and the colonizers. They were picked up from Samalpur jail and transported to Assam tea gardens.

The immigration of indentured labourers to Assam became slow towards the beginning of 20th century. The opening of Tata Iron Works at Sakchi[present Jamshedpur] in 1907 and the opening of the mining sector had slowed the labour migration to Assam. Now the labourers from West Odisha mostly landless, locally called Sukhbasi preferred to work in iron plant and mines.[21] Towards the end the second decade of 20th century cocoon rearing had become totally unprofitable.[22] Hence the iron work and mines had absorbed the surplus labour from Samalpur region.

Post script

Dadan or migrant labourer issue is a major problem in Odisha today. Every year tens of thousands of labourers migrate to A.P, Tamil Nadu etc. southern states to work in thebrickklins.They are also known as Pathrias. Frequent drought, decline in the traditional weaving industry, closure of a few spinning mills and deforestation etc have pushed the marginal communities to the walls. Though today they are not going to Assam tea gardens as indentured labourers as they used to do but today they are leaving their villages for the south bound trains.

References:

1. LSSO Malley - Bengal District Gazeteer 1909.
2. Cobden Ramsay – The Feudatory States of Orissa 1910. Firma KLM 1982.
3. Sunani, B – Dalita sanskrutira Itihasa (Odia) 2009. Eeshan Ankit Prakashani, Nuapada P-262-282.
4. Cobden Ramsay – P-323.
5. Girban Biswas – A Tale of Two Leaves and a Bud. IHC Proceeding 2005 P-584.
6. Deepak Ku. Panda – Sambalpur Itihas (un published manuscript) P-95.
7. Irfan Habib – Indian Economic (1858-1914) A people's History of India (28) 2006, P-80.
8. Ibid- P-80.
9. Ibid – P-80.
10. Ibid – P-80.
11. Deepak Ku. Panda, P-95.
12. Ibid – P-95.
13. Ibid – P-95.
14. Cobden Ramsay – P-322.
15. Ibid – P-323.
16. Ruma Chatterjee The Tasar Silk Industry and its decline in Bengal and South Bihar-1872 – 1921 in the Indian Historical Review (ICHR) Vol-XVII No.1-2 July-1990 and January-1991 P-182.
17. Ibid – P-185
18. Ibid – P-185.
19. Ibid – P-293.
20. Bharat Chandra Nayak – Mora Purba Sruti Katha (Odia) 1966 P-91-92.
21. Ibid – P-92.
22. Ruma Chatterjee – P-191.
23. Ibid – P-191.

(15)
The Real in Reel Presentations: Bangladesh Liberation Movement (1971): An Evaluation.

Dipankar Chakrabarti

During the war there were widespread killings and other atrocities – including the displacement of civilians in Bangladesh (East Pakistan at the time) and widespread violations of human rights began with the start of Operation Searchlight on 25 March 1971. The Bangladesh liberation war witnessed widespread atrocities committed mainly on the Bengali population of East Pakistan, at a level that Bangladeshis maintain is one of the worst genocides in history.

The actual extent of the atrocities committed is not clearly known, and opinions vary. However, there is little doubt that numerous civilians were tortured and killed during the war. There are many mass graves in Bangladesh, and newer ones are always being discovered, such as a recent one in a mosque in Dhaka located in the non-Bengali region of the city. The first night of war on Bengalis, which is very well documented, saw indiscriminate killings of students of Dhaka University and other civilians. The number of people that died in the liberation war of Bangladesh is not known in any reliable accuracy. There has been a great disparity in the casualty figures put forth by Pakistan on one hand (26,000) and India and Bangladesh on the other hand (3 million). International media has also had different views. Due to the lack of records and the long time that has since passed, an accurate number is hard to get, though various arguments for and against certain numbers have been put forward. Most guesses fall somewhere between a few hundred thousand and two million. Pakistan has maintained that only 26,000 people died in the war. Though most researchers do not support such a small number, many are inclined to believe that the real number was still a far cry from the 3 million put forward by Bangladesh and other sources. Some maintain that the real number of casualties was closer to 300,000 and was wrongly translated. On the other hand, though the figure of 3 million is unsubstantiated, many believe that the real number is still exceedingly high (more than 1 million) and the killing can clearly be termed a genocide. This view gets support from the aforementioned reports in international media, which were reported during the war before the 3 million figure was put forward. Supporters of this view would also point out to the enormous influx of refugees into India (8 million seems to be a widely accepted number), and reason that killings numbering as low as the Pakistanis would like to claim would not have caused such a large number of people to leave their homes. Some say that the Bangladesh claim might have had roots in a statement by Yahya Khan. According to Robert Payne in *Massacre* [1973], on February 22, 1971 Yahya Khan told a group of generals, "Kill three million of them, and the rest will eat out of our hands." Numerous women were tortured, raped and killed during the war. Again, exact numbers are not known and are a subject of debate. Bangladeshi sources cite a staggering figure of 200,000 women raped. Some other sources, for example Susan Brownmiller, refer to an even higher number of 400,000. Pakistani sources claim the number is much lower, though having not completely denied rape incidents.

There has been evidence of not only rape (and usually subsequent murder) of women, but of sex slaves kept captive by the Pakistan army. During the last periods of war, when the Pakistani army was retreating, the Mukti Bahini and Indian forces reported freeing numerous such women. Apart from Brownmiller's, another work that has included direct experiences from the women raped is *Ami Virangana Bolchhi* ("I, the heroine, speak") by Nilima Ibrahim. The work includes in its name from the word *Virangana* (Heroine), given by Sheikh Mujibur Rahman after the war, to the raped and tortured women during the war. This was a conscious effort to alleviate any social stigma the women might face in the society. How successful this effort was is doubtful, though. The minorities of Bangladesh, specially the Hindus, were the biggest targets of the Pakistan army. There was widespread killing of Hindu males, and rapes of women. In public places, men were often made to undress to prove that they have been circumcised and hence were Muslim.

More than 60 percent of the Bengali refugees that had fled to India were Hindus, and many never returned. It is not exactly known what percentage of the people killed by the Pakistan army were Hindus, but it is safe to say it was disproportionately high. This widespread violence against Hindus was motivated by a policy to purge East Pakistan of what was seen as Indian influence. The West Pakistani rulers identified the Bengali culture with Hindu and Indian culture, and thought that the eradication of Hindus would remove such influences from the majority Muslims in East Pakistan. The Pakistani ruling class had long formed distaste for Bengali intelligentsia and students. They viewed them, correctly, as one of the main proponents of the rise of Bengali nationalism in East Pakistan. This group had been instrumental in the 1952 uprising called the Language movement, which ended in Pakistan accepting Bangla as one of its national languages. The famed six-point demand put forward by Mujib, which became the rallying point for Awami League in the years before the war, was derived from the earlier 11-point program penned by the students. In an attempt to undermine the rising Bengali identity, Pakistan had variously tried to have Bangla written in roman letters, ban singing the songs of Rabindranath Tagore, mostly in vain. The rulers, again correctly, also found a growing leftist sentiment in the intelligentsia and studentbodies which they vowed to crush. Hence during the war, a planned effort was made to void Bangladesh of its most enlightened people. In addition to the killings committed at the beginning and all throughout the war, a meticulously planned execution was carried out on December 14, 1971. Professors, journalists, doctors, artists, writers of unknown numbers were rounded up in Dhaka, blindfolded, taken to Rajarbag in the middle section of the city, and executed en masse. This day is now honored in Bangladesh as *Buddhijibi Hotta Dibosh* ("Day of Martyred Intellectuals").

Militias:

*According to political scientist Peter Tomsen, Pakistan's **secret service**, in conjunction with the political party Jamaat-e-Islami, formed militias such as Al-Badr ("the moon") and the Al-Shams ("the sun") to conduct operations against the nationalist movement. These militias targeted noncombatants and committed rapes as well as other crimes.*

Local collaborator known as Razakars also took part in the atrocities. The term has since become a pejorative akin to the western term 'Judas'. Members of the Muslim League such as Nizam e- Islam, Jamaat-e-Islami and Jamiat Ulema Pakistan, who had lost the election, collaborated with the military and acted as an intelligence organisation for them. Jamaat-e-Islami members and some of its leaders collaborated with the Pakistani forces in rapes and targeted killings. The atrocities by

Al-Badr and the Al-Shams garnered worldwide attention from news agencies; accounts of massacres and rapes were widely reported.

Killing of intellectuals:

During the war, the Pakistan Army and its local collaborators, mainly Jamaat-e-Islami carried out a systematic execution of the leading Bengali intellectuals. A number of professors from Dhaka University were killed during the first few days of the war. However, the most extreme cases of targeted killing of intellectuals took place during the last few days of the war. Professors, journalists, doctors, artists, engineers and writers were rounded up by Pakistan Army and the Razakars militia in Dhaka, blindfolded, taken to torture cells in Mirpur, Mohammadpur , Nakhalpara, Rajarbagh and other locations in different sections of the city to be executed en masse, most notably at Rayerbazar and Mirpur . Allegedly, the Pakistani Army and its paramilitary arm, the Al-Badr and Al-Shams forces created a list of doctors, teachers, poets, and scholars.

During the nine-month duration of the war, the Pakistani army, with the assistance of local collaborators systematically executed an estimated 991 teachers, 13 journalists, 49 physicians, 42 lawyers, and 16 writers, artists and engineers. Even after the official ending of the war on 16 December there were reports of killings being committed by either the armed Pakistani soldiers or by their collaborators. In one such incident, notable film-maker Jahir Raihan was killed on 30 January 1972 in Mirpur allegedly by the armed Beharis. In memory of the persons who were killed, 14 December is observed in Bangladesh as Shaheed Buddhijibi Dibosh ("Day of the Martyred Intellectuals").

Several notable intellectuals who were killed from the time period of 25 March to 16 December 1971 in different parts of the country include Dhaka University professors Dr.Govinda Chandra Dev (Philosophy), Dr. Munier Chowdhury (Bengali Literature), Dr.Mufazzal Haider Chaudhury (Bengali Literature), Dr.Anwar Pasha (Bengali Literature), Dr.M. Abul Khair (History), Dr.Jyotirmoy Guhathakurta (English Literature), Humayun Kabir (English Literature),Rashidul Hasan (English Literature), Ghyasuddin Ahmed, Sirajul Haque Khan, Faizul Mahi ,Dr. Santosh Chandra Bhattacharyya Dr and Saidul Hassan (Physics), Rajshahi University professors Dr. Hobibur Rahman (Mathematics), Prof Sukhranjan

Somaddar (Sanskrit), Prof Mir Abdul Quaiyum (Psychology) as well as Dr.Mohammed Fazle Rabbee (Cardiologist), Dr. AFM Alim Chowdhury (Ophthalmologist), Shahidullah Kaiser (Journalist),Nizamuddin Ahmed (Journalist), Selina Parvin (Journalist), Altaf Mahmud (Lyricist and musician),Dhirendranath Datta (Politician), Jahir Raihan (novelist, journalist, film director) andRanadaprasad Saha (Philanthropist).

Violence against women: The generally accepted figure for the mass rapes during the nine-month long conflict is 200,000. Numerous women were tortured, raped and killed during the war. Again, exact numbers are not known and are a subject of debate. Bangladeshi sources cite a figure of 200,000 women raped, giving birth to thousands of war-babies. The Pakistani Army also kept numerous Bengali women as sex-slaves inside the Dhaka Cantonment. Most of the girls were captured from Dhaka University and private homes.

Among other sources, Susan Brownmiller refers to an even higher number of over 400,000. Pakistani sources claim the number is much lower, though having not completely denied rape incidents. Brownmiller quotes:

Khadiga, thirteen years old, was interviewed by a photojournalist in Dacca. She was walking to school with four other girls when they were kidnapped by a gang of Pakistani soldiers. All five were put in a military brothel in Mohammedpur and held captive for six months until the end of the war.

In a New York Times report named 'Horrors of East Pakistan Turning Hope into Despair', Malcom W. Browne wrote:

One tale that is widely believed and seems to come from many different sources is that 563 women picked up by the army in March and April and held in military brothels are not being released because they are pregnant beyond the point at which abortions are possible.

The licentious attitude of the soldiers, although generally supported by their superiors, alarmed the regional high command of the Pakistani army. On 15 April 1971, in a secret memorandum to the divisional commanders, Niazi complained,

Since my arrival, I have heard numerous reports of troops indulging in looting and arson, killing people at random and without reasons in areas cleared of the anti state elements; of late there have been reports of rape and even the West Pakistanis are not being spared; on 12 April two East Pakistani women were raped, and an attempt was made on two others.

Another work that has included direct experiences from the women raped is *Ami Birangona Bolchhi* ("I, the heroine, speak") by Nilima Ibrahim. The work includes in its name from the word *Birangona* (Heroine), given by Sheikh Mujibur Rahman after the war, to the raped and tortured women during the war. This was a conscious effort to alleviate any social stigma the women might face in the society. How successful this effort was is doubtful, though. In October 2005 Sarmila Bose, published a paper suggesting that the casualties and rape allegations in the war have been greatly exaggerated for political purposes. A number of researchers have shown inaccuracies in the work, including flawed methodology of statistical analysis, misrepresentation of referenced sources, and disproportionate weight to Pakistan army testimonies.

A 2014 film titled Children of War focussed on the harrowing condition in the 'rape camps' set up by the Pakistan Army.

Violence against minorities:

The minorities of Bangladesh, especially the Hindus, were specific targets of the Pakistani army. There was widespread killing of Hindu males, and rapes of women. Documented incidents in which Hindus were massacred in large numbers include the Chuknagar massacre, the Jathibhanga masscre, and the Shankharipara. More than 60% of the Bengali refugees who fled to India were Hindus. It is not exactly known what percentage of the people killed by the Pakistan army were Hindus, but it is safe to say it was disproportionately high. This widespread violence against Hindus was motivated by a policy to purge East Pakistan of what was seen as Hindu and Indian influences. The West Pakistani rulers identified the Bengali culture with Hindu and Indian culture, and thought that the eradication of Hindus would remove such influences from the majority Muslims in East Pakistan. Buddhist temples and Buddhist monks were also attacked through the course of the year.

According to R.J.Rummel, Professor of Political Science at the University of Hawii,

The genocide and gendercidal atrocities were also perpetrated by lower-ranking officers and ordinary soldiers. These "willing executioners" were fuelled by an abiding anti-Bengali racism, especially against the Hindu minority. "Bengalis were often compared with monkeys and chickens. Said General Niazi, 'It was a low lying land of low lying people.' The Hindu among the Bengalis were as Jews to the Nazis: scum and vermin that [should] best be exterminated. As to the Moslem Bengalis, they were to live only on the sufferance of the soldiers: any infraction, any suspicion cast on them, any need for reprisal, could mean their death. And the soldiers were free to kill at will. The journalist Dan Coggin quoted one Pakistani captain as telling him, "We can kill anyone for anything. We are accountable to no one." This is the arrogance of Power.

Violence against Biharis

In 1947, at the time of partition and the establishment of the state of Pakistan, Bihari Muslims, many of whom were fleeing the violence that took place during partition, migrated from India to the newly independent East Pakistan. These Urdu-speaking people were averse to the Bengali language movement and the subsequent nationalist movements because they maintained allegiance toward West Pakistani rulers, causing anti-Bihari sentiments among local nationalist Bengalis. When the war broke out in 1971, the Biharis sided with the Pakistani army. Some of them joined Razakar and Al-Shams militia groups and participated in the persecution and genocide of their Bengali countrymen including the widespread looting of Bengali properties and abetting other criminal activities. It is alleged that Awami League-aligned militias carried out large scale massacres of Biharis and other ethnic groups, but these claims are disputed. R.J.Rummel estimated that 150,000 non-Bengals were massacred, with a low estimate of 50,000 and a high estimate of 500,000. According to *The Minorities at Risk Project* the number of Bihari killed is about 1,000. There are many reports of massacres of Biharis and alleged collaborators that took place in the period following the surrender of the Pakistani Army on 16 December 1971. In an incident on 19 December 1971, captured on camera and attended by members of the foreign press, Abdul Kader Siddiqui and Mukti Bahini guerrillas under his command bayoneted and shot to death a group of prisoners of war who were accused of belonging to the Razakar paramilitary forces. But Siddiqui later stated on his book *Swadhinota'71* that he bayoneted those persons who were Bengali and they were kidnapping two non-Bengali girls. Because no court or other judicial system was there, they were executed.

In 1996, *Muktir Gaan* (Songs of Liberation) a documentary film was released in Bagladesh. It was shot in 1971 by the American photographer Lear Levin. Tareque and Catherine Masud, two documentary filmmaker retrieved these reels from Lear Levin's cellar in New York and released it as *Muktir Gaan* in Bangladesh. The film documents the activities of the Bangladeshi Freedom struggle, cultural squad, a group of young middleclass men and women who during wartime toured various refugee camps, tracing centers of liberation fighters and liberated zones and sang songs to provide moral support and inspiration to the refugees and liberation fighters. More importantly the film could sensitize the citizens about the ongoing torture on the women folk vis-à-vis the patriarchal womanliness in the form of torturing their dishonoured wives by the aliens.

During the nine month span of the war, the Pakistani army with the assistance of the local collaborators killed some three million men and women from all section of the society – intellectuals, journalists, students, workers, villagers and others. About 2-3 lakhs of women were raped. As the war was being waged and nearly one crore refugees infiltrated from across the border into India, East Pakistan was suddenly catapulted from relative obscurity into the headlines of the International press. The atrocities commuted by the Pakistani regulars and their Bengali collaborators were widely viewed as the human right abuses by the international community. This was highlighted with the 'Help Bangladesh concert' held by George Harrison and Joan Baez in Madison Square Garden, New York in August 1971. After the war various aid agencies, charities, doctors and medical personnel from several western countries came to Bangladesh in order to pool their resources and services to help the newly created nation. In the documentary *Dateline Bangladesh* (1972) the Prime Minister of India Mrs. Indira Gandhi justified the Indian military support to Bangladeshi struggle by commenting 'Shall we sit and watch their women get raped?'. The newborn state valorised the raped women in the post war period by declaring them as war heroine. Ostensively, this was an attempt to reduce social ostracism towards these women and enable their smooth social re-absorption, but the hard reality was that they were diseased, malnourished and traumatized, and many were killed by their husbands as they had been dishonoured. The state also assumed the role of a patriarch when the newly elected Prime Minister; publicly denounced the children born of the raped Bangladeshi women-citizen as alien. As the first president of Bangladesh, he decided to give up the more than 30,000 'war babies' for adoption, in many cases against the wishes of their mother. The babies, in many cases, had been mishandled and nourished the houses of dishonoured practice. It may be safely assumed that a healthy society is a by-product of a binary called public-private interphase. The films, in our postulation, provided a different perspective. For the first time, the aggression had been visualized as a psychological battle. To dismantle the organized Bengalee intelligentsia Pak regulars decided to molest the Bengali women folk of the region so that their men folk, may automatically, be demoralized. But they might not have imagined that a military assistance to the distressed from the Indian side may freeze their effort.

The films, in our standard, were the active narrator of the genocide and successfully sensitizing the people against all wrongs done mainly to the women by the aggressor. The films also raised the issue of patriarchal injustice done to the women war victims. The husband or the nation may not have the right to torture or kill their wives or subject on the plea of their being dishonoured in the turmoil rather their masculine entity may be doubted for inefficiency as they could not protect their private counterpart . The event thus demands a neutral enquiry. The study is also important in the current occasion for perspective that even today, in the post partition Democratic Tripura, 80% of the local Folk-lore, 76% of the art and craft forms, 78% Bengali attenuate, 82% food habit, 84% conjugal practice, a great deal of sentiments and finer sensibility, intelligentsia and political awareness etc. are directly linked with the lost domain of approximately 6.5 lakhs of war refugees in Tripura. Hatred for betrayers and refugee-mentality may also be counted as its negative effects. Thus without a pre-conception of the liberation movement our effort for knowing the behavior of inhabitants of Tripura en-masse will prove to be an incomplete study.

References:

1. Agnew, John A.; Mamadouh, Virginie;Secor, Anna and Sharp, Joanne (Eds.) (2015), The Wiley Blackwell Companion to Political Geography, Oxford: John Wiley & Sons.
2. Bhaumik, Subir (2007), *Insurgencies in India's Northeast: Conflict, Co-option & Change*, Working Paper, East-West Center, Washington.
3. Chapman, Graham P. (2012), The Geopolitics of South Asia: From Early Empires to the Nuclear Age, Burlington: Ashgate Publishing, Ltd
4. Clad, James and McDonald, Sean M. (Eds.), (2011), The Borderlands of Southeast Asia: Geopolitics, Terrorism, and Globalization, Washington, DC: National Defense University Press.
5. Cohen, Saul Bernard (2003), Geopolitics of the World System, New York: Rowman& Littlefield.
6. Cohen, Saul Bernard (2014), Geopolitics: The Geography of International Relations, New York: Rowman& Littlefield.
7. Dalby, Simon, and Gearóid Ó Tuathail (eds.) (1998), *Rethinking Geopolitics*, New York: Routledge.
8. Flint, Colin (2012), Introduction to Geopolitics, London: Routledge.
9. Hazarika, Joysankar(1996), Geopolitics of North East India: A Strategical Study, New Delhi: Gyan Publishing House.
10. Jones, Terry-Ann andMielants, Eric (2015), Mass Migration in the World-system: Past, Present, and Future, *Volume 31 of Political economy of the world-system annuals*, New York: Routledge.
11. Kumar, Satish (Ed.) (2013), India's National Security: Annual Review 2010, New Delhi: Routledge.
12. O'Hanlon, Michael E. (2015), The Future of Land Warfare, Washington, DC:Brookings Institution Press.
13. ThongkholalHaokip (2010), "India's Northeast Policy: Continuity and Change," *Man and Society*, Vol. VII, winter 2010, pp. 86–99.
14. Report (2012), The Other Burma? Conflict, counter-insurgency and human rights in Northeast India, 11 October 2012.

15. Singh, Atom Sunil (2009), Notorious "Golden Triangle": India's Golden Opportunity? *IPCS Artilce,* New Delhi: 2806 (11 February 2009).
16. Twentieth Century Population Thinking: A Critical Reader of Primary Sources edited by The Population Knowledge Network (2015), New York: Routledge.

(16)
Partition of India and the Forgotten History of Namasudra Community

Dr. Dipankar Biswas

Namasudra jatakhyata sampradaya samvedadhikari!
Dashadishabadhya souchya palanang purusanakramena arjhyrate!
Tirthe pravashe grehavashe cha sraddhadi karjhya!
Tena pakkanna pindadang bidhi drishyte!!

--- Manu's Doshakosh Pangika

Throughout 1947 of India ended up being partitioned into nominally "Hindu" of India and "Muslim" Pakistan. That generated physical violence, and the is broad displacement of around 10 million people, together with rates involving 75 thousand women raped, and 1 million people killed. Partition features still left an older involving politics competition, huge sociable trouble, and the expected on-going sociable backlashes involving a really huge level displacement of folks. Some of those out of place have been Dalits; ex-untouchables as well as reduced caste Hindus exactly who fled via Far East Pakistan, right now Bangladesh, to Western Bengal between 1947 and 1951. Roughly 3.7 million Dalits had forgotten his or her properties and livelihoods, heading for Western Bengal, Assam and Tripura. Although partition is effectively examined, it's grasped while caused by elite national politics. Story of the unique group of people (Dalits) has been comparatively silent. The history has been sunken inside legacy of music connected with partition.

Now we have to understand that the forms of discrimination against the untouchables in Bengal differed from that in Maharashtra or South India. In Bengal, caste rigidities were never strong enough to keep the untouchable population in a state of perpetual servitude. In this context, the types of discrimination faced by depressed or scheduled caste leaders like Jogendranath Mandal were not the same as those experienced by Ambedkar in Maharashtra.

The Namasudra Movement of East Bengal had been the most powerful and politically mobilized Dalit movement in India during the colonial period that had kept the Bengal Congress Party in opposition from the 1920s, in alliance with the Muslims. However partition resulted in the loss of bargaining power of the Dalits because, being divided along religious lines of Hindus and Muslims, they became political minorities in both countries.

Who are Namasudras?

The Namasudras claim Brahmin descent and one historical account seems to confirm this. According to the account this Bengali Brahmin community was asked to perform the wedding ceremony of a king who was marrying outside his caste (to a Dom bride). The community refused to comply and the king ordered his soldiers to execute their leaders and reduce the community to Sudras (or manual labourers). Today the Namasudra earn their living as boatmen, fisherman and carpenters. They are not regarded as an occupational caste (with one particular occupation generally characterizing the group), but are essentially labourers-for-hire, capable of serving in a wide variety of capacities. Though a poor, uneducated community they exhibit a strong desire to improve themselves.

Subsequently the 1950s, '60s and '70s saw the influx of Bengali Hindus from what had become East Pakistan (and later Bangladesh) to West Bengal, who came here with the hope of settling down. They were, however, sent to various uncongenial areas outside West Bengal with the assurance that they would eventually be relocated to West Bengal. The first wave of refugees consisted of traditional upper caste elites. Of the 1.1 million who had arrived by June 1948, 350,000 were urban middle class, 550,000 were rural middle class, a little over 100,000 were agriculturalists, and almost 100,000 were artisans (Chakrabarti 1990).

If the richest of them found a haven amongst relatives and friends in Calcutta, the poorer sections squatted on public and private lands and tried to resist eviction. In the 1960s and '70s – and especially after the Bangladesh War of Liberation in 1971, Mujibur Rahman's assassination in 1975 and Zia-ur-Rahman's coming to power – communal agitations started to be directed against the poorest and low caste Hindus who had remained in East Bengal. They now sought refuge in West Bengal and Tripura.

Chandal to Namasudra

Starting in 1901, various castes sent representations to the Bengal government demanding a name change and a higher status in the hierarchy. In 1911, the pile of such representations weighed 1.5 maunds (about 57 kilograms). Babhans (who now call themselves Bhumihar) wanted to be called Brahmarshi Brahmans, Bengali Kayastha thought they deserved the Kshatriya status and Baidyas sought the Brahman tag. All these demands were turned down. Two representations – one from Chandals seeking to be renamed Namasudra and the other from the Kaibarttas to be declared Mahishya – were accepted. The Chandals had put in a lot of effort to make this happen. F. B. Peacock, commissioner, Presidency Division, observed in a communication (No 87, dated 18 July 1881): "The improvement of the Chandals who are in the chief agriculturists [in Narail subdivision, in Jessore district] has led them to aspire to a superior status in the Hindu caste system. They call themselves Namasudra and profess to be Baishnab"(A.K. Biswas, 2016).

Indian independence movement and Namasudra community

The Chandals, who in 1911, were officially re-designated as Namasudras, observed a 'general strike' in 1872-73 in protest against their caste men, when in jails as prisoners, being exclusively compelled to perform conservancy services, while prisoners of other castes and Muslims were exempted. The strike lasted for over at least four months, exerting ruinous repercussions on the life of 5.5 million people of Faridpur, Backarganj and Jessore, now in Bangladesh.

The Superintendent of Police, after an inquiry, reported on March 18, 1873, to the District Magistrate, Faridpur, which was the theatre of the strike, that "...Chandals are not only agriculturists, but they are also boatmen, porters, carpenters, potters, and fishermen; on them devolve all the occupation and trades practised by other castes in more settled tracts". Unfailingly the strike by such a community brought life of the rural economy to a standstill. The district Magistrate too conducted an inquiry and found its repercussion "ruinous".

The Lieutenant Governor, Sir George Campbell, had passed order that "the Chandals in jail should not in future be forced to do the work of sweepers, but that any of them who chooses to do it when its comparatively easy nature is pointed out, may be allowed so to work". Unfortunately, the order, for mysterious reason(s), remained unimplemented. This remains as an illustration of standing shame for the failure of the colonial bureaucracy to implement orders of His Excellency the Lieutenant Governor of the Lower Provinces of Bengal.

After 35 years, the Bengal Provincial Congress at Pabna in 1908, passed a resolution calling for an end to the discriminatory practice of engagement of Chandals, as Guru Chand Thakur, a Namasudra patriarch, social reformer and religious leader of Faridpur stood firmly on the partition of Bengal and against the *Swadeshi* movement in 1905. Sir Surendra Nath Banerjea wrote a letter to the Namasudra leader, urging to join the *Swadeshi* movement with his lakhs of followers, known as Matuas. Rabindranath Tagore participated in an annual conference of Namasudras held in Mymensingh in 1905. The Hindu intellectual class has consciously suppressed this fact.

But Guru Chand Thakur turned down his request with an interjection that the upper castes were consumers of luxurious goods imported from abroad and hence the movement should remain confined within them. Deprived of their political right, he wrote back, the Namasudras were victims of oppression and discrimination in their own homeland. So the upper castes, his letter further disclosed, would do well to learn a lesson on how to fraternize with the untouchable and the depressed classes; otherwise they would never participate in the *Swadeshi* movement. The Namasudras are still bereft of political rights and are oppressed and exploited ruthlessly in their own homeland. High caste Hindus are deadly opposed to grant of any political rights to them. They must, therefore, inculcate a feeling of brotherhood for the low castes; else, the degraded and low castes will never join the high caste Hindus in any agitation against the British."

A number of memoranda were submitted by All-Bengal Namasudra Association and All-Bengal Depressed Classes Association. A joint delegation of these two Associations gave oral evidence to Simon Commission in 1929 at what was then Calcutta and ventilated their grievances under the leadership of Mukunda Behary Mallick, a Namasudra. The memorandum of the Namasudras stated that "the literacy of the Brahmans is 48 per cent, that of the Vaidyas 65 per cent and that of the Kayasthas 41 per cent. It is a matter of history that for reasons known to them; these communities have practically shut the doors of schools against the members of the depressed classes during the pre-British rule in India". According to the All-Bengal Depressed Classes Association, "denial of admission in Medical College and Hospital, Calcutta, for treatment" of untouchable patients was a reality in Bengal.

Subhas Chandra Bose held a black flag demonstration, saying, "Go back Simon" in then Calcutta. The memorandum read like charge sheets against the minuscule upper castes, against the vast majority of their own country.

The Namasudra community submitted two memoranda before the Simon Commission. In February 1928, the All Bengal Depressed Classes Association submitted a memorandum and adopted the memoranda submitted by the Namasudra community as representing their interests too. The presentations of nine leaders of the two bodies, who jointly met the Commission on 29 January 1929 in Calcutta, were recorded. The representatives focused on the realities of socio-economic and cultural life in Bengal and their aspirations. One of their demands was that "appointments be made out of qualified candidates of different communities in proportion to their numerical strength". They added that only candidates of the depressed classes and others, including Muslims, should be appointed until "an equalization of these classes is secured to those who have already filled these services". Their aim was to end the unhealthy monopoly of the 'Bhadralok' in administration. Domination of the judiciary by a minuscule minority was a bane for India, they said, and proposed setting up of service commissions for appointment of personnel in central and provincial governments – the central commission to be headed by a European member of the Governor General's Executive Council, and provincial commission by Governor's European executive member. They thus made it clear that they didn't trust the upper-caste Indians. They wanted "free and compulsory elementary education" in the country. In what was a scathing indictment of the 'Bhadralok', the leaders of the depressed classes said the upper castes "have assumed the position of the heaven-born guardians of the masses".

They also believed that the term "efficiency and competence are absolutely a misnomer and have absolutely no scope in public service".

Protagonists of efficiency and competence actually divided the country on this plank.

Guru Chand Thakur campaigned against zamindars and their exploitation. In 1921, Mukunda Behari Mallick and Bhishmadeb Das, both members of the Bengal Legislative Council, demanded a law that granted two-thirds of the crop to the sharecropper. This was the genesis of that Tebhaga movement, which was later usurped by the Bengali communists in support of the peasantry. In the Bengal Assembly elections 1937, there were 30 reserved constituencies and 12 Namasudras won – 10 were followers of Guru Chand and two represented the Congress. All of them carried an imprint of Guru Chand's personality. Dr C. S. Mead paid his tribute to Guru Chand thus: "With a liberality of thought, a courage and foresightedness uncommon among men of orthodox school he has sought the uplift of the great Namasudras caste. They owe a great deal to him. So do I." (A.K. Biswas, 2016).

The election of Dr B. R. Ambedkar to the Constituent Assembly from Bengal in 1946 was an example of political sagacity and foresight on the part of Bengali Untouchables' representatives like Jogendra Nath Mandal, Mukunda Behari Mallick, Dwarikanath Barui, Nagendranath Roy and Kshetranath Singh from the districts of Faridpur, Jessore, Khulna and Barisal, now in Bangladesh. The Bengali Dalits suspect these districts with large numbers of Namasudras were parcelled out to Pakistan for electing Dr Ambedkar to the Constituent Assembly. The crucial behind-the-scenes role of these Untouchables in Constitution making has yet to be recognized (A.K. Biswas, 2016).

In 1945 the Namasudra leader Jogendra Nath Mandal started the Bengal provincial branch of Dr. B.R. Ambedkar's Scheduled Caste Federation. He believed that the Dalit and Muslim peasants in east Bengal had similar interests, and so, a Dalit-Muslim political alliance was in the best interest of the Dalit. But his pro-Muslim League stance was not acceptable to many of his fellow Dalit leaders, who were wary of their future in a Muslim majority Bengal. The history of Dalit and Muslim peasant relationship was not an uninterrupted story of harmony and co-operation; it was regularly interrupted by violent riots. So, around this time, there were two other rival Scheduled Caste organisations: the Depressed Classes League, headed by another Namasudra leader Pramatha Ranjan Thakur, supported the Congress, while the Depressed Classes

Association, led by yet another Namasudra leader Birat Chandra Mandal, was more directly aligned with the Hindu Mahasabha. In other words, the Scheduled Castes, and the Namasudra community which represented them, remained intensely divided on the Partition issue in 1946-47, and were also strategically aligned with various mainstream political parties, such as Muslim League, Congress and the Hindu Mahasabha.

The 1946 riots in Calcutta and Noakhali brought further rift that went beyond the ranks of the Dalit leadership and caused even greater damage to their identity politics. Mandal remained a minister in the Muslim League ministry of H.S. Suhrawardy, widely believed to be the mastermind behind the Great Calcutta Killing, and this made him intensely unpopular among the caste Hindus. Mandal, and the Bengal branch of the Scheduled Caste Federation which he was leading, continued to oppose Partition and advocated a united sovereign Bengal. In a situation like this, when the Hindu Mahasabha launched its campaign to partition Bengal in order to create a Hindu majority province of West Bengal within the Indian Union, and Congress endorsed it after the Tarakeswar Convention in April 1947, many Namasudras became actively associated with this movement. Their major concern at this stage was to keep their habitat – the districts of Bakarganj, Faridpur, Jessore, and Khulna – within the Hindu majority province of West Bengal. However, it will be wrong to conclude that Dalit protest was lost in the quagmire of Partition politics – one need not in this context undermine the importance of class in shaping their political protest. In 1946, when the communist-led share-croppers' movement, known as the Tebhaga movement, started, the Rajbansis in north Bengal and the Namasudras in east and central Bengal were its main protagonists.

Partition and Namasudra Community

The partition of British India and the emergence of the independent states of India and Pakistan in 1947 are linked to the largest recorded population dislocation in history. The two-nation solution negotiated by the competing nationalist movements led by the Congress Party and the Muslim League produced a territorial settlement linked to the principle of religious majoritarianism. Pakistan came to consist of the North West Frontier Provinces, Baluchistan, Sind, and West Punjab, separated by nearly thousand miles from East Bengal and the Sylhet district of Assam. Though two-third of India's Muslims became

Pakistanis, both nations included numerically large yet vulnerable minorities. In Punjab, nearly 12 million Sikhs, Muslims and Hindus were displaced and 1 million lost their lives (Zolberg et al 1989) during the so-called "exchange of populations". In the case of Bengal however, Partition was predated by sectarian violence in 1946 which spurred the initial two-way movement of Hindus to West Bengal and Muslims to East Pakistan, and unlike the situation in Punjab, the flight of Hindu refugees eventually overtook that of Muslims and has continued sporadically through the brutal civil war in Pakistan in 1971 and the birth of Bangladesh into the present.

Suffering came in many forms. Once the Namashudras used to be ill-treated by the so-called higher caste Hindu people, they never got equal rights, but ironically they also had to leave their motherland because of being Hindu. They became refugees, ill-fed, ill-clothed, ill-housed. Places like Andaman-Nikobar, Nainital, Dandkaranya etc were their new destination. Even there, they made land fertile by virtue of their inheritance, honest labour as most of them used to have their livelihood by farming. The history of Marichjhanpi is the history of the loss of identity of the suffering humanity.

After partition in 1947 when millions of Hindus migrated from the eastern part of Bengal to its western part, few lower caste people could manage to migrate since they lacked necessary means to cope with immediate dislocation. For the Namasudras, the Partition did not solve their problems, as, despite their intense protestations, all the districts which the Namasudras lived in went to East Pakistan. But most of them did not or could not migrate immediately. The Namasudras who mostly remained in Pakistan faced violence and discrimination and were ultimately forced to migrate.

Very few Namasudra peasants migrated at this stage or could afford to move, because migration required resources which they lacked. Also leaders like Mandal and the Federation advised them to stay put, because they were assured by Jinnah that they would get a fair deal in Pakistan, where 'every man would be equal.' In a celebratory message on Jinnah's birthday in December 1947, Prime Minister Khwaja Nazimuddin repeated that solemn pledge: 'Pakistan is not the state of Muslims alone, it belongs to all peoples and communities who live in it and who are loyal to it.' Many Scheduled Caste peasants who stayed back in East Pakistan believed him.

But as the situation gradually unfolded itself, those Namasudras soon found that the growing power of Islamic nationalism of the Pakistani state unmistakably ascribed to them a 'Hindu' minority identity. Jogendra Nath Mandal chose to remain in Pakistan and joined the Liaquat Ali Khan ministry as its Labour and Law Minister. He remained in this position until 1950, and all this time, he alternated between representing the larger Hindu minority interests on the one hand and championing the specific Scheduled Caste identity on the other. As for the Namasudra peasants, they were subjected to a process of 'Othering' initiated by the Pakistani state as it moved towards greater Islamization of the polity. The projected 'Other' of the Pakistani nation was the 'Hindu' – a category that tended to collapse the differences between all non-Muslims and incorporated the Dalit. And, therefore, even when the Namasudra peasants fought for social justice under communist leadership in 1948, the state in Pakistan represented the Namasudra peasant rebels as 'Hindu' miscreants. This process of 'Othering,' not only tended to exclude them from the Pakistani nationhood by imposing on them a 'Hindu' identity, but also helped the corresponding Hindu nationalism in India in trying to appropriate them as oppressed Hindu minority. This changed situation in January-February, 1950, when, at last, the Namasudra peasants in large numbers decided to leave Pakistan.

After the final breakdown of the Dalit-Muslim alliance in East Pakistan as the Dalit peasants were deliberately targeted in this post-Partition upsurge of violence. At the Bongaon railway station, the first batch of Namasudra refugees of about 500 families arrived in the first week of January 1950, and since then, thousands of them began to arrive every day. Either they came through Bongaon and then moved on to the Sealdah station in Calcutta, from where they were despatched to various refugee camps, or they arrived at the border districts of Nadia or 24-Parganas, where they began to settle down as the local Muslims began to flee across the border. As one report suggests, in the early months of 1950, about 10,000 refugees were arriving everyday through Bongaon and settling down in Gaighata, Baduria, Habra and other places.20 By the beginning of 1951, following the disturbances in Khulna, about 1.5 million refugees had arrived in West Bengal. Majority of them were Scheduled Caste peasants. 'About 95 per cent of the refugees are Namasudras', reported a police intelligence report in June 1952. They were mostly cultivators or day-labourers, or belonged to various professions, like washermen, fishermen, weavers, petty businessmen and small jotdars and talukdars.

The Namasudra peasants, who just crossed the border on foot or by boat, there was no one waiting to welcome them with a handsome rehabilitation package; they had to fend for themselves. The horrific experience of displacement obviously led to retaliatory violence on the Muslims in the border districts of West Bengal.

When, after 1950, the Namasudra peasant refugees began to arrive in large numbers, there were targeted attempts to mobilize them. For example, Manohar Roy, who claimed himself to be a right hand man of Jogen Mandal, started a Purba Banga Bastuhara Samiti in Chandmari Camp and started mobilizing the Namasudra refugees. Similarly, one Ramendra Kishor Mullick, who claimed to be close to P. R. Thakur, began to mobilise Namasudra refugees in Bagula and Dhubulia, asking them not to join any political party. In largely attended meetings, he discussed ways and means of rehabilitating peasant refugees who had just migrated from East Bengal. But sometimes they also mobilised under non-Dalit local refugee leaders. For example, when a storm destroyed 300 huts in Cooper's Camp in April 1952, more than 200 residents of the camp, under the leadership of Jyotish Mukerjee and Bimal Biswas (a Brahmin and a Namasudra consecutively), travelled by train without ticket to Calcutta to communicate their grievances to Chief Minister and Relief Commissioner. They were arrested at Sealdah Station and sent back to Cooper's, while their leaders were prosecuted and convicted. A few days later, about 800 refugees of the Dhubulia Camp squatted on the railway tracks for the whole day to ventilate their complaints against the Camp Administration.

But the refugees' main grievance was against the official rehabilitation policy. The government argued that there was not enough vacant land in West Bengal to rehabilitate these agriculturists. So it decided to rehabilitate them in the neighbouring provinces of Assam, Bihar and Orissa, and further off in the Andaman Islands and in early 1956 announced the Dandakaranya Scheme of rehabilitating them in a region consisting of 78,000 square miles of inhospitable unirrigated land in the tribal areas of Orissa and Madhya Pradesh. From January 1950, groups of Namasudra families were being secretly shipped off to Anadaman Islands. From 1953, there was a more explicit policy of selecting only the Namasudra peasants for resettlement in Andaman.

Many of Namasudra community moved to Tripura and Assam from East Pakistan. In Tripura according to the census of 2011 of India Namasudra is the largest sub group in Scheduled Caste. The Namasudra Community are basically the main powerhouse behind organised Scheduled Caste movement in the colonial period. For a long period of time after independence the community was struggling to settle down in different parts of India where the political and social situations are different in different parts of India. The Government of India also don't have specific settlement plan for the refugees.

Conclusion

Partition changed Namasudra community's political and community perception. As they migrated from the eastern part of Bengal to escape religious persecution in the hands of a communal regime they now saw themselves primarily as Hindus, pitted against their projected other-the Muslims. This collapsed the difference between outcastes and caste Hindus in the Dalit consciousness. This change in their political outlook is the key to understanding the absence of caste based interest and grievance articulation in the initial decades after partition in 1947 even when there was an enough hint of an upper caste conspiracy to dismantle the Dalit solidarity. While the upper caste Hindu migrants were allowed to settle in Calcutta and its thriving suburbs, the Namasudra refugees were mostly sent outside the state of West Bengal, mainly to Dandakaranya in Chattisgarh and Andaman and Nicobar Islands and few of them were resettled in districts far away from Calcutta, the seat of power and prosperity. It is difficult to conclusively prove that the lower caste unity and political regrouping of the Namasudras were prevented at the behest of the upper caste dominated parties and this is also not to deny that caste Hindu political elite everywhere in India sought to dominate public space and monopolise political power, and they preferred to see an internally homogenised nation. The people in India little talked about history of Namasudra Community who was the strong force behind Sudra movement in undivided India.

Bibliography

1. Anandabazar Patrika, 1 January 1948.
2. Bandyopadhyay, S. 1998. *Caste, Politics and the Raj*, Calcutta, 1990; Namasudras, London,
3. Bandyopadhyay, S. 2004. Caste, Culture and Hegemony: Social Dominance in Colonial Bengal, Sage publications,New Delhi.
4. Bandyopadhyay, S. 2009. Partition and Ruptures in Dalit Identity Politics in Bengal, *Asian Studies Review*, 33, 459-461,
5. Bandyopadhyay, S. 2014. The Scheduled Caste Movement in West Bengal after Partition, *Mahanirban Research Group*, Kolkata.
6. Biswas, A. K. 2000. The Namasudra of Bengal, Blumoon Books, New Delhi, P.3.
7. Biswas, U.N. 2004. The Strike, NCMB Memorial Trust, Kolkata, P. 48.
8. Bose, S. 1986. Agrarian Bengal: Economy, Social Structure and Politics 1919-47, Cambridge: Cambridge University Press, p. 258.
9. Confidential report of 4.4.52 regarding the arrival of the refugees of Ranaghat Cooper's Camp, at Sealdah Railway Station on 3.4.52', GB, IB Records, F.No. 982/48-Sealdah, WBSA.
10. Confidential report of Sealdah Railway station, dated 8/5/52, GB, IB Records, F.No. 982/48-Sealdah, WBSA.
11. Ghatak, N.K. 1987. Namasudra of Bengal through the Ages, Bulletin of the Cultural
12. Ghuyre, G.S. 1996. Caste and Race in India, Popular Prakashan, Bombay, P. 52.
13. Kamal, A.H.A. (2007), 'Peasant Rebellions and the Muslim League Government in East Bengal, 1947-54', in From the Colonial to the Postcolonial: India and Pakistan in Transition, eds. D. Chakrabarty, R. Majumdar and A. Sartori, New Delhi: Oxford University Press. pp. 203-4, 217.
14. Report of the Bengal Boundary Commission', Government of India, Reforms Office, File No. 68/47-R, National Archives of India, New Delhi.
15. Report on refugee situation for week ending 5/2/50, GB, IB Records, F.No. 1838/48, Part III, WBSA.

16. Report on the refugee situation for the week ending 19/11/50, GB, IB Records, F.No. 1838/48, Part III, WBSA.
17. Report on the refugee situation for the week ending 19/2/50, GB, IB Records, F.No. 1838/48, Part III; Copy of a report of a D.I.O of Nadia District, dated 3/7/50, GB, IB Records, F.No. 1809-48, Nadia, WBSA.
18. Report on the refugee situation for the week ending 22/1/50, GB, IB Records, F.No. 1838/48, Part III,WBSA.
19. Report regarding influx of East Bengal refugees at Sealdah R/S dated 3/6/52, GB, IB Records, File No.982/48-Sealdah, WBSA.
20. Report regarding influx of East Bengal refugees at Sealdah R/S dated 3/6/52, GB, IB Records, File No.982/48-Sealdah, WBSA.
21. Report regarding influx of East Bengal refugees at Sealdah R/S dated 3/6/52, IB Records, File No. 982/48-Sealdah, WBSA.
22. Research Institute Vol. XVII, No. 3-4, Govt. of West Bengal,P 18.
23. Sarkar, G. 1995. Jatitattwa Sangraha, (Bengali) Hiranmoy Sarkar, North 24 Paragana, West Bengal, P. 25.
24. Sarkar, S. 1382 (Bengali Year). Namasudrai Parsav Bipra, Khulna Press, Khulna, Bagladesh, P. 81.
25. Singh, K.S. 1995. The Scheduled Castes, Oxford University Press, Delhi, P. 978.
26. Thakur, K. K. (2007), 'Dalits of East Bengal: Before and After the Partition', in B. Chatterjee and D. Chatterjee (eds.), Dalit Lives and Dalit Visions in Eastern India, Kolkata: Centre for Rural Resources, p.33.
27. The Statesman, 21 January 1950.
28. The Statesman, 5 November 1946, cited in Jagadish Chandra Mandal, Mahapran Jogendranath o Babasaheb Ambedkar, Kolkata, Biswas Publisher,1999, p. 112.
29. Usuda, M. (1997), 'Pushed towards the Partition: Jogendra Nath Mandal and the Constrained Namasudra Movement', in H.Kotani (ed.) Caste system, Untouchability and the Depressed, New Delhi: Manohar, pp. 221-74.

Bibliography:

Acharya, Agni Kumar – *Tripura Prashasanik Bibartaner Itikatha,* Parul Prakashani, Agartala, 1998

Acharyya, R.K. (2007), Development of Tribal Languages: A hope for the Mission, TRCI, Govt. of Tripura.

Agnew, John A.; Mamadouh, Virginie; Secor, Anna and Sharp, Joanne (Eds.) (2015), The Wiley Blackwell Companion to Political Geography, Oxford: John Wiley & Sons.

Ahmed, Salahuddin & others (ed)- Bangladesher Mukti-Sangramer Itihas, 1947-71,(History of Bangladesh Liberation War), Agamee Prakashani, Dhaka, Third Reprint: 2002.

Ao, Temsula. *These Hills called Home*. New Delhi: Penguin Books, 2006. Print.

__________________, "Gender and Power Women- Centred Narratives from Ao-Naga Folklore." *Ethno- Narratives.* Bhattacharjee, Sukalpa & Dev, Rajesh. (ed.), Delhi: Anshah Publishing House, 2006.

Barooah Nirode K. and Bordoloi, Gopinath, '*The Assam Problem' and Nehru's Centre,* Bhabani Print and Publications, Guwahati, 2010.

Bhattacharyya, Gayatri, (1988), *Refugee Rehabilitation and its Impact on Tripura's Economy*, Omsons Publication, New Delhi.

Bhattacharyaa, N., *Predicaments of Secular Histories*, Public Culture Vol. 20, No. 1.

Bhattacharya, Ruma & Deepak, Pradeep Kumar (2014) *Tripura* .Noida :Vikas Publishing House Pvt. Ltd.

Bhaumik, Subir (2007), Insurgencies in India's Northeast: Conflict, Co-option & Change, Working Paper, and East-West Center, Washington.

_________________, (1996), *Insurgent Crossfire: Northeast India*, New Delhi: Lancer Publishers.

__________________, (2007), *Insurgencies in India's Northeast: Conflict, Co-option & Change*, Working Paper, East-West Center, Washington.

Boehmer, Elleke. *Colonial & Postcolonial Literature*, New Delhi: OUP, 1995.

Chakma, Bindu Ranjan, (2013), *Stateless people in the New Global Order: The Experience of the Chakmas,* New Delhi: Lakshi Publishers and Distributors.

Chakravarti, Mahadev, (2008), "Redcliff Award and Partition Historiography: Assam and Tripura", *SOCIAL CHANGE IN NORTH-EAST INDIA Partition, Ethnicity, Revivalism, Globalization*, NEIHA, Shillong.

________________, (2007), 'Documentation of the process of Integration of princely Tripura with the Indian Union' in S.Nag, T. Gurung and A. Choudhury, *Making of The Indian Union*, Akansha Publishing House, New Delhi.

________________,(ed.), Administration Report of Tripura State, Vol.-III.

_________________, (1994), *.Administration Reports of Tripura State (In 4 Volumes).* New Delhi: Gyan Publishing House.

Chakraborty, S.K. (1994), Goutami Sahitya Samskriti Bishaka Patrika, Dasaratha Dev's Article: No.3, Murdha Mlan Muk Mokhee Ditee Habee Bhasha, Sudhanna Debbarma Smaree Sankhya, Govt.of Tripura, Kyuik Print , Agartala.

Chandra, Bipan, Mukherjee, Mridula & Mukherjee, Aditya (2008). *India Since Independence.* New Delhi: Penguin Books.

Chapman, Graham P. (2012), The Geopolitics of South Asia: From Early Empires to the Nuclear Age, Burlington: Ashgate Publishing, Ltd.

Choudhury, Jitendra (2006), Minister of Tribal Welfare Dept.)'S Presidential Speech In The Seminar Of "Development Of Tribal Languages: Sharing Of Experiences' On 27th -28th May.

Clad, James and McDonald, Sean M. (Eds.), (2011), The Borderlands of Southeast Asia: Geopolitics, Terrorism, and Globalization, Washington, DC: National Defense University Press.

Cohen, Saul Bernard (2003), Geopolitics of the World System, New York: Rowman & Littlefield.

Dalby, Simon, and Gearóid Ó Tuathail (eds.) (1998), Rethinking Geopolitics, New York: Routledge.

Dasgupta, Anindita, (2001), *Denial and resistance: Sylhet Partition 'Refugees' in Assam,* Contemporary South Asia.

Dastidar, Sachi Ghosh, (2008), *Empire Last Casuality: Indian Subcontinent's Vanishing Hindu and other Minorities,* Kolkata:

De, R.K., Merger and Princely Tripura's Political Transition:1947-1949' in S.Nag, T. Gurung and A. Choudhury, (2007) *Making of The Indian Union*, Akansha Publishing house, New Delhi.

________________, (ed.) *Report On The Administration Of Tripura State, (1898-99, 1899-1900, 1943-46*), Varanasi.

Deb, R., (1997), *Srihatta Parichoy*, Kallayni.

Debbarma, K. N. (2013), An Article: Kokborok O Anyaanya Sanyaloghu Bhasa Unnayana O Tripura, In Sikha Samachara, Smaranika, 52th Sikhak Dibasha, Dept. of School Education, Govt. of Tripura.

Debbarma, M., Debbarma, N., Debbarma, A & Roy R.,(2007) Theatre Song, Referred By Debbarma S.L., His Article- An Evolution of Kokborok Language And Literature, R.K. Acharyya, (Editor) Development of Tribal Languages: A hope for the Mission, T.R.I., Govt. of Tripura.

Debbarma, N., Kokborok Bhasha Sahityeer Cramabikash, Naba Chandana Pukasani, Agartala, Tripura.

Debnath, Jayanta, (2001), *Santrasklanta Tripura,* Agartala: Dainik Sambad Publishers.

Dutta, Binayak , (2013), Violent Parting: Recovering the History of Violence in Sylhet on Partition and After. (1947-50) in *The Heritage*, Vol-IV, Issue-1..

________________, 'The Past as Present: Partition in Assam politics during independence and beyond', in *Dialogue, Volume-16 No.1.*

Flint, Colin (2012), Introduction to Geopolitics, London: Routledge.

Hazarika, Joysankar (1996), Geopolitics of North East India: A Strategical Study, New Delhi: Gyan Publishing House.

Gassah, L.S., (1984), 'Effects of Partition on the Border Markets of Jaintiya Hills', in *Marketing in North East India (Problems of Rural Markets)*, New Delhi.

Gangoli, J.B., (2006), *An Economic History of North East India, New Delhi.*

Gogoi, Rupam. (2011) "Outliving turbulence: An Analysis of These Hills Called Home". *Matrix of Redemption* .Das, Nigamananda. Ed. New Delhi: Adhayan Publishers.

Grierson, G., Linguistic Survey Of India, New Delhi, Vol V, Part-1.

Guha Thakurta, S.N. (1999), *Tripura*. New Delhi: National Book Trust.

Gupta, Ashoka, East is East,West is West, Seminar, No.510.

Kumar, Krishna, Prejudice and Pride, R. C. Majumdar, *History of the Freedom Movement*, Vol. I & III.

Habib, Harun (1992), *Mukti-Yuddha: Dateline Agartala, Jatiya Sahitya Prakashani*, Dhaka.

Hobsbawm, Eric, (1998), *On History*, London: Abacus.

Jena, Kashinath and Chakma, Bindu Ranjan, (2008), *Ethnic Unrests and India's Security Concerns,* New Delhi: Abhijeet Publications.

Jha, D. N (2015), "The Cow was Neither Unslayable nor Sacred in the Vedic period", *Frontline*, October 30. .

Jones, Terry-Ann and Mielants, Eric (2015), *Mass Migration in the World-system: Past, Present, and Future*, Volume 31 of Political economy of the world-system annuals, New York: Routledge.

Karim, Nehal (1992), *The Emergence of Nationalism in Bangladesh,* University of Dhaka, Dhaka, 1992

Kumar, Satish (ed.) (2013), *India's National Security*, Annual Review 2010, New Delhi: Routledge.

Menon, V.P., (1998), *Transfer of Power,* New Delhi, 1967, Re-Print 1998.

Misra, Tilottoma (ed.), Writings from North-East India .New Delhi: OUP, 2011.

Misra, Udayan. *The Periphery Strikes Back.* Shimla: IIAS, 2000.

Mohsin, Amena, (1997), *The Politics of Nationalism: The Case of Chittagong Hill Tracts, Bangladesh,* Dhaka: The University Press Limited.

Mukhia, Harbans (2015)"Distorting History Won't Help", *India Today*, October12.

Leary, Brendan O', Analyzing Partition: Definition, Classification and Explanation, *Working Paper 27,* Queen's University, Belfast.

Nehru, B. K., Nice Guys, *Finish Second Memoirs*, Penguin Books, Delhi, 1997.

O'Hanlon, Michael E. (2015), The Future of Land Warfare, Washington, DC: Brookings Institution Press.

Pahari, G.K., *Bharater Itibritya*, Vol.-II

Parthasarathi, G. (ed) *Letters to Chief Ministers*, Vol.1.

Raina, Badri (2015),"The Lynchings", *Mainstream*, October10.

Ray, Samiran (ed) (2003), *Tathya Panji and Nirdeshika,* Tripura Darpan.

R.K. Acharyya, (Editor) Development of Tribal Languages: A hope for the Mission, T.R.I., Government of Tripura.

Roy, Kaushik (ed.). 2012. *Partition of India Why 1947?* New Delhi: Oxford University Press.

Rustomji, Nari, (1997), Enchanted *Frontiers*, Oxford University Press, Delhi.

Rymbai, R.T., (1997), 'Integration of the Khasi States', in *The Shillong Times,* Shillong.

Sachar, Rajindar (2015),"Don Not Play With Fire", *Mainstream*, October17..

Syiemlieh, David R., *RESPONSE OF THE NORTH EAST HILL TRIBES OF INDIA TOWARDS PARTITION, INDEPENDENCE AND INTEGRATION: 1946-1950,*

Saha, Palash (ed.). 2013, *Tripura* Year Book. Agartala: Tripura Info.com

Sankarnarayanan, Vijayan (ed.). (2007). *Themes in Indian History Pt III.* New Delhi: N.C.E.R.T.

Sen, Chandra, *Tripura in Transition*, Times Press, Agartala, 1970.

Singh, Atom Sunil (2009), Notorious "Golden Triangle": India's Golden Opportunity? IPCS Artilce, New Delhi: 2806 (11 February 2009).

Sur, H.K., (1986) *British Relations with the State Of Tripura 1763-1947,* Agartala.

Thakur, Amrendra Kr (2011), "The Curriculum in History in Modern India: An Overview", in Sagar Boruah (ed.), *Historical Studies in the Context of Globalisation: Rationale for Restructuring Curriculum*, Khagarijan College, Nagaon, Assam.

Singh, Anita Inder (2006), *The Partition of India.* New Delhi : National Book Trust.

Singh, Chandrika. *North-East India Politics and Insurgency,* New Delhi: Manas Publishers, 2009.

Thakurta, Meghna Guha, (2002), *Uprooted and Divided*, Seminar, No.510, February.

Thongkholal Haokip (2010), "India's Northeast Policy: Continuity and Change," Man and Society, Vol. VII, Winter.

Zakaria, Rafiq (2004).*The man who divided India.Mumbai* :Popular Prakashan Pvt.Ltd.

Census of India, 1951, Vol.XII, Part I-A.

The Times of India, September 27, 2007.

Mainstream, Dec 25, 2010.

Governor's Secretatiat, File No. GS/ MISC.215/45 G.Sectt. Dept.,Meghalaya State Archives, Shillong.

Report (2012), The Other Burma? Conflict, Counter-insurgency and human rights in Northeast India, 11 October.

Twentieth Century Population Thinking: A Critical Reader of Primary Sources edited by The Population Knowledge Network (2015), New York: Routledge

Directorates of Census (2011), Agartala, States Primary Census Abstract For Individual Scheduled Tribe.

Index